THE GITA AS IT WAS

THE GITA AS IT WAS
Rediscovering
the Original Bhagavadgita

PHULGENDA SINHA

OPEN COURT

La Salle, Illinois

OPEN COURT and the above logo are registered in the U.S. Patent and Trademark Office.

First printing 1987.

Printed and bound in the United States of America.

Library of Congress Cataloging-in-Publication Data

Sinha, Phulgenda, 1924–
    The Gita as it was : rediscovering the original Bhagavadgita / Phulgenda Sinha
    p.   cm.
    "Text of the original Gita": p.
    Bibliography: p.
    Includes index.
    ISBN 0-8126-9024-9 : $28.95.   ISBN 0-8126-9025-7 (pbk.) : $16.95
    1. Bhagavadgītā—Criticism, interpretation, etc.
I. Bhagavadgītā.   II. Title.
BL1138.66.S57 1987
294.5'924—dc19   87-27700

Dedicated to
THE HEIRS OF INDIAN CIVILIZATION

TABLE OF CONTENTS

PREFACE

My search for the original Gita was inspired by my personal experiences of living in India and elsewhere. The idea for the project did not come suddenly but crystallized over a period of 15 years. Since the story of my rediscovery of the Gita is very closely related to other events in my life, it may be informative to review some of my background.

After receiving a Ph.D in political science from The American University, Washington, D.C., I returned to India in 1968 with the ambition to work for the betterment of the nation. Though I had been active in Indian politics from 1946 to 1957 and knew most of the prominent socialist leaders, I did not join any political party upon my return. The decision to remain outside active politics took shape during work on my dissertation, 'The Praja Socialist Party of India'. During my research for the thesis, I concluded that the building of a better India cannot be accomplished by the politicians of any party. I expressed this belief at the first opportunity upon returning to India. About a hundred people came to the Patna Airport to greet me. Among them were several political leaders of Bihar and other prominent men of Patna. I told this group: "I will not join any political party. I have come back to work for the uplifting of the country, but I will work as a non-political person."

Another occasion for expressing my views came on the way to my village in northern Bihar. About a half-mile from the village, at a market place known as Parihar, about ten thousand people had assembled to welcome me. It was the most touching scene of my life. I was wondering what these people expected from me that they had waited for hours to see and hear me. They had arranged a public meeting for me in the compound of a local high school. The warmth of their reception made me cry. The school-children sang, and a young man delivered an oration about what I had accomplished, how I had transformed myself, and what I could do for the people. The moment came for me to say a few words, and I said, "Brothers, sisters, friends and children! I am very deeply touched by your affection and warmth. I have returned to serve you and will work to make a better India. But I will work without joining any political party." This declaration disappointed many of my long-time political associates, who had expected me to work with them upon my return.

I had strong feelings about working for the betterment of India, but I was very wary about the fragmented political leadership of that time. I was convinced that making a better India could not be achieved by the political parties, the government, the social activists, or any foreign assistance. The country could only be made better by the people themselves. What I had found during the research for my thesis and what I felt upon returning to India convinced me that the political parties spent much of their time in rivalry, manipulation and gaining political power and that they had very little interest in reconstructing the nation.

Faced with these feelings, I planned to organize programs of voluntary service in which villagers would carry out projects involving simple manual labor. I held some meetings with the local village leaders and political and social activists and presented my ideas to them. My plan was well received. An organization was formed under the name Bharat Sundar Banao (Make India Beautiful). I wrote a booklet explaining the aims of this organization; selected five villages of the neighboring area as demonstration projects; organized volunteers in each village; and set up village committees and a central committee to guide and co-ordinate the work in all the model villages.

For a few months the work went very well in all the villages. But I was soon disappointed. Political party workers became unco-operative, criticizing and creating conflict among the volunteers, organizers, and village leaders. This disheartening experience with the villages strengthened my conviction that *there is something basically wrong with the thinking and action of the Indian people*. But I could not identify the source of the problem.

I pondered some of the basic facts and problems related to India. Its people are no less intelligent, strong, and healthy than those of other nations. Its climate and natural resources are ideal for national growth and prosperity. The country has the basic technological knowledge for industrial and agricultural excellence. But having all these, why does India remain an impoverished country in which millions cannot eat well, cannot afford shelter, and cannot get adequate education and health services? In a country where millions can survive only by begging and where millions live an inhuman life in the midst of abundant resources and vast manpower, there must be a deep-rooted cause acting as a binding or limiting force. But up to that point, I did not have any clear understanding of the reason for this national incapacity.

Finding myself unsuccessful in my effort to work in the villages by organizing voluntary manpower, I looked for other means of service to the people. I decided to teach Yoga because of my experience in the U.S.A. from 1964 to 1968. I had founded the Yoga Institute of Washington in 1965 in Washington, D.C., and had taught there until 1968.

During the period of my teaching in America I had found it difficult to interpret certain philosophical concepts of the ancient thinkers. This difficulty arose primarily because, prior to the 1960s, Yoga was mostly taught as an offshoot of Hinduism and not as a system of secular thought. Since in my teaching I had tried to present it as a rational system, there were various points where I clashed with the traditional presentation and interpretation.

To my surprise, even those few books which described Yoga as a rational system did not maintain a spirit of objectivity. With rare exceptions, Yoga continued to be presented as a mixture of religious, mystical, and cultic beliefs and practices.

I tried to find out if Yoga was truly a rational system in all its assertions —practical and theoretical. Since almost all the secondary source materials on Yoga presented it mixed with religious-spiritual values, I had to go to the original writings of Kapila, Patanjali and Vyasa. During the period 1965–1968 while teaching Yoga in Washington, I conducted research at the Library of Congress and built up a personal collection of books. From my studies, it became very clear to me that Yoga had been well-developed as a rational system of practice and philosophy in India and that it had reached maturity in the writings of Vyasa.

After my return to Patna I began making a thorough study of all the available primary source materials to determine (i) what this rational system was and its relevance for mankind today; (ii) whether we can critically examine all the assertions of Yoga from an objective standpoint; and (iii) what caused the degeneration of Yoga into mysticism and superstition.

By studying primary and secondary source materials on the Vedas, ancient Indian history, the explorations at Harappa and Mohenjodaro and other recently excavated historic sites in India, and by going through the works of Kapila, Buddha, Mahavira, Patanjali, Vyasa, and other prominent thinkers and writers, such as Bal Gangadhar Tilak and Swami Vivekananda, I came to the following conclusions:

(i) The basis of Yoga as a discipline and as a system is known as Samkhya Darshan (Samkhya philosophy). This philosophy was established by Kapila, who lived about 700 B.C. Surprisingly, he anticipated by 200 years certain ideas of the most renowned thinkers of the ancient world, such as Plato, Confucius, Buddha, and Mahavira.

(ii) Though Yoga was practiced during the period of the Harappa and Mohenjodaro civilization (generally dated around 3000 B.C.), we do not have any deciphered writing on Yoga from that period. The first known and comprehensively discussed book on Yoga is Patanjali's *Yoga Sutra*, dated about 400 B.C. In *Yoga Sutra*, Patanjali accepted everything taught by Kapila in his Samkhya Philosophy, and added more to make a comprehensive system for achieving a healthy, happy, and creative life.

(iii) Yoga reached its highest and most glorious stage in the work of Vyasa in about 400 B.C. Vyasa wrote the *Gita* by incorporating all the basic theories and concepts of Kapila and of Patanjali and by adding much original thought of his own. Thus, by 400 B.C. India as a civilization had produced a matchless philosophical work presented in the simple form of song, telling how *dukha* (sorrow) can be eliminated and how *sukha* (happiness) in life can be achieved. This philosophical work was the *Gita*.

(iv) In the post-Vedic period, up to about 800 A.D., the thinkers and writers of India were men of rational outlook. They did not accept the idea of a single, almighty deity. A close study of all available records indicates that theistic concepts were non-existent in India prior to about 800 A.D.

(v) In a surprising way, the thought pattern of India changed after 800 A.D. Monotheism made sudden inroads into India.

Considering the whole history of India from the most ancient to the contemporary period, I found a distinct dividing line in the literary and philosophical heritage of the country, making it appear as if there were two Indias—one which existed from ancient times to 800 A.D., and another which came after 800 A.D. Let me point out some of the salient features of these two Indias.

India prior to 800 A.D. produced philosophers and writers who accepted Man as the supreme being. They talked about two main entities: *Purusha* (Man) and *Prakriti* (Nature). Change in these two entities occurs due to the ever-present and everlasting work of three *Gunas—Rajas, Tamas,* and *Sattva.*[1] Ignorance, lack of proper knowledge and improper action cause *dukha* (sorrow or unhappiness). Man can liberate himself from *dukha* and can attain *sukha* (happiness) by acquiring proper knowledge, mastering certain teachings, following certain practices, and by working according to the Samkhya-yoga theory of action.

India after 800 A.D. adopted quite a different outlook. The ideas proposed by writers and commentators were now mostly matters of belief and faith, colored by religion, mysticism, and caste. Not Man but God was held to be supreme. Man could do only what was predestined by God. There was Heaven and Hell. Man possessed a soul which did not die but was reincarnated according to past and present deeds. The Brahmans were superior to all castes and the word *Brahman* was synonymous with *Brahma* (one of the post-Vedic gods) and all the divinities. Indian thought in this period bore certain resemblances to the teachings of Judaism, Christianity, and Islam. I became determined to find out why these seemingly alien con-

---

[1] For details on Gunas, see Chapter one on Samkhya Philosophy.

cepts came to India and to discover who brought them. What added to my curiosity was the fact that, though I had found similarities between Hindu belief and the doctrines of Jews, Christians, and Moslems, there was quite a difference in the mode of worship. Let me elaborate on this difference.

We know that whoever believed in a monotheistic god (the Almighty, the Supreme Being) built a place of worship in His name, without having any image or idol. Accordingly, we see that the synagogues of the Jews, the churches of the Christians, and the mosques of the Moslems do not have any idols in them. This is not the case with the Hindu religion. The Hindu religion, which believes in the concept of God as presented in the Bhagavadagita, did not build a place of worship for Him but for *purusha* such as Rama, Krishna, and Shiva.

This observation suggested that the concept of God as almighty and supreme is of foreign, not Indian, origin. It seems likely that the concept of God was introduced into a culture where polytheism had been long established. Since the temples for deities were built long before the invasion of the God concept, they were left untouched. But changes did occur on philosophical and literary levels. It was easy to revise the few handwritten books of that time. Since the Gita was the most outstanding book of philosophy, it was changed to appear as an authentic scripture. It will be explained later who brought this change, when and why, and what has been the impact of this change on Indian society and culture.

Here I wish to raise another pertinent question which also motivated me to go into the details of this change. For a long time I had been trying to find out why certain nations are rich, prosperous, well-developed, and better-governed than others. To put it differently, why have certain nations achieved prosperity even when their circumstances were unfavorable and resources meagre, whereas others have been unable to prosper even in the most favorable circumstances and with rich resources at their disposal?

I compared several major nations of the world, looking for the common factor which enabled some to achieve prosperity, while progress in others was blocked. I offer the following tentative explanation:

As is the level of thought in a nation, so is the level of its progress. The rate of progress is the same as is prevalence of thought. This holds true for a nation, a society, a community, a group, or a single individual. Where the level of thought does not rise, the society, the nation or the entity does not prosper.

This idea can be tested by taking any nation as an example. Ask who were or are the philosophers, the writers, the thinkers, the inventors, and the scientists whose work has been known to people of that country and what had or has been the level of their work. The nature and quality of their thought will be reflected in the nature and quality of the accomplishments of that society. The level of performance will be equal to the level of thought.

Keeping this hypothesis in mind, I began looking for the dominant thought-pattern of present-day India. I tried to determine what were the thoughts commonly shared by the people in general, be they rural or urban. My effort was to isolate the thought-pattern that could be called the national thought-pattern of India today.

This national thought pattern can be summarized in the following words:

Work without caring for the results.

Act, but do not look for the fruits of action.

Desires cause *dukha* (sorrow); therefore, do not have them.

You get only what fate dictates.

Material wealth is inferior; spiritual life is superior.

You should strive to achieve unity with God for a happy life, to go to ,heaven, and to be reincarnated.

Man is predestined and cannot do anything unless it is willed by God.

Sorrow, pain, and misery can be removed only by God, not by human effort.

This thought-pattern of India appeared to me quite contrary to that which characterized the Vedic and post-Vedic ages. From what source did the Indian people derive this thought-pattern? The source is what we know as the Bhagavada Gita. Since this Gita is the most revered book of the Hindus today, its teachings are accepted with obedience and sincerity by the Hindu people. It can safely be stated that the national thought-pattern of India is represented by the Bhagavada Gita.

After identifying the present Gita as the source of the changed thought pattern in India, I began questioning: Is this Bhagavada Gita the same as that written by Vyasa in 400 B.C.? Or is it an altered document composed at a later date by someone acting alone, in a cabal, or in consort with some alien agents? If the present Gita is an interpolated version, where is the original Gita?

I had become convinced from my study that the original Gita was different and that the present Gita is the work of a later period. Prior to 800 A.D., the Indian thought-pattern was conditioned and shaped by Vedic and post-Vedic traditions, norms, practices, teachings, and philosophy. The motivational traits during this era, whether expressed through rituals or in philosophy, evolved around the theme of: (i) fulfillment of desire; (ii) proper knowledge; and (iii) right action.

In the Vedic period, these traits were expressed in rituals, sacrifices, prayers and oblations to deities. All of these necessitated knowing which deity to invoke and what forms of rituals or prayers to offer for obtaining the desired result. In this way, knowledge, desire, and action remained an integral part of human expression.

In the post-Vedic period the mode of expression changed. Ritualistic ways were devalued and a philosophical and intellectual outlook towards problems of life was highlighted. This is evident from the original teachings of all the reformers, thinkers, and philosophers of the post-Vedic period. Beginning with Kapila, we find the basic themes of desire, knowledge, and action comprehensively taught and discussed by all the subsequent thinkers, such as Buddha, Mahavira, Gautama (Nyaya Darshan), Kanada (Vaisesika Darshan), Patanjali (Yoga Sutra) and Vyasa (original Gita).

Because of the prevalence of this rational teaching which culminated in the composition of the original Gita, India achieved progress and prosperity in many fields of human endeavor. But when this original Gita was reworked, and rationalistic thought was distorted by changing all the ancient books of philosophy, India as a nation developed a pattern of thought which had its roots not in Indian soil but in another culture.

India fell into a Dark Age whose prolongation for over a millennium strangled the sources of motivation, knowledge, and action.

It was in this period of darkness that the original Gita and all other prominent philosophic and Yoga texts were altered and suppressed. With the rediscovery of the original Gita, I hope that the people of India will once again come to know their actual treasure and will be inspired to adopt it. When India realizes the value of desire *(bhava)*, rational thought, proper knowledge, and right action, as highlighted in the original Gita, India will find ways, on its own, towards progress and prosperity.

Phulgenda Sinha
October, 1986

ACKNOWLEDGMENTS

This book was written under personally difficult circumstances. A health problem which began some years ago in India became acute during my stay in the United States. Intensive medical treatment and prolonged hospitalization forced me to discontinue Yoga teaching, which was my sole means of livelihood. A number of friends came to my assistance, enabling me to regain my health, cope with financial hardship, and remain in the States long enough to bring the book to its completion. I owe thanks to all of them.

I am especially grateful for the medical care provided by Dr. Mark I. Singer, M.D. and Dr. Eric D. Blom of Head and Neck Surgery Associates, Indianapolis, Indiana; to Dr. Benjamin Blatt, M.D., George Washington University, Washington, D.C.; and to Dr. Patrick A. Coyne, M.D., Washington D.C. Their efficient and skillful treatment has enabled me to regain my health and resume regular work. I express my gratitude to them and their associates.

It was equally important for me to find a place to stay. Lodging was provided by Rev. Jertha O. Love and my student Rev. Murial J. Love, the founders of the Ascending World Community Church. I shall ever be grateful to them and to all the members of this church for offering me shelter and allowing me to conduct Yoga classes at their church.

I must express my heartfelt thanks to my long-time student and friend Laverne Myren for her constant help, care, and affection during this stressful period. I can never forget those moments when she would visit me daily in the hospital and make sure that everything was going well. I am very much obliged to her and our mutual friends, T. Max Cvetnick, Ruby Smith, and Catherine V. Coleman.

I wish to extend heartfelt thanks to my long-time friend, attorney Stephen D. Keeffe, and his associate Mary Herlihy, for taking care of all the requirements concerning my visa, the legal status of the Yoga Institute of Washington, and my health care, and also helping me financially whenever I became hard-pressed.

As regards the completion of the manuscript, the most valuable help came from my long-time friend, Raymond L. Johnson, and my student, Jane Whitington. Raymond edited the manuscript in its several drafts, and offered valuable suggestions and criticisms which have helped me to improve the quality of its final presentation. Jane typed the manuscript over and over again, edited it, and extended valuable suggestions. In their own ways, they have both contributed greatly to the completion of this book. I am most thankful to each of them.

During this long period of my research and preparation for the manuscript, I had the opportunity to discuss various aspects of the original Gita with my students and friends in India, Europe, and the U.S.A. I have greatly benefitted by exchanging views with these varied groups of people. Their interest, criticism, and probing questions have proven a source of great inspiration and encouragement. And therefore, I wish especially to thank Paul de Wolde, Holland; Lilo Wagner, Ibiza, Spain; and in Washington, D.C., Joseph T. Nocerino, Patricia C. Hyorth, Billy Hall, Jesse E. Vaughan, Jr., Christan M. DiFrisco, Richard Lovell and Buddy Rossi.

Several scholars and friends have read this manuscript, in part or in full, and have given me valuable suggestions. Amongst them I am thankful to George Fernandes (India), Dr. Vidya Nand Singh, Dr. Sada Nand Singh, Dr. William F. McLoughlin, and Dr. K. D. Mathur.

I wish to express my heartfelt thanks to the staffs of the Research Facilities Section and the Loan Division of the Library of Congress, Washington, D.C., U.S.A., for offering me research facilities and providing all the source materials I needed to complete this work.

And lastly, let me express my appreciation and thanks to my wife, Shanti Devi, for managing the family responsibilities during my long absence, and to my elder son, Vinay Sinha, for efficiently running the Indian Institute of Yoga, Patna, India, during these years. I wish also to thank Girindra Mohan Bhatta, Din Dayal Prasad 'Arya', and all the members and staff of the Indian Institute for maintaining it well and rendering its various services to the people.

THE GITA AS IT WAS

PART ONE

1
RELIGIOUS PRACTICES AND TRENDS OF THOUGHT IN ANCIENT INDIA TO 800 A.D.

A striking feature of India prior to 800 A.D. is that the concept of God as almighty and supreme did not have any place in religious practice or thought. The concept of a monotheistic God entered India during the revival of Brahmanism around 800 A.D. In order to understand this change and its repercussions on the civilization as a whole, we need to examine the cultural, literary, and philosophical heritage of India from its earliest period to 800 A.D.

There was a time when it was not easy to talk about ancient India in a historical sense. Lack of a well-established chronology compelled us to guess at the dates in almost all aspects of ancient Indian life. This condition has improved in the last fifty years or so due to the labors of both Indian and western scholars. Disagreements on dates and periods have narrowed. The differences over dating among the historians are not of centuries or millenniums but of decades, and in many instances such differences have been eliminated altogether. Many events of ancient India are now being dated with precision and accuracy.

The Stone Age

The archaeologists have divided the pre-historic settlers of India into two classes: Paleolithic and Neolithic. The Paleolithic were the Old Stone Age people who lived around 35000 to 10000 B.C. The Neolithic were the New Stone Age people who lived around 10000 to 5000 B.C.[1]

---

[1] V.D. Mahajan, *Political & Cultural History of Ancient India* (New Delhi: S. Chand & Co., 1962), p. 36. See also Mahajan, *Ancient India*, Ch. III, The pre-historic people and Ch. IV, Pre-historic races and cultures in India; Bridget & Raymond Allchin, *The Birth of Indian Civilization* (England: Penguin Books, 1968) pp. 52–157.

Paleolithic sites have been found in several parts of India, such as Madurai, Tanjore, Kadur, around Madras in the South and also in the states of Hyderabad (now Andhra), Gujarat, Uttar Pradesh, Bengal, Bihar, Orissa, and Madhyapradesha. Mahajan is of the opinion that "there must have been some connection between the Paleolithic peoples of different parts of India as the finds are similar in different parts."[2]

Paleolithic men lived near rivers, lakes, and caves. They ate roots, fruits, nuts, and the flesh of wild animals. Cave paintings representing hunting scenes, drawings of animals, and human dancing postures have been found near Raigarh in Madhyapradesha and in the Mirzapur district of Uttar Pradesh.

Neolithic settlements have been found throughout India. The Neolithic people made sketches of birds, beasts, and human beings. They hunted, fished, and domesticated animals. In their later period, they developed agriculture and began growing fruits, vegetables, and crops. They consumed animals, fish, and milk.

The Neolithics worshipped ancestral spirits and performed rites on the occasion of death. Stone-worship was common among them. But they also worshipped the phallus. They performed both animal and human sacrifices.

Some of these Neolithic people were driven into the hills and forests by latter-day invaders, and their descendants still live in those places. They are known as Gonds, Bhils, and Santhals.[3]

Mahajan writes that "we have inherited a number of superstitions from the Neolithic period, such as the use of amulets, beads, sacred threads, shells, stones, etc. for curing diseases and keeping away evil spirits."[4] The New Stone Age period gradually ended when these people began making tools from metal. F.E. Zeuner in his *Prehistory in India* writes that "the Late Stone Age continued in some parts of India while city civilizations like that of the Indus Valley were flourishing."[5]

The metal age emerged in a gradual way out of the New Stone Age. While the use of some stone tools was still in practice, the people of northern India began making axes, swords, spear-heads, and various other implements from copper. Iron working came much later.

According to Mahajan, there was a difference in the sequence of change from stone age to metal age between North and South India. In northern India, stone was replaced first by copper and then by iron. But in southern India, stone tools were directly replaced by iron tools. Another historian, Waryam Singh, is of the view that "copper tools were in use in India as early as 2000 B.C. and iron was brought into use about a thousand years

[2] *Ibid.*, p. 32.
[3] Mahajan, *Ancient India* (Delhi: S. Chand & Co. 1962), p. 27.
[4] *Ibid.*
[5] F.E. Zeuner, *Prehistory in India* (Poona: Deccan College, 1951), p. 3.

later, i.e., in 1000 B.C."[6] Mahajan agrees with this view by saying, "the Copper Age probably started about 4,000 years ago."[7]

There is some difference of opinion among the historians in identifying the most ancient people of India. Most historians agree that the Kolarians were the first inhabitants of India. Their descendants are scattered in several parts of the country even now, and are known by different tribal names. Bhils live in Rajputana and in the Vindhya hills, Gonds live in Central India, and Santhals live in Orissa and in certain parts of Bihar.

The most significant aspect of the life of the Kolarians is that they are still regarded as primitive. Their way of life has not changed much. They have not made any contribution to the advancement of Indian civilization.[8]

Besides the Kolarians, there is another group of people called Dravidians who are also regarded by many historians as among the original inhabitants of India. They were spread all over India and had developed a rich civilization in certain areas before the coming of the Aryans. Therefore, let us examine their cultural life in some detail.

The Dravidians

There is a difference of opinion about the origin of the Dravidians. "There are many theories about their origin. Some historians believe that they were the original inhabitants of India, while others opine that they were the earliest invaders from the northwest."[9]

Mahajan's view is that the Dravidians came to India from the eastern Mediterranean and that there were at least three varieties of them. All of them were speakers of the Dravidian language. They were long-headed and of dark complexion. They had attained a fairly high level of civilization at the time of their coming to India. Eventually, the Dravidian culture spread all over India. As there was no solid concentration of Dravidians in Northern India, the invading Aryans found it easy to impose their own culture in that region.[10]

The religion of the Dravidians differed from the Kolarians. They worshipped earth, stone, and trees.[11] Mahajan gives a detailed description of the religious life of the Dravidians and points out that the puja ceremonies

[6] Waryam Singh. *History of Ancient India: From the Earliest Times to the Muslim Conquest* (Lahore: Sikh University Press, 1943), p. 22.

[7] Mahajan, *Ancient India*, p. 28.

[8] Waryam Singh, *op.cit.*, p. 22.

[9] Waryam Singh, *op. cit.*, p. 23. See also Gilbert Slater, *The Dravidian Element in Indian Culture.* (New Delhi: E. E. Publications, 1976), pp. 22–25.

[10] Mahajan, *op. cit.*, p. 32. For a historical account of the Dravidian race and culture see E. L. Tambimuttu, *Dravida* (Bombay: International Book House, 1945).

[11] Waryam Singh, *op. cit.*, p. 23.

(religious rituals) using flowers, leaves, fruits and water are of Dravidian origin. In course of time, the puja rites were adopted by the Hindus.[12] The worship of snakes and the *linga* (phallus) was common among the Dravidian, as was the worship of *grama devatas* (village divinities).

These divinities of the Dravidians had no temples or priests. The sacrifices and oblations were made at sowing and harvesting time for rain, fair weather, or the prevention of diseases. Grama devatas were represented by a heap of stones, generally in a grove or at a quiet spot near every village. Some village deities were smeared with black and some of them with red color.[13]

The details of the Dravidian civilization are known from the findings of the Harappa and Mohenjodaro excavations. Since the Indus Valley civilization is pre-Aryan, it is commonly regarded as Dravidian.

The Indus Valley Civilization

Since the date of this civilization is generally accepted to be 3000 B.C., its excavation has revealed a great deal about various aspects of human life in ancient India. The centers of this civilization have been found near the Indus River, now in Western Punjab. The earliest excavations began at Harappa and Mohenjodaro during 1922–1924 and continued for several years. In recent years, more than 60 further sites of this civilization have been excavated. According to Walter A. Fairservis, Jr., nearly 1,000 Harappan sites have been located. Some of the prominent excavations at Rupar, Rangpur, Lothal, Chanhudaro, Kot Diji, and Kalibanga have added much to our knowledge of the Indus Valley civilization. These excavations prove that this civilization occupied various parts of India, in a wide arc from Western India in the vicinity of the Narmada River northward across Gujarat and Kutch through Sind, Rajasthan, and up to the vicinity of New Delhi and the Ganges Valley. [14]

As regards the date of this civilization, there is still some disagreement among historians. Though a majority of historians seem to accept the view of John Marshall, who put the date at 3000 B.C., there are a few who consider 2500–1500 B.C. as the more accurate date. But according to Chandler, "masterpieces of Harappan city planning were the culmination of towns and villages which date from 6000 B.C. to 7000 B.C."[15]

[12] Mahajan, *op.cit.*, p. 33; Slater, *op.cit.*, pp. 82–117.
[13] *Ibid.*, p. 34.
[14] *Ibid.*, p. 36–38. See also Dr. Phulgenda Sinha, *Yoga for Total Living* (New Delhi: Orient Paperbacks, 1977), p. 19; Walter A. Fairservis, Jr. 'The Script of the Indus Valley Civilization', *Scientific American*, March 1983, p. 58.
[15] Wayne B. Chandler, 'The Jewel in the Lotus', *African Presence in Early Asia* (Oxford, U.K.: Transaction Books, 1985), p. 82.

The findings of these excavations reveal that it was a highly developed urban civilization. The city was well planned, with paved roads, underground drainage and sewage systems, public bathing places, double-storied brick buildings, and a stable system of government. Though iron was not used by the people of this civilization, they could make weapons of bronze and copper. They used clay and stone for making seals.

Practice of Yoga and Forms of Religion
in the Indus Valley Civilization

One major difficulty in knowing all the details of this period is our inability to decipher what has been written by the people of the Indus Valley civilization. They had developed a script found on various seals and copper tablets. From what is available, we can speculate about their religious beliefs and practices.

Two seals of the Harappa-Mohenjodaro civilization reveal that the people knew and practiced Yoga. One of the most remarkable things about these two seals is that the Lotus Pose depicted on them is practiced today the same way.[16] Further, by looking at the photo plates of this period at the library of the Archaeological Survey of India, New Delhi, one can see several seals resembling Yoga postures. This finding establishes the fact that Yoga practices were known by the people of the Indus Valley civilization.

Since the script depicted on these two seals and various others cannot be read as yet, we do not know what is written there. The recent decipherment by Fairservis, though incomplete, does reveal some predominent features of the socio-cultural life of this civilization. Some of the seal inscriptions which have already been deciphered reveal that there were powerful chiefs, noble householders, and even noble first ladies. Surprisingly, religious references are scarce. In the light of these evidences, it can be ascertained that Yoga was practiced by the noble families, not as a religion, but as a science. Since the Indus Valley civilization is pre-Aryan, it can safely be said that the origin of Yoga is rooted in the most ancient culture of India.

As regards the religious practices of this civilization, Indian historians seem to agree that the *pipal* (a kind of tree) god was the major deity of the Indus age.[17] Mahajan is of the opinion that the Indus people worshipped *linga* (phallus) and *yoni* (vulva). This view is based upon some polished stones found in the forms of the phallus and some pierced stones identified as yoni. The people had faith in amulets and charms.[18]

---

[16] Phulgenda Sinha, *op. cit.*, p. 20. See also Chandler, *op.cit.*, pp. 96–100.

[17] Mahajan, *op. cit.*, p. 47. Note: It needs to be mentioned that the pipal tree is still worshipped in Northern India, and it is one of the village deities (grama devatas). The script decipherment of Fairservis has not revealed evidence of religious practices, though certain seals are interpreted to signify religious practices. For more on religious practices of this period, see K. N. Dikshit, *Prehistoric Civilization of the Indus Valley* (Madras: University of Madras, 1967), pp. 31–39.

[18] *Ibid.*, p. 49.

Indian historians do not accept the view of John Marshall that a mother-goddess was worshipped by the Indus Valley people. A seal showing a male deity with three faces and seated in Yoga posture is interpreted by some historians as 'Pasupati', lord of animals.

There are several views regarding the disappearance of the Indus Valley civilization. Some hold the view that it was destroyed by flood, and some are of the opinion that invaders destroyed this culture and subjugated the people. When this civilization vanished, the Aryans arrived.[19] But Fairservis, and Chandler hold the view that the Harappan culture did not disappear: it is the parent of the present-day villages of India.

The Aryans

There is still great controversy among historians about who the Aryans were and from where they came. One long-held view has been that the Aryans originally lived in Central Asia.

F. Max Müller, the German scholar, highly respected for his pioneering study of comparative languages, pointed out that the ancestors of the Indians, Greeks, Persians, Romans, Germans, and Celts must have lived together originally. This was based upon his study of the languages of these people.

Bal Gangadhar Tilak, in his book *The Arctic Home of the Aryans*, put forth a theory that the Aryans came from the Arctic regions.

There are a number of historians who support the view that the Aryans were of Indian origin and that they came from the Punjab area. Mahajan expresses the view that the nature of the Aryan invasion of India cannot be satisfactorily solved.

Carrying fire and sword, the Aryans exterminated many of the original inhabitants. There is a reference to the wars between Aryans and non-Aryans in the *Rig Veda*.

Mahajan's view is that when the Aryans came to India, they conquered the inhabitants and spread to the East and Southeast. They made the women and children slaves. Racial mixture resulted when Aryans marrried the enslaved women.

As we have seen, prior to the coming of the Aryans, the non-Aryans were already settled all over India. The non-Aryans of Magadha, Anga, Vanya, and Kalinga were very strong and could not be absorbed by the Aryans. It was in this environment that Buddhism and Jainism took root.

---

[19] Steven Warshaw and C. David Bromwell, *India Emerges* (California: Diable Press, 1974), p. 16; Fairservis, Jr. *op. cit.*, p. 79; and Chandler, *op. cit.*, pp. 93–104.

The number of Aryans who went to South India was not very large, and, as the people were not Aryanized, the Dravidian culture there remained dominant.[20]

There is a difference of opinion among historians regarding the date of the Aryans' arrival in India. Some hold that they might have entered India sometime between 2500 and 1500 B.C.[21] The earliest work of the Aryans is called Vedas; and it may have been composed between 1200 and 600 B.C.[22] The exact period when these hymns were composed is a matter of conjecture. According to Macdonell, all that we can say with any approach to certainty is that the oldest of them cannot date from later than the thirteenth century B.C.[23]

The Vedas

The word Veda is derived from the Sanskrit root *Vid* which means 'to know'. Veda means knowledge. The Vedas were composed by the ancient *Rishis* (learned men) and were handed down from generation to generation through oral transmission from teacher to students. Dasgupta believes that "it is not improbable that some of them were composed before the Aryan people entered the plains of India."[24] When the Aryans settled down, the Vedic hymns were compiled into books and given their present form. The Vedic hymns were written at different times by different people.[25] The Vedas are collections of hymns, chants, and prayers; and there are four in number: the *Rig Veda,* the *Sama Veda,* the *Yajur Veda,* and the *Atharva Veda.*

The Rig Veda is the oldest. Originally it contained 1,017 hymns (eleven more were added at a later date), which have been divided into ten mandalas or chapters. Its hymns and prayers address aspects of nature as gods and were meant for recitation aloud. Mahajan says that "the oldest hymns are to be found in mandalas from 2 to 9. The first and the tenth Mandalas seem to be later additions",[26] they "do not belong to the period when most of the Rigveda was written."[27]

According to Macdonell, six of the ten books, II to VII, are homogeneous in character. The hymns contained in each of them were composed by

[20] Mahajan, *op. cit.,* p. 66.

[21] Waryam Singh, *op. cit.,* pp. 30–31.

[22] Warshaw and Bromwell, *op.cit.,* p. 17.

[23] Arthur Anthony Macdonell, *A Vedic Reader* (London: Oxford University Press, 1965), p. XI.

[24] Surendranath Dasgupta, *A History of Indian Philosophy* (Cambridge: University Press, 1932), p. 15.

[25] Mahajan, *op. cit.,* p. 67.

[26] Mahajan, *op. cit.,* p. 68.

[27] *Ibid.,* p. 82. See also Deshmukh, *Religion in Vedic Literature,* p. 202.

poets of the same family, which handed them down as its own collection. The tradition is borne out by the internal evidence of the seers' names mentioned in the hymns. On the other hand, books I, VIII, and X were not composed by a distinct family but rather by unrelated individuals.[28]

Macdonell gives a detailed account of these later additions saying that "the earliest of these additions appears to be the second half of Book I, which consisting of nine groups, each by a different author, was prefixed to the family books, the internal arrangement of which it follows." The ninth book was added as a consequence of the first eight being formed into a unit." The tenth book was the final addition. Its language and subject matter show that it is later in origin than the other books; its authors were, moreover, clearly familiar with them. Both its position at the end of the Rig Veda and the fact that the number of its hymns (191) is made up to that of the first book indicate its supplementary character.[29]

The Sama Veda hymns are mostly taken from the Rig Veda, and it is called 'Book of Chants.' It has 1,549 hymns. There is nothing original in this Veda. Being entirely based on the Rig Veda, it possesses practically no independent value.[30] It is regarded as the song book of the priests.

The Yajur Veda hymns are sacrificial prayers, most of them taken from the Rig Veda, but also having original prose sections explaining the details of various ceremonies. There are two schools of the Yajur Veda: the Black and the White. The Black school presents the hymns and prose in a mixed form, whereas the White school calls the hymns *Samhita* and the prose *Brahmana*.

The Atharva Veda hymns relate to magical spells or incantations directed against hostile forces such as illness, demons, and enemies. There are formulas for witchcraft and sorcery. Atharva Veda is divided into 20 books and has 731 hymns. "It presents an interesting and unparallelled picture of primitive popular belief and superstition current among the lower strata of the early Indo-Aryans."[31] It is a much later collection than the other three.

The texts of these Vedas are called Samhitas. Besides the Samhitas, other literature of the Vedic period includes the Brahmanas, the Aranyakas, and the Upanishads. Though the earlier Upanishads belong to the Vedic period, many of the others are post-Vedic, and some were composed during the medieval period.

The Brahmanas explain the meaning and methods of performing sacrifices. Each Brahmana is attached to one of the Vedas. They are commentaries on the various hymns in the Vedas. The Brahmanas are regarded as theological prose dealing with the ceremonial aspects of religion.

[28] Macdonell, *op. cit.*, p. XIV. For more on the Rig Veda, see his Introduction, pp. XII–XXXI.
[29] *Ibid.*, p. XV–XVI.
[30] P.S. Deshmukh, *Religion in Vedic Literature* (London: Oxford University Press, 1933), p. 190.
[31] Mahajan, *op. cit.*, p. 191.

The Aranyakas are considered to be the 'Forest books' separated from the concluding section of the Brahmanas. They were separated from the Brahmanas for guidance to those hermits who lived in the forests. They were written between 1000 B.C. and 800 B.C.[32]

The Upanishads

When we move onward from the Brahmanas and the Aranyakas into the Upanishadic literature, we notice a marked change. Whereas the Brahmanas and the Aranyakas originated amongst the Brahmans and were linked to Vedic tradition and ritual, the early Upanishads originated amongst the Kshatriyas and were primarily concerned with intellectual speculations centering around such themes as the nature of man, reality, truth, Brahman, Atman, and meditation. In the early period, these philosophers appeared to be in opposition to the priestly class. In later times, "this philosophy became in the fullest sense the property of the Brahmans and has been cultivated by them for twenty-five centuries, down to the present day, so that it is still regarded as the orthodox doctrine of Brahmanism. But this does not alter the fact that it took its rise in the ranks of the warrior caste."[33]

Scholars give different interpretations of the nature and origin of the Upanishads. According to Dr. Radhakrishnan, "The Upanishads form the concluding portions of the Veda, and are therefore called the Vedanta or the end of the Veda, a denomination which suggests that they contain the essence of the Vedic teaching. They are the foundations on which most of the later philosophies and religions of India rest."[34]

This view is rejected, however, by S.K. Belvalkar and R.D. Ranade. While discussing "Transition from the Brahmana to the Upanishad Period", the authors express the view that the priestly ratiocinations had very limited scope and were incapable of satisfying the quest for a more profound understanding. The practice of metaphysical speculations could not be kept, like the knowledge of the Vedic sacrificial technique, a monopoly of the priestly class or caste. People of non-Aryan and non-Brahmanic origin did not subscribe to the doctrines of the Brahmana cult, but preserved and enriched a rival philosophical tradition which made "its distinct mark upon the sacerdotal and theological speculations of the day." Belvalkar

---

[32] Waryam Singh, op. cit., p. 33.

[33] Richard Garbe, The Philosophy of Ancient India (Chicago: Open Court Publishing Company, 1897), p. 78. For a comprehensive view of Kshatriya origin of Upanishads, see Nicol Macnicol, Hindu Scriptures (London: J.M. Dent & Sons, 1938), pp. XVII to XXIV and 127.

[34] Dr. Radhakrishnan, Indian Philosophy (London: George Allen & Unwin Ltd., 1966), Vol. I, p. 138.

and Ranade hold the view that "the Upanishads may be said, in a sense, to constitute a 'revolt' against the old Brahmana way of belief and practice."[35]

The nature of this revolt is revealed in a passage of the Chhandogya Upanishad, which is commonly accepted as one of the earliest. The twelfth khanda (section 12) of this Upanishad likens a procession of priests, marching to perform Vedic rituals, to a procession of dogs, each animal holding in its mouth the tail of the dog in front and crying, "Om, let us eat! Om, let us drink!"[36]

According to Garbe, the doctrine of the All-One "did not have its origin in the circle of the Brahmans at all."[37] Garbe cites historical evidence to show that the Brahmans sought ultimate knowledge from the Kshatriya kings. A few such instances are noted below:

In the second *Adhyaya* (book) of Brihadaranyaka Upanishad, there is a story of a learned Brahman Gargya Balaki who goes to Ajatsatru, the prince of Kashi (Banaras), to learn what is Brahman. He becomes a royal disciple. Thereupon, Ajatsatru explains at great length the value of Self and Brahman, saying:

> As the spider comes out with its thread, or as small sparks come forth from fire, thus do all senses, all worlds, all Devas, all beings come forth from that Self. The Upanishad (the true name and doctrine) of that Self is 'the True of the True.'[38]

There is another story of a Brahman and his son seeking knowledge from a Kshatriya king, Pravahana. The sixth Adhyaya (Book VI) of Brihadaranyaka Upanishad relates this story.

Stories of Brahmans seeking metaphysical wisdom from Kshatriya kings are found in several Upanishads. Rangachar notes that King Janaka of Videha and King Ajatasatru of Kashi (Banaras) are acclaimed in several stories as the accredited repositories of the highest metaphysical wisdom. They are often found presiding over many great philosophical councils and seminars. Many Brahmans approach King Asvapati Kaikeya and request to become his pupils.[39]

The foregoing discussion indicates that philosophic deliberations and uninhibited free thinking were deeply rooted practices amongst the Kshatriya kings and their families. This profound curiosity about life, birth, death, and the universe among the Kshatriyas continued for centuries and subsequently gave birth to several systems of rational thought. It was

[35] Belvalkar and Ranade, *History of Indian Philosophy* (New Delhi: Orient Books Reprint Corp., 1974), p. 86. For more about this opposition, see Ch. III, pp. 77–145.
[36] Translation quoted from Nicol Macnicol, *Hindu Scriptures, op. cit.,* p. 127. See also, pp. XVI–XXI for Macnicol's views on the Upanishads.
[37] Garbe, *op. cit.,* p. 68.
[38] Translation quoted from Macnicol, *op. cit.,* pp. 58–60. For full discussion of Gargya and Ajatsatru, see *Brihadaranyaka Upanishad,* second adhyaya, Number 1–20.
[39] S. Rangachar. *Early Indian Thought* (Mysore: Rao and Raghavan, 1964), pp. 52–53.

against this background that the Samkhya philosophy of Kapila, Nyaya philosophy of Gautama, Vaisesika philosophy of Kanada, Lokayata, and the philosophy of Buddha and Mahavira emerged and flourished.

There are still divergent opinions about the date of the early Upanishads. The most commonly held view is that they were written between 800 B.C. and 500 B.C.[40] Dasgupta tells us that "though the earliest Upanishads were compiled by 500 B.C., they continued to be written even so late as the spread of Mahommedan influence in India."[41] But according to Dr. Radhakrishnan, "The accepted dates for the early Upanishads are 1000 B.C. to 300 B.C." [42]

There are 108 Upanishads written by various sages and learned men. Again, there is a difference of opinion about the exact number of these Upanishads. Belvalkar and Ranade have noted that there are between two and three hundred texts calling themselves "Upanishads" which have been handed down to us.[43]

Likewise, there is no unanimity of opinion about what the Upanishads teach. "Different commentators, starting with particular beliefs, force their views into the Upanishads and strain their language so as to make it consistent with their own special doctrine."[44] It is true that the Upanishads do not present any consistent system of philosophy, but their philosophical speculations, even in their most rudimentary form, did prove to be the seeds which gave birth to the most refined rational philosophy of Kapila in 700 B.C.

The main theme of the Upanishads centers around two words: Brahman and Atman. According to Dasgupta, Brahman is used to signify the ultimate essence of the universe, and Atman is used to denote the inmost essence in man. The Upanishads are emphatic in their declaration that the two are one and the same. In other words, the essence in man and the essence of the universe are one and the same, and it is Brahman.

The word Upanishad means 'sitting down near' the teacher to receive instruction. It connotes receiving secret doctrine. Upanishad is comprised of three words: *Upa* (near) + *ni* (devoutedly) + *shad* (sitting).

One significant point about these Upanishads is that only the following six are considered truly ancient: Brihadaranyaka, Chhandogya, Taittiriya, Aitareya, Kena, and Kaushitaki.

Belvalkar and Ranade have said that "we have no reason to suppose that the present form of an Upanishadic text is the original form in which it

[40] Mahajan, *op. cit.*, p. 70.
[41] Surendranath Dasgupta, *A History of Indian Philosophy* (Cambridge: The University Press, 1932), Vol. I, p. 39; also see 41–50.
[42] Dr. Radkhakrishnan, *op. cit.*, pp. 141–142.
[43] Belvalkar and Ranade, *op. cit.*, p. 87.
[44] Dr. Radhakrishnan, *op. cit.*, pp. 139–140.

was revealed . . . What we have in our Upanishads is the improved form by an author whose identity could no longer be established."[45] Macnicol expresses a similar view when he says, "no doubt all or most of the Upanishads have undergone more or less revision and interpolation."[46]

We have noticed how, after the composition of the Rig Veda, other literary forms developed. During the later Vedic period, mystical tendencies along with the growth of philosophic speculations emerged and continued, as evident from the hymns of the Atharva Veda and from the contents of the Upanishads.

Commenting on the later Vedic literature, Max Müller writes, "In the songs of the Rigveda, we find but little of philosophy, but we do occasionally meet with wars of kings, with rivalries of ministers, with triumphs and defeats, with war songs and imprecations. The active side of life is still prominent in the genuine poetry of the Rishis, and there still exists a certain equilibrium between the two scales of human nature. It is only after the Aryan tribes had advanced southward and taken quiet possession of the rich plains and beautiful groves of Central India, that they seem to have turned all their energies and thoughts from the world without them to that more wonderful nature which they perceived within."[47]

Max Müller quotes from Megasthenes's account of India in which he describes the passive and abstract character of the Brahmans throughout the whole post-Vedic literature. Then Müller goes on to say, "A people of this peculiar stamp of mind was never destined to act a prominent part in what is called the history of the world. This exhausting atmosphere of transcendental ideas could not but exercise a detrimental influence on the active and moral character of the Indians."[48]

Before going into the post-Vedic literature, let us consider the religious beliefs and practices of the people during the Vedic period.

The Religion of the Vedic People

The Vedic people worshipped a large number of gods representing natural phenomena. "The Vedic poets divided their thirty-three gods into three groups according to the three-fold division of the universe: heaven, atmosphere and the earth."[49] They believed in terrestrial gods like *Prithvi*, *Soma*, *Agni* and *Rivers*. They prayed to atmospheric gods like *Indra*, *Maruts*,

[45] Belvalkar and Ranade, *op. cit.*, p. 136.
[46] Macnicol, *Indian Theism* (Delhi: Munshiram Manoharlal, 1969), p.77.
[47] F. Max Müller, *A History of Ancient Sanskrit Literature* (Edinburgh: Williams & Norgate, 1860), p. 25.
[48] *Ibid.*, p. 29.
[49] Deshmukh, *op. cit.*, p. 211.

Vayu and *Vata*, *Rudra* and *Parjanya*. Their heavenly gods were *Varuna*, *Surya*, *Dyaus*, *Savitr*, *Mitra*, *Vishnu*, *Vivasvat*, *Adityas*, *Ushas*, *Asvins*, and *Pushan*.

They offered prayers and sacrifices to particular gods to obtain special favors. They worshipped Surya (sun) for overcoming darkness and its evil spirits; Indra for preventing thunderstorms and giving rain; Agni as god of fire; Prithvi the mother earth, and so on. "The Vedic people believed that gods and goddesses behaved like human beings. They ate and drank and had feelings and emotions like the ordinary human beings."[50]

Sacrifices were an important part of the Vedic religious practices. The *Ashvamedha Yagya* (horse sacrifice) was the great sacrificial offering. "One very noteworthy feature of the Vedic religion is that there were no temples and no idols. People said their prayers in the open air and worshipped nature-spirits with simple sacrificial rites."[51]

As mentioned earlier, the Vedic people worshipped thirty-three gods. "Each of the gods is on the whole, regarded as quite independent and not in any way subordinate or inferior to any other god. The idea that the various gods are but different forms of the same divine being, however, never undermined the influence or importance of the individual gods and consequently they never merged into one god, so as to develop a monotheistic belief. More or less equal importance and independent sovereignty of each god was, indeed, one of the most fundamental ideas of the Rigveda from a very early period."[52]

Expressing his views on the Vedic gods in general, Deshmukh says, "The main purpose of the hymns was to please the god invoked by praising his power and greatness. It does not constitute a distinct type of religious thought."[53] According to Dasgupta, "this stage can neither be properly called polytheistic nor monotheistic, but one which had a tendency towards them both, although it was not sufficiently developed to be identified with either of them." While discussing 'Religion of the Rigveda,' Macdonell observes, "It is thus essentially a polytheistic religion, which assumes a pantheistic colouring only in a few of its latest hymns."[54]

When we talk of Vedic religion, we try to evaluate it on the basis of our familiarity with religions of our time. This leads us to misinterpret and distort what was in fact a simple form of praise to move the powers of nature. The prayers, chants, and hymns of the Vedas do not constitute any religious doctrine, such as we see in the organized religions. While talking about theism of the Rig Veda, Macnicol has rightly observed, "it is obvious that the religion of which those hymns are the utterance cannot

[50] Mahajan, *op. cit.*, p. 87.
[51] Waryam Singh, *op. cit.*, p. 35.
[52] Deshmukh, *op. cit.*, p. 321.
[53] *Ibid.*, p. 320. See also Dasgupta, *op. cit.*, p. 19 and pp. 16–27.
[54] A.A. Macdonell, *op. cit.*, p. XVIII.

be described as strictly theistic or monotheistic in the sense in which today we understand those words."[55]

Some people refer to Brahma and some to Prajapati as the supreme deity of Vedic origin. "This supreme being is sometimes identified with Viswakarma, sometimes with Prajapati, sometimes with Brihaspati, and some other times with Hiranyagarbha."[56]

Deshmukh points out that "Brahma was never universally worshipped, and his acknowledgment as the Supreme God is not even true, still less a prominent characteristic of Brahmanical religion and sects."[57] He further comments, "the word has indeed, so far as we know, originated among, and is more or less confined to, the Western scholars of Sanskrit, and is hardly found to be in Indian literatures."[58]

As regards Prajapati, we find a very comprehensive discussion about him by Deshmukh in his *Religion in Vedic Literature*. He states that in the Satapatha Brahman, Dyasu and Prithvi are counted as the thirty-third and Prajapati is added as the thirty-fourth god. The addition of Prajapati among the gods, thus, dates from a much later period, and even then he was not given the status of a supreme god. He remained one of the thirty-four gods even in the Brahmana.

Deshmukh goes on to say that "it should be noted that Prajapati is often identified with Brahman and the whole Brahman. He is also said to be *Visvakarman*, the *Purusa*, the *Dhatr* and to have been born out of the golden egg."[59] In the words of Mahajan, Prajapati stands for Purusha. During the later Vedic period, Rudra and Vishnu came into prominence. Then Rudra took the place of Prajapati.[60]

It is not uncommon to find scholars arguing that monotheistic concepts existed during the Vedic period and the doctrine of one supreme god was implied in such names as Prajapati (Lord of creatures), Dhatr (creator or supporter), and *Tratr* (Protector). At times, these scholars refer to several hymns of the Rig Veda to prove their point. The hymns often cited are: RV. X 90 (purusa-sukta); RV. X 129 (hymn of creation); RV. X 81, 82 addressed to Viswakarman (as all creating deity); and also RV. X 121 addressed to *Hiranyagarbha* (as lord of all existence).

A.A. Macdonell clarifies this point very well with his explanation of the religious beliefs and practices of the Vedic people. According to Macdonell, the gods of the Rig Veda had not yet become dissociated from the physical phenomena they represented; their figures were indefinite in outline and deficient in individuality. Having many attributes such as power, brilliance,

[55] Nicol Macnicol. *Indian Theism, op.cit.,* p. 7.
[56] Rangachar, *op. cit.,* p. 30.
[57] Deshmukh, *op. cit.,* p. 350.
[58] *Ibid.*
[59] *Ibid.,* p. 362.
[60] Mahajan, *Political and Cultural History of Ancient India,* pp. 89 and 90.

benevolence, and wisdom in common with others, each god exhibited few distinctive attributes. Clear characterization was further hampered by the practice of invoking deities in pairs—giving gods a sort of dual identity.

The idea that various deities are but different forms of a single divine being, however, never developed into monotheism, for none of the regular sacrifices in the Vedic period were offered to a single god. Finally, in some later hymns of the Rig Veda, we find the deities Aditi and Prajapati identified not only with all the gods, but with nature as well. This brings us to that pantheism which became characteristic of later Indian thought.[61]

As pointed out earlier, there have been interpolations in the Rig Veda. But as yet it is not fully established when these interpolations were made. The interpolations are so obvious that details about them can be unambiguously determined. For example, the Purusa Sukta of Rig Veda (X, 90.12) mentions how the four castes emerged. By determining the period when the caste system was vigorously promulgated, the period of interpolations in the Rig Veda can be established.

Likewise, several concepts such as Purusa (Purusa evedam sarvam), sat (existent), asat (non-existent), kamah (desire) as the first seed of mind, resemble the concepts expressed in Samkhya philosophy. Inclusion of these concepts in the last section of the Rig Veda appears no different in intent than interpolations made in the Yoga Sutra, Samkhyakarika, Upanishads, and the original Gita. It's reasonable to conjecture that final interpolations in the Rig Veda were made at about the period when the original Gita was altered into the Bhagavadgita. It appears, though, that the additions in the Veda preceded other prominent recensions.

Another point which deserves attention is that no god of the Veda is worshipped or recognized as God (the supreme) by the Hindus of present-day India. If any of the Vedic gods had been truly recognized as God, there is every reason to believe that that name would have survived through subsequent generations, especially when the monotheistic ideas gained prominence. But it did not happen.

On the contrary, we find that all the names used to address God (the supreme) as depicted in the Bhagavadgita are non-existent in the Rig Veda. For example, the monotheistic concept related to one supreme God is addressed by the following names in the Bhagavadgita and also by the common people of India: *Isvar, Isvaram, Isam, Parmatma, Parmeshwar, Prabhu (Prabho), Maheshwar,* and *Bhagavan.*

From these it is evident that the concept of one supreme God, as depicted in the Bhagavadgita, did not exist in the Veda. Rather, it came as a new concept and was adopted by the Indian priestly class to revive their religious authority. It is not surprising that the exponents of the new doctrine felt

[61] Macdonell, *op. cit.,* p. xix.

it necessary to declare Vedanta (end of Veda) and Advaita (no twoism or pairs of gods). The door of the Veda was closed when a new door was announced opened.

As mentioned earlier, in the later Vedic period various kinds of literature were created either as commentary or as guidelines for prayer and sacrificial rites. The chanting of the Vedic hymns and the performance of the rites necessitated acquiring and mastering a special skill. Those possessing the knowledge and skills of Vedic rituals began to be called *Brahmans*, which, in due time, became a caste.

Likewise, professional skill was needed to wage warfare. Those possessing the skill began to be called *Kshatriyas*. Similarly, those engaged in trade and commerce began to be called *Vaishyas;* and those doing menial work were called *Sudras*. Thus a system of social division, on the basis of occupational and professional skill, took the form of caste identification. Though the caste system was declared abolished after independence, its practices prevail all over the country except the southern part.

The Caste System

The caste system was not well established during the early Vedic period. Though reference to it is made in the Purusa Sukta in the Tenth Mandala (chapter) of the Rig Veda, this Mandala is an addition of a later period to the original Rig Veda.[62] The caste system in its rigid form developed in the post-Vedic period because of social, racial, ethnic, and occupational differences of the people. To understand this change and development, we must consider the socio-political composition of the people of that time.

We have already discussed that, before the coming of the Aryans, the Dravidians were already settled in various parts of the country. The Dravidians differed from the Aryans in many ways. The Dravidians were dark-skinned, snub-nosed, spoke a different language, had different forms of worship, did not believe in the Vedic gods, and did not perform sacrifices. The Aryans were fair-skinned, warriors, worshipped Vedic gods, and performed sacrifices. The Aryans had to fight the Dravidians in order to conquer and subjugate them.

The Aryans looked down upon the Dravidians and called them by such degrading names as *dasyus* (slaves), *asuras* (uncultured), *pishachas* (demons), and *rakshasas* (monsters). The Aryans separated themselves from the non-Aryans by using the term *varna,* which means colour, kind, class or order. In due time *varna* became a synonym for caste. Since the Aryans were the victors, they enslaved most of the vanquished Dravidians and put

---

[62] *Ibid.*, p. 82. For a comprehensive discussion on the origin of the caste system and views of Indian and Western scholars see J.H. Hutton, *Caste in India* (London: Oxford University Press, 1963 ed.), pp. 170–191.

them to do menial work. These manual laborers began to be called Sudras (the untouchables). In the caste hierarchy they remained at the lowest level.

On the other hand, the Aryan king had to appoint a large number of priests to perform sacrifices and sacred rituals.These appointed priests began to be called *Purohitas,* though selected from the Brahmans. The Purohitas became a class of professionals who knew the Vedas, sacrifices, mode of worship, and also the inner working of the kingship. They became an integral part of the kingship and gradually began to be appointed as ministers, advisers, and counsellors to the king. Thus, as a social group, the Brahmans now controlled both the religious and political centers of power of the society. They began dominating both the social and political spheres and consequently raised their position to the highest level by maintaining the rigidity of the caste system and by creating literature to support their superiority.

In the early stage, the caste system was flexible, and one could change from one to another.[63] Parshurama, a Brahman by birth, became Kshatriya by profession, and Vishvamitra, a Kshatriya by birth, became a Brahman Rishi. There are numerous instances of Vaishyas and Sudras becoming Brahman because of marriages, professional skill, or acquired knowledge.

But the distinction between the upper and lower classes became more marked in the period of the later Vedic texts and the sutras. Mixed dining and intermarriage began to be looked upon with disfavour and eventually were banned outright.[64]

Along with the distinction of the caste system, a form of religion completely dominated and controlled by the Brahmans developed. In the post-Vedic period, the Brahmans as a caste achieved a status superior to all the other castes. They now became the sole masters, deciding what was right and what was wrong, and all the remaining castes had to obey without question.

R.C. Dutt, in his book *Ancient India,* describes very well the repercussions of this changing condition during the post-Vedic period: "The literature of a nation is but the reflection of the national mind; and when the nation turned its religion into forms and ceremonials, religious literature became to some extent inane and lifeless. We miss in the voluminous Brahmans of this age the fervency and earnestness of the Vedic hymns. We find, on the other hand, grotesque reasons given for every minute rite, dogmatic explanations of texts, penances for every breach of form and rule, and elaborate directions for every act and movement of the worshipper. The

---

[63] *Ibid.* See the growth of the caste system and later days position, pp. 118–123; Hutton, *op.cit.,* pp. 92–110.

[64] Sudhansu Bimal Mookherji, *India's Empire of Mind* (Agra: Lakshmi Narain Agarwala, 1973), p. 27.

works show a degree of credulity and submission on the part of the people, and of absolute power on the part of the priests."[65]

The domination of the Brahmans in all aspects of life provoked opposition and revolt. This came in a very bold and courageous way. Before I discuss these developments, here are a few observations on the whole Vedic period.

Observations on the Vedic Period

A notable aspect of Vedic life is that from its earliest period it perpetuated the notion of Man's helplessness and his total dependence on the mercy of some power. The power of Man was not recognized. People believed themselves to be wholly dependent upon deities to whom chants and sacrifices were offered.

The idea that Man has the capability to find solutions for his problems was never expressed in either the Vedic or later-Vedic literature. The central theme running through all this period appears to be that man on his own can do little. Man remained a passive recipient of favor and mercy from various deities.

Second, those who claimed to know how to placate the gods proclaimed their supremacy not only by becoming advisers and ministers to the kings, but also by creating a vast and very often meaningless literature to prove their superiority over all the rest.

With these, a belief was promulgated that a man was born to be either superior or inferior and the status could not be changed. The resultant caste system not only separated people according to profession but condemned the lowest to remain such for life.

Third, we do not find an organized philosophy in Vedic literature. "The songs of the Veda contained but little of philosophy or theosophy, and what the Brahmans call the higher knowledge is not to be sought for in the hymns of the Rishis."[66]

Fourth, we find that the Brahmans were devious. They acquired a habit of interpolating, changing, and interpreting the major works from the Vedic period onward. We will see how this practice was used to alter the original Gita.

Further, we find that instead of creating original literature, they merely revised and reworked the old literature and called it new. For example, they created Sam Veda by taking it from Rig Veda, and made Brahmana by taking a part from the Yajur Veda, which in iteself was taken mostly from the Rig Veda. They wrote commentaries on Vedas and called it Upanishads but did not say who wrote them and when they were written.

[65] Romesh Chunder Dutt, *Ancient India (2000 B.C. to 800 A.D.)* (London: Longmans, Green and Co., 1893), p. 64–65.
[66] Max Müller, *op. cit.*, p. 319.

The Brahmans became an organized, closely linked group, specializing in altering or interpreting the literature which appeared to them necessary for strengthening their position as a class or for supporting their belief system. Their habit continued even during the medieval and modern period. This is evidenced by the countless number of Upanishads created during these periods but claimed to be very, very old.

And lastly, the Brahmans as a caste acquired a sort of monopoly in matters of religious life and practices. "They encouraged superstition and tried to extort as much as they could from the people. Every attempt was made by the Brahman priests to multiply the number of sacrifices which were required to be performed by every householder. The Brahman priests began enriching themselves by extracting money and possessions on various pretexts. The Hindu religion began to be presented in a confusing mass of things which was beyond the comprehension of the man in the street. Due to this acquired wealth, the Brahman priests began living a life of vice and corruption."[67]

These conditions created opposition among the non-Brahman people, especially the Kshatriyas, who did not consider themselves inferior to Brahmans and as a caste were rulers at that time. The opposition to Brahmanic domination expressed itself in a philosophical form which many historians call the Sutra (aphoristic) period of Indian history. I prefer to call this period the Age of Philosophy. We now come to consider the major thinkers and philosophers of the post-Vedic period, whose works are in the Sutras, which means "precise statements."

Max Müller described the significance and the marked difference in this change from Vedic to Sutra: "In the Sutras we see that a change has taken place. Their authors seem to feel that the public which they address will no longer listen to endless theological swaggering. There may have been deep wisdom in the Brahmanas, and their authors may have sincerely believed in all they said; but they evidently calculated on a submissiveness on the part of their pupils or readers which only exists in countries domineered over by priests or professors. The authors of the Sutras have learnt that people will not listen to wisdom unless it is clothed in a garb of clear argument and communicated in intelligible language."[68]

The Age of Darshan (Philosophy)

The proper English translation of Darshan is philosophy. There are six recognized schools of thought in ancient India: *Samkhya Darshan*, *Yoga Darshan*, *Nyaya Darshan*, *Vaisesika Darshan*, *Mimansa Darshan*,

---

[67] Mahajan, *op. cit.*, pp. 131–132.
[68] Max Müller, *op. cit.*, p. 258.

and *Vedanta Darshan*. Besides these widely known philosophies, there is now growing recognition that *Lokayata* (Materialism) was also one of the earliest established schools of rationalistic thought.

The oldest of all these Darshanas is the Samkhya Darshan. It was founded by Kapila, whose period is now generally accepted to be 700 B.C. His philosophy is regarded "as the earliest recorded system of philosophy."[69] We will discuss in detail the contents of this philosophy shortly after describing briefly the other philosophies.

Yoga as a system of philosophy and practice is based on the Samkhya Darshan of Kapila. The earliest major systematic work on Yoga is by Patanjali, whose period is believed to be 400 B.C. Yoga as a system of philosophy is considered to be an expansion of the Samkhya philosophy. To this philosophic base, Patanjali added his own Yoga system.[70] We will discuss the details of this philosophy after describing the Samkhya philosophy.

Nyaya Darshan is called the science of logic. It was founded by Gautama, who lived a century or two after Kapila.[71] According to Nyaya, logic is the basis of all studies. It is a science of acquiring right knowledge through proof based upon perception, inference, analogy, and testimony. This philosophy covers all the basic tenets of Samkhya and recommends Yoga and meditation for acquiring true knowledge.

Vaisesika is the system of atomic philosophy expounded by Kanada. This philosophy came after the Nyaya philosophy of Gautama.[72] The basic theme of this philosophy is that all material substances are aggregates of atoms. The atoms cannot be destroyed; they only take different shapes. This philosophy considers the cause-effect principle of Kapila in depth and explains the origin and functioning of the universe. Neither Nyaya nor Vaisesika accepted the existence of God.

As a reaction to these rational philosophies, the orthodox Hindus "started two new systems of philosophy in consonance with their ancient practices and faith. The Mimansa School insisted on the performance of the ancient Vedic rites, and the Vedanta school proclaimed once more the belief in a Universal Soul, which was first inculcated in the Upanishads."[73]

Lokayata, known as materialism, is now recognized to be very old. Though Brihaspati is generally considered to be the founder of this school, the name of Charvaka is popularly known and many consider him to be

[69] R.C. Dutt, *Ancient India*, p. 96.
[70] *Ibid.*
[71] *Ibid.*, p. 97. See also Ganganath Jha, *Gautama's Nyayasutras* (Poona: Oriental Book Agency, 1939), pp. V–IX.
[72] *Ibid.* For details of this philosophy see Nandalal Sinha, *Vaisesika Sutras of Kanada* (Trans.) (Bahadurganj, India: The Panini office, Bhuvaneswari Asrama, 1911), pp. I–XX.
[73] *Ibid.*

its founder. His period is dated as 550 B.C.[74] Riepe considers that the golden period of Indian philosophical thought "extended from 500 B.C. or slightly earlier to A.D. 500 or slightly later" and it was in this period that "naturalistic" or "protoscientific" thoughts were prevalent in India.[75]

According to Chandradhar Sharma, "No original work of this school is extant. It is therefore very difficult to have a correct idea of this school. Our chief sources of information are the accounts which are given in the works of the other schools. But this is done only to refute materialism. Thus, we find the tenets of materialism often misrepresented. The weak points in this school are exaggerated and the good points are omitted. So we get only a faint caricature and not a true picture of this school."[76] Debiprasad Chattopadhyaya expresses the view that "in the ocean of uncertainty concerning the lost Lokayata the only piece of definite information is that we are left with no original work on it. Modern scholars do not agree among themselves even on the question whether any such work ever existed at all."[77]

Considering the historical evidence available, it cannot be denied that Lokayata as a system flourished in ancient India. This is evident from the fact that the Buddhist text Divyavadana refers to Lokayata "as a special branch of study which had a *bhasya* (commentary) and a *pravachana* (annotations) on it." Likewise, the Arthashastra (300 B.C.); Katyayana (300 B.C.) the author of Varttika Sutra; Chandrakirti in his Prajna Shastra; and Aryadeva's Satasastra have all referred to Lokayata.[78] There are references to this doctrine in the Mahabharata (Santiparva, verses 1414 and 1430–1442; and Salyaparva 3619).[79] According to Radhakrishnan, "The classic authority on the materialist theory is said to be the sutras of Brihaspati, which have perished. Our chief sources are the polemical works of other schools."[80]

The main tenets of Charvaka philosophy, as we know them, can be genuinely summarized: "There is no heaven, no final liberation, nor any soul in another world. Perception *(pratyaksha)* is the only means of valid knowledge. The validity of inference is rejected, as it is a mere leap in the dark. Testimony is not a valid means of knowledge as inference would become dependent on it. Induction is uncertain and deduction is argument in circle."[81]

---

[74] See Dale Maurice Riepe, *The Naturalistic Tradition In Indian Thought* (Seattle: University of Washington Press, 1961), p. 14. A comprehensive presentation on Lokayata and Charvaka is given by Debiprasad Chattopadhyaya in his *Lokayata: A Study in Ancient Indian Materialism* (Delhi: People's Publishing House, 1959).

[75] *Ibid.*, p. 6.

[76] Chandradhar Sharma, *Indian Philosophy* (Banaras: Nand Kishore & Bros., 1952), pp. 41–42.

[77] Chattopadhyaya, *op. cit.*, p. 6ff.

[78] *Ibid.*

[79] See Radhakrishnan, *Indian Philosophy* (London: George Allen & Unwin Ltd., 1966), Vol. I, p. 278.

[80] *Ibid.*

[81] Sharma, *op. cit.*, pp. 40–50.

Charvaka did not espouse the idea of soul, God, and heaven. It admitted the existence of only four elements: earth, water, fire, and air. It did not accept ether as the fifth element. It rejected the authority of Veda and denounced the priesthood of the Brahman. According to it, "Life is the end of life." Death alone is liberation.

Commenting on materialism, Radhakrishnan writes, "The materialist theory had a good deal to do with the repudiation of the old religion of custom and magic . . . Materialism signifies the declaration of the spiritual independence of the individual and the rejection of the principle of authority. Nothing need be accepted by the individual which does not find its evidence in the movement of reason."[82]

Now that the major schools of philosophy have been reviewed, we will discuss in depth the Samkhya philosophy, which is not only the earliest of all but also the foundation of Yoga as a cohesive system. A comprehensive discussion of Kapila is imperative because all his basic ideas together with the major concepts of Yoga were presented in the original Gita. Without a proper understanding of Kapila, one would not be able to discern the contents of the original Gita.

It is necessary to use numerous Sanskrit words, many of which cannot be satisfactorily translated into English. I will attempt to provide roughly equivalent words in parentheses.

Samkhya Darshan (Philosophy)

There have been countless books written by both Indian and Western scholars on Samkhya philosophy, but only a few have done justice to it. Some have tried to see theism in it; others have called it atheistic.

The most noteworthy of the early scholarly work on Samkhya philosophy is by German scholars. Likewise, some recent works by American scholars are very objective and reliable in terms of an accurate presentation of the philosophy.

Larson in his book *Classical Samkhya* tells us that "from the end of the nineteenth century and continuing into the first decades of the twentieth, the most distinctive work in regard to the history and interpretation of the Samkhya was that of Richard Garbe, the German scholar. His work included a number of definitive editions and translations of key Samkhya texts, as well as some major studies regarding the interpretation of the Samkhya system."[83] Let us see what Garbe has to say about the origin of Samkhya philosophy and about Kapila, its founder.

[82] Radhakrishnan, *op. cit.*, p. 283.
[83] Gerald James Larson, *Classical Samkhya: An Interpretation of its History and Meaning* (Delhi: Motilal Banarsidass,1979), pp. 15–16.

Garbe cites Kautilya's Arthasastra, which refers to three systems of 'philosophy' or 'science' current at that time. The Arthasastra period is about 300 B.C. The three philosophies cited in Arthasastra are: Samkhya, Yoga, and Lokayata (materialism). Garbe says that Samkyha is one of the oldest philosophies of the Indian tradition and points out that other systems such as Nyaya, Vaisesika, Mimansa, and Vedanta had not at that time been elaborately formulated. He goes on to say that the sage Kapila was the historical founder of the system and that the doctrine of Kapila is a Kshatriya philosophy.[84]

Garbe points out that none of the ideas of Samkhya can be found in the Brahmanas and Aranyakas or in any pre-Buddhistic or Brahmanical literature.[85] He asserts that these ideas originated in non-Brahmanical circles. Garbe cites evidence for the kshatriya origin of the Samkhya system and says that "in the Bhagavata Purana (III, XXI 26) Kapila is said to descend from a Rajarsi" (royal kshatriya sage).[86]

According to Garbe, Kapila did his work in Kapilavastu (where Gautama Buddha was born), and the Samkhya system is the work of one man.[87] Commenting on those who have tried to link Kapila with Brahmanical thought, Garbe states that ". . . the doctrine of Kapila, although later numbered as a part of the great wisdom or knowledge of Brahmanism, was yet originally unbrahmanical —i.e., a kshatriya philosophy."[88]

While discussing the special features of Samkhya philosophy, Garbe points out:[89]

(i) A god or gods play no part in the system of Kapila;
(ii) it seeks to solve the problems of the universe and man simply by means of reason;
(iii) Samkhya is much closer to naturalism and rationalism in the history of thought.

In *The Philosophy of Ancient India*, Garbe expresses great admiration for Kapila, saying, "In Kapila's doctrine, for the first time in the history of the world, the complete independence and freedom of the human mind, its full confidence in its own powers were exhibited."[90] Macdonell, in *A History of Sanskrit Literature,* observes that "of the six systems which are accounted orthodox, no less than four were originally atheistic, and one remained so throughout. The strangeness of this fact disappears when we reflect that the only conditions of orthodoxy in India were the recognition

[84] *Ibid.,* p. 17.
[85] *Ibid.,* p. 19.
[86] Richard Garbe. *Die Samkhya-Philosophie* (Leipzig: H. Haessel Verlag, 1917), p. 13.
[87] *Ibid.,* see Ch. II, pp. 46–51.
[88] The original is in German in Garbe's *Die Samkhya Philosophie*, p. 13. The translation is quoted from Larson, *op. cit.*, p.17.
[89] Garbe, *op. cit.*, p. 253–260.
[90] Richard Garbe, *The Philosophy of Ancient India* (Chicago: Open Court Publishing Company., 1897), p. 30.

of the class privileges of the Brahman caste and a nominal acknowledgment of the infallibility of the Veda, neither full agreement with Vedic doctrines nor the confession of belief in the existence of God being required. With these two limitations the utmost freedom of thought prevailed in Brahmanism. Hence the boldest philosophical speculation and conformity with the popular religion went hand in hand, to a degree which has never been equalled in any other country."[91]

It was against this background of free thinking that Kapila developed his Samkhya philosophy. Expressing his admiration towards Samkhya, Macdonell asserts that for the first time in the history of the world it "asserted the complete independence of the human mind and attempted to solve its problems solely by the aid of reason."[92]

With this background, let us now consider in depth what this Samkhya philosophy is and how it relates to universal man.

The Theme of Samkhya Philosophy

Kapila himself states the theme of his philosophy in the first verse (sutra) of Samkhya Darshan. Indeed, the central concern of Samkhya philosophy is how to liberate the individual from threefold misery (dukha) and enable him to achieve happiness (sukha).

Kapila points out that there are three types of sorrow (dukha): (i) personal (atmika), (ii) worldly or social (bhautika) and (iii) cosmic, originating in the forces of nature (daivika). "That is to say, suffering is brought about by factors relating to the bodily or mental make-up of man himself, by factors coming from man's social environment, and by factors coming from the forces of nature."[93]

After identifying the sources of sorrow, Kapila provides the means of eliminating them. At the outset of his treatise, Kapila rejects the Vedic premises that ritualistic compliance will eliminate sorrow (dukha), saying that they do not provide reliable or genuine relief.

Since in the Vedic tradition it was customary to drink soma (a kind of alcohol distilled from indigenous herbs) and slaughter animals in sacrificial ceremonies, Kapila considered these methods of removing sorrow to be impure, destructive, and excessive.

Kapila claims in sutra II that a superior method for terminating sorrow is to acquire scientific knowledge (vijnanata) of the manifest (vyakta), the unmanifest (avyakta), and the knower (purusha).

Kapila expounds two theories for achieving liberation from sorrow: (i) the theory of samyak Jnana (proper knowledge); and (ii) the theory of

[91] Arthur Anthony Macdonell, A History of Sanskrit Literature (New York: Haskell House Publishers Ltd., 1968), p. 385–386.
[92] Ibid.
[93] Larson, op.cit., p. 155.

satkaryavada (right action). To present clear understanding of Kapila's theories, I will first discuss his basic concepts of prakriti (nature), purusha (man, the knower) and gunas (the forces or constituents of nature).

Prakriti (nature) is singular, eternal, unconscious, and uncreated by any power or entity. Kapila describes nature as *mulaprakriti*, which can be translated as primordial, basic, or original. It is impartial and non-intelligent. It is generative and works for the benefit of purusha.

Purusha (the individual) is numerous, mortal, conscious, and non-generative (i.e., cannot cause the emergence of things). Kapila does not go into any discussion about the origin of man. He accepts man's existence as he accepts the existence of nature.

Purusha witnesses in a subjective manner and observes the various manifestations of prakriti. The presence of purusha renders meaningful the manifestations and workings of nature. Purusha and prakriti cooperate with one another like a blind man and a lame man: each one benefits from the capabilities of the other. The basic reason nature functions is because of the presence of purusha.

Gunas can be translated as qualities or forces of nature. They are indestructible constituents of nature and function in a state of constant flux and change, eternally at work in nature and also in man. Gunas exist in three forms: *sattva, rajas,* and *tamas.* Each of these gunas possesses a distinct and separate quality of its own.

Sattva is characterized by harmony, equilibrium, perfection, clarity, goodness, quietness, and illumination. In man, its presence is demonstrated by knowledge, virtue, and the possession of power.

Rajas is characterized by activation, mobility, stimulation, passion, and pain. Rajas can be understoood as the source of all activity. When a man is dominated by this quality, he is on the move most of the time, engages in restless effort, and seeks a life of enjoyment which results in pain. Unless opposed by other gunas, it creates disorder and suffering.

Tamas is characterized by heaviness, darkness, torpor, and insensibility. When dominated by tamas, a man resists activity and is indifferent and apathetic. He is lazy, dull, and ignorant.

These gunas are invisible. We have to understand their nature and functioning through inference. Since the gunas are opposed to one another, they are in an eternal process of transmutation. They dominate, support, activate, and interact with one another.

Though in constant flux, the gunas attempt to reach a state of equilibrium which is called *samyavastha.* The constant opposition among the gunas disrupts the state of equilibrium, and this instability gives rise to creation in its many forms.

The concept of guna is comparable to the atom with its proton, electron, and neutron. Sattva can be said to resemble the proton, rajas the electron, and tamas the neutron. The modern scientific conception of the construction of the atom has been compared by Catalina with the three forms of the gunas. As "the proton provides the coalescence or form of the atom, the electron gives us energy and the neutron provides the mass."[94] The gunas fulfill similar funtions.

Catalina explains the interaction of the gunas by referring to water, which is "composed of the atoms of hydrogen and oxygen in the ratio of two to one, and is generally written with the symbols H_2O = water. The two different atoms act quite differently when independent of each other. Also, if the ratio of these atoms is changed, we find that we have a new product such as hydrogen peroxide (H_2O_2), etc."

Let us now return to Kapila's two theories for achieving liberation from sorrow.

The Samkhya Theory of Knowledge

According to Samkhya there are three modes of obtaining correct knowledge: perception *(pratyaksha)*, inference *(anumana)*, and reliable authority *(aptavachana)*.

Perception involves the operation of five sense organs and three internal organs: intelligence *(buddhi)*, self-awareness or self-consciousness *(ahamkara)*, and mind *(manas)*. It is the act of ascertainment of objects through contact with sense organs. The three internal organs function simultaneously when any of the sense organs perceives an object.

With respect to that which is not present in perception, the function of the three (buddhi, ahamkara, and manas) internal organs is based upon a prior perception. The external and internal organs and the senses accomplish their own particular function in coordination with one another. The only motive is to serve the purusha. There is no other reason that motivates the thirteen-fold instrument (buddhi, ahamkara, manas, five sense organs, and five action organs) (sutra XXXI). While the external organs (five sense organs and five action organs) function in the present time, the internal three organs *(antahkarana)* function in all the three temporal phases —past, present and future.

The way these instruments function is explained in sutra XXXV. The senses perceive objects without interpretation or judgment and bring such percepts to the mind, which synthesizes them and takes them to self-awareness (ahamkara), which in turn refers them to purusha (self), and as objects of self-consciousness they come before intelligence (buddhi), which ascertains their nature. Since the buddhi together with the other internal organs (ahamkara and manas) comprehend every object, this threefold

[94] Dr. Francis V. Catalina, *A Study of the Self Concept of Sankhya Yoga Philosophy* (Delhi: Munshiram Manoharlal, 1968), pp. 32–33.

internal instrument functions as a door-keeper, and the remaining ten (external organs) are like the doors.

These organs are different from one another and they are distinct specifications or modifications of the gunas. They are like a lamp disclosing all the objects. The ahamkara, manas, and the ten senses present the whole (of the object perceived) to the buddhi and illuminate it like a lamp for the sake of the purusha (sutra XXXVI).

Inference is derived from experience. Though Kapila does not discuss kinds of inference, ancient logicians generally drew three distinctions : antecedent *(purvavat)*, subsequent *(sheshvat)* and analogous *(samanya)*. The knowledge of things beyond the senses is by means of inference based on analogy. For example, by seeing the rising clouds, rain is inferred (antecedent); by tasting some milk from its container, the quality of the rest of the milk is inferred (subsequent); by noticing apple trees in blossom at one place, it is inferred that apple trees elsewhere have also blossomed (analogous).

Reliable authority means unimpeachable verbal testimony or a trustworthy source. According to Larson, reliable authority "is probably used primarily with respect to the tradition of Samkhya teachers."[95]

Perception may be impaired for various reasons. Kapila gives eight reasons for the obstruction of perception (sutra VII): because something is too far away; or is too close; because of an injured sense organ; because of non-steadiness of the mind; because something is exceedingly minute or subtle; because of some intrusion between an organ and the object to be perceived; because of masking (as when one cannot see the planets because of the brightness of the sun); and because of confusion with what is similar.

Kapila goes on to explain (sutra VIII) that the failure to perceive nature (prakriti) is because of its subtlety but not because it does not exist. Nature is perceived through its effects. The intellect, self-consciousness, and the subtle elements (tanmatras) are the effects of nature, but they work also as nature. The process of emergence of various organs and the way they work is explained by the principle of twenty-five elements (to be discussed shortly).

After describing the three means of acquiring knowledge, Kapila explains prakriti (nature), purusha, and the gunas. By understanding these fundamentals, the purusha would acquire proper knowledge of himself, the forces of nature, and the social environment in which he lives. Based on this knowledge, he would act properly to derive the desired result and thus ward off suffering. Let us now consider how the universe of man operates in relationship to nature.

Kapila is not concerned with explaining how purusha and nature came into contact with one another. Larson clarifies this point by saying, "The

---

[95] Larson, *op. cit.*, p. 159.

task is not to explain how *prakriti* and *purusha* first came together. The task, rather, is to describe the nature of human existence and suffering in view of the fact that *prakriti* and *purusha* are together, and then to offer a solution."[96]

According to Kapila, there is complete separation of purusha and nature. They are in proximity to one another, but not in actual contact. Because of the proximity, a kind of interplay or dialectic occurs. Primordial nature (mulaprakriti) begins to undergo transformation or modification which is manifest in the world, and the purusha begins to witness this transformation.[97]

The reason prakriti functions is because of the presence of purusha. Though prakriti functions for the benefit of purusha, the latter's proximity to the former causes conditions, such as seeing the manifestations of nature and changes in self and society, which lead to suffering. The suffering arises because the purusha feels as if he is responsible for all those changes, which in fact he is not.

Kapila, in his sutra LV, explains that pain is in the nature of things. The purusha experiences suffering arising out of decay and death until his deliverence from bodily existence. In sutras LVI to LX Kapila explains how mulaprakriti functions for the enjoyment and liberation of purusha. As milk benefits the calf without having conscious intent to do so, similarly prakriti works unconsciously to benefit purusha.

In order to make us understand the relationship of prakriti and purusha, Kapila explains certain qualities of both. Prakriti is non-intelligent. Therefore, prakriti does not exist for its own sake. There must be someone else, some intelligent being, for whose benefit prakriti manifests itself and undergoes transformation. This intelligent being is the purusha. What is thus witnessed by the purusha is the manifest world of nature.

Therefore, purusha is held responsible for both his suffering and his release. By understanding the process of change and by acting in accordance with cause-effect principles, he can eliminate suffering. Thus, purusha by his own effort *(purusartha)* achieves liberation from suffering. When purusha acquires this knowledge and acts accordingly, his suffering ceases.

As mentioned earlier, purusha and prakriti cooperate like a blind man and a lame man, each one benefitting from the capacities of the other. From this association of the conscious (purusha) and unconscious (prakriti), a process of creation emerges which is explained by the principle of 25 *tattvas*, which can be translated as elements, constituents, or primary substances. (For details see the illustration on the following page.)

---

[96] *Ibid.*, p. 172.
[97] *Ibid.*, p. 173.

The Principle of Twenty-Five Tattvas

Nature (prakriti) when in proximity to man (purusha) undergoes trans-formation, and from this process intellect (buddhi) emerges. Buddhi is characterized by exertion and resolution *(adhyavasaya)*.

Virtue, knowledge, motivation, and possession of power constitute its sattva quality. In opposition to these are its tamas quality (sutra XXIII). Buddhi produces or brings about every enjoyment of the purusha and, moreover, it distinguishes the subtle difference between the prakriti and purusha.

As the transformation continues, ahamkara (self-consciousness, self-awareness) emerges from buddhi. Ahamkara signifies one's personal iden-tity or opinion about one's own ability. Up to this point, evolution is successive as each element (tattva) emerges from a prior element.

From ahamkara, a group of sixteen tattvas emerges which are of two categories: (i) the group of eleven; (ii) the group of five. The group of eleven includes the mind *(manas)*, the five sense organs (buddhi-indriyas) and the five action organs *(karma-indriyas)*. The group of five includes the five subtle elements *(tanmatras)*: sound, touch, form, taste and smell.

The Chart of Twenty-Five Tattvas (Elements) of Kapila

(1)
PURUSHA

Consciousness, intelligence. The one
who witnesses the manifestations
of nature.

(2)
PRAKRITI

Non-consciousness, non-intelligence.
It has three constituents: rajas,
tamas, sattva; and two states:
unmanifest (avyakta) and manifest
(vyakta).

(3)
BUDDHI (intellect)

emerges due to proximity of
purusha and prakriti

(4)
AHAMKARA (self-awareness)

emerges from buddhi

group of eleven (5–15)
(emerges from ahamkara)

(5)
MANAS
(mind)

functions as sense organs
and action organs

(6–10)
BUDDHI-INDRIYAS
(sense organs)

eyes, ears, nose,
tongue, skin

(11–15)
KARMA-INDRIYAS
(action organs)

hands, feet, speech,
excretory organ,
generative organ

group of five (16–20)
(emerges from ahamkara)

(16–20)
TANMATRAS
(subtle elements)

sound (shabda)
touch (sparsha)
form (rupa)
taste (rasa)
smell (gandha)

(21–25)
MAHABHUTAS
(gross elements)
(emerges from tanmatras)

space (emerges from sound)
wind (emerges from touch)
fire (emerges from form)
water (emerges from taste)
earth (emerges from smell)

Before going further, a clarification of two words is necessary: prakriti and *vikriti*. We know that prakriti is generative, but purusha is not. What is generated or what emerges from prakriti is called vikriti by Kapila (sutra III). Purusha is neither prakriti nor vikriti. There are certain vikritis (products of nature) which also generate and thereby work as nature. In other words, certain of the tattvas work both as vikriti and prakriti.

With this clarification, we can easily understand that buddhi, which is a product of nature (vikriti), generates ahamkara (self-awareness), and therefore it works as prakriti. Likewise, ahamkara, though itself a vikriti, generates a group of sixteen and thereby functions as prakriti.

The significant point to note here is that, out of this group of sixteen, the group of eleven (mind, five sense organs, and five action organs) is not generative. No element (tattva) emerges from any of them. But the group of five from the group of sixteen does generate and thereby functions as prakriti.

The group of five which emerges from ahamkara is called tanmatra (subtle elements). They are: sound, touch, form, taste, and smell. This group of five tanmatras generates five gross elements which are called *mahabhutas*. Each tanmatra generates a single mahabhuta. Thus, sound generates space, touch generates wind, form produces fire, taste produces water, and smell produces earth.

The tanmatras (five subtle elements) are non-specific, as they are non-differentiated. The mahabhutas (five gross elements) are specific. The distinctions of the subtle elements are not observable by us, and therefore they have been called non-specific *(avishesha)* (sutra XXXVIII). These five non-specific subtle elements produce five specific gross elements *(pancha bhutta)* which are the objects of the senses of men and are characterized as soothing, turbulent, and delusive or deprived of sensibility. That which is soothing *(shanta)* is of sattva guna kind; that which is turbulent *(ghora)* is of rajas guna kind; and that which is delusive *(mudha)* is of tamas guna kind.

This whole creation—from buddhi (intellect) down to the specific gross elements—is brought about by prakriti (nature) for the sake of the liberation of each purusha. Prakriti does it as if it were working for its own benefit. Kapila says in sutra LVIII that, just as a man in the world engages in actions for the fulfillment of a desire, so also does the prakriti function for the sake of the release *(vimoksha)* of the purusha.

As a dancer ceases from the dance after having performed for the audience, so also prakriti ceases after having manifested herself to the purusha. Kapila goes on to explain (sutras LXI to LXIII) that no one, therefore, is bound; no one is released; and no one transmigrates. Only prakriti in its various forms transmigrates, is bound, and is released. Prakriti binds herself by means of seven forms (rupa); she releases herself by means of one form for the sake of each purusha.

With the cessation of prakriti, the purusha, on attaining separation from the body, attains liberation *(kaivalya)* which is both certain and final (sutra LXVIII). Kapila devotes a number of verses to explaining how the life (the existing body) comes to an end. These verses can be summed up by saying that, when nature ceases to function in our bodies, they come to an end. The tanmatras (subtle elements) go to tanmatras and the gross body mixes with the gross elements. The existing body at the end takes just another form (rupa).

Before discussing another important theory of Kapila, it needs to be pointed out that "the doctrines of Samkhya philosophy are inextricably involved with one another, and one must take them together in order to get the full force of the Samkhya point of view."[98] The basic ideas of the preceding pages should be remembered when considering the theory of right action.

The Samkhya Theory of Right Action (Satkaryavada)

The basic assumption of this theory is that the effect exists (before the operation) in the cause. The theory discusses various aspects of the cause-and-effect relationship and shows its relevance to purusha (man). For a better understanding of this theory, let us first be clear about the meanings of its two major concepts, cause and effect.

The cause is what produces an effect or result. It could also mean the reason, motive, or purpose for an action. What is done to bring about something can be considered a cause. Or we can say that from which something is produced is the cause. In short, that which makes is the cause and that which is made is the effect.

The cause could be material or non-material. When something is produced from certain material, it is a material cause. For example, when butter, yogurt (curd), or cheese is produced from milk, the milk is primary in this case and the agent who produces some product from it is secondary. In this case, the tools, knowledge of production and its quality, all depend on having the milk first. Therefore, in the case of material cause, having the proper material is primary.

There are things whose production does not depend upon this or that material but primarily on the knowledge, talent, skill, and power of the individual. For example, when an athlete competes in some sport or game, when a musician sings a song or an artist paints a picture, that production or performance (effect) is due to that person's respective human qualities.

[98] Larson, *op. cit.*, p. 166.

Here the availability or absence of any material thing is secondary. What is primary is the quality and the talent of the person concerned. In such cases, the cause is the human cause.

Whether material or non-material, there is always an agent of the cause who brings the effect. The agent of a certain cause may vary from one person to several. When a collective effort of a group is involved in achieving some result (effect), the cause is corporate.

Likewise, there could be areas (fields of operation) where the material cause and the human cause are both instrumental in achieving the effect, such as farming. Here the quality of material, such as seed, is as important as the knowledge of farming. There could be numerous materials, such as fertilizer, pesticide, water, proper soil, etc., which will have some impact on the production (effect). In such cases, the agency of operation has to consider the material cause and the human cause together for a desirable effect.

With these clarifications, let us now consider the fundamentals of the theory of right action (satkaryavada). Kapila explains the basic tenets of his theory in sutra IX. (The examples are mine):

(i) *Asat akarnat*: That which does not exist cannot be brought into existence by any means. For example, oil cannot be extracted from sugar cane, or sugar cannot be produced from salt.

(ii) *Upadana grahanat*: An appropriate material cause must be selected for any given effect or product. For example, for making yogurt, milk must be used and not water.

(iii) *Sarva sambhava abhavat*: There is no production of all by all. Production of everything is not possible by every means. For example, a garment cannot be woven from clay or gold cannot be produced from silver.

(iv) *Shaktasya shakya karnat*: The agent can produce only what he is capable or competent of producing. This refers to the capability of the agent and his tools. For example, a tailor or his tools cannot produce a clay water pot, nor can a potter with his tools produce a garment.

(v) *Karana bhavat*: Like is produced from like. As is the character of the cause so is the character of the effect. For example, wheat flour from wheat, rice flour from rice.

After describing the basic principles of the theory, Kapila points out the variability in action of the individuals because of the variability in their *bhavas*. Bhava can be translated as disposition, mental inclination, motivation, nature, or temperament. According to Kapila, these bhavas subsist in the intellect of the purusha; they are inborn and also acquired.

These bhavas are eight in number.[99] They are noted below together with their meanings:

(i) Dharma
(virtue, duty, responsibility, justice)

(ii) Adharma
(vice, evil)

(iii) Jnana
(knowledge)

(iv) Ajnana
(ignorance)

(v) Raga
(attachment, affection, joy, desire, passion)

(vi) Viraga
(disinclination, discontent, disaffection, absence of desire)

(vii) Aishvarya
(power, affluence, wealth or supremacy)

(viii) Anaishvarya
(impotence, feebleness)

Kapila explains the consequences of these bhavas (motivations) in sutras XLIV and XLV, saying: when people work with dharma bhava (virtuous motive), there is upward movement (betterment, prosperity); when working with adharma bhava (vice or evil motive), there is downward movement (degradation). When people work motivated by jnana bhava (knowledge), there is liberation; but when working with ajnana bhava (ignorance), there is bondage. When working with raga bhava (desire), there is activation and creativity; when people work with viraga bhava (without desire), it is like merging with nature or passively following nature. When people work with aishvarya bhava (power), there is destruction of obstacles; its reverse, obstruction, is the result when working with anaishvarya bhava (feebleness).

Kapila explains another important aspect of this theory in sutra LVIII saying that one takes action for the fulfillment of a desire (autsukya nivritt-yartham). According to Kapila, just as people in the world engage in various actions for the fulfillment of their desires, so also does prakriti function for the sake of liberation of purusha.

The fulfillment of a desire depends upon the fruit of action. If the result of action (effect) is satisfactory, fulfillment of desire comes, which means happiness. When the result of action (effect) is unsatisfactory, there is unfulfillment of desire, which means unhappiness. In other words, happiness (sukha) depends on obtaining satisfactory fruits of action. In the absence of beneficial fruits of action, there is misery (dukha).

---

[99] Kapila has mentioned only eight bhavas. The interpolators made it fifty in number. For details on original and interpolation, see the section on "Interpolation in Samkhya Karika."

The purusha of Kapila, having knowledge of himself, of the world around him, and of nature, can improve, modify, and inculcate what is pertinent and necessary for creating desirable effects in whatever he is engaged. If, by selecting or modifying the material cause, the fruits of action can be bettered, he possesses the ability to do so. He should know that prakriti works for the sole purpose of enjoyment, nourishment, and happiness of every purusha. Therefore, in selecting, altering, or modifying the material cause, he will be supported by prakriti.

If the fruits of action depend upon improving, correcting, developing, acquiring certain skills, knowledge, and technique, then he possesses the power and ability to do so. It has already been mentioned that all three of his internal organs (intellect, consciousness, and mind) and all ten of his external organs (five sense organs and five action organs) work co-operatively for the sole purpose of providing him enjoyment and betterment.

It should also be remembered that the three gunas (rajas, tamas, and sattva), prakriti, and all the faculties of the purusha work and function to fulfill one aim, the happiness of the purusha. When the purusha, armed with the proper knowledge of self, society, and nature, acts in accordance with the theory of satkaryavada, he produces the desired results. Then he is capable of finding solutions to human problems and thereby is able to eradicate suffering. Man, on his own, then achieves happiness.

An Observation on Samkhya Philosophy

The most significant aspect of Samkhya philosophy is that it considers the problems of man as man. It does not differentiate men from one another on the basis of birth, race, or beliefs. Every man is equal, can acquire proper knowledge, and can be educated to act in accordance with the principles of right action (satkarya-vada).

On the other hand, in the absence of proper knowledge and right action, a man is bound to suffer from the misery arising out of the three sources of sorrow: self, nature, and society. Therefore, man himself is responsible for both suffering as well as release.

If we consider the problems of people around the world, it would be found that the three basic sources of suffering remain unchanged. It will remain so in the future. What Kapila raised as a problem remains even now a valid universal question, and the remedy he offered is a valid solution today. Therefore, the study of Samkhya in its undistorted form is very relevant and becomes an important endeavor, regardless of who we are and where we reside. Since "Samkhya seeks to find an answer to the problem of suffering in human life",[100] its study is of enduring value and relevance.

[100] Larson, *op. cit.*, p. 196.

Interpolation in Samkhya Philosophy

Before we move on to other thinkers, it is appropriate to consider inter-polation in the Samkhya philosophy and also the authenticity of its text-books. The most authentic text on Samkhya philosophy is Samkhya Karika written by Ishvarkrisna.

"The Samkhya-Karika is the oldest systematic manual which has been preserved. As it was translated into Chinese by a Buddhist monk, Pa-rmartha, between 557 and 569 A.D. (the date of his death), this translation has fortunately been preserved and proves the authenticity of the Sanskrit text as it now stands."[101] "It cannot belong to a later century than the fifth, and may be still older."[102]

There are altogether 73 sutras (verses) in this Samkhya Karika. Thirteen sutras have been interpolated. The interpolated sutras occur at two places: nine in the latter part of the treatise and four at the end of it.

The interpolation of four sutras (LXX to LXXIII) at the end of the treatise is so obvious that it does not require any explanation. There is no philosophic discourse in these four verses. They talk about the succession of Samkhya teachers and make a defensive claim that the contents of the Karika are not defective. The contents of these verses are in no way a part of Samkhya philosophy, nor is there any reason to accept their version of Samkhya teachers. Because of this, there are scholars who do not accept these four verses (from 70 to 73) and consider only the remaining 69 verses original.[103]

Among the remaining nine interpolated verses, six are related to the concept of bhavas. These six verses (XLVI–LI) have been interpolated to enlarge the basic idea of bhavas discussed by Kapila in sutras XLII to XLV. As we have already mentioned, Kapila talks about eight bhavas (basic strivings of man, or motivation) and explains their impact on human modes of action and their resultant consequences.

The eight bhavas were later expanded to 50. The verses enumerating the 50 bhavas are XLVI (46) to LI (51). In these six interpolated verses, the bhavas are described as: five kinds of ignorance, error (viparyaya); twenty-eight kinds of incapacity (asakti); nine kinds of complacency or satisfaction (tusti); and eight kinds of perfection (siddhi).

The enlargement of the numbers of bhavas and their categorization do not provide any convincing and understandable notion about them. They are meaningless terms and do not fit into the theme of Samkhya. According to Larson, "The six intervening verses discuss fifty bhavas, but the doctrine in these intervening verses is decidedly different from the doctrine of eight

---

[101] A.B. Keith, *A History of the Samkhya Philosophy* (Delhi: Nag Publishers, 1975), pp. 78–79.
[102] Dr. Catalina, *op. cit.*, pp. 14–15.
[103] T.G. Mainkar, *The Samkhya Karika of Isvarakrisna* (Poona: Oriental Book Agency, 1964), pp. 29–32.

bhavas. This peculiar contradiction in the text led Keith to suggest that *Karikas* XLVI–LI represent a later interpolation."[104]

Keith goes into much detail in describing the contents of the interpolated verses and concludes saying that "the verses (46–51) which deal with them are a later interpolation, added at or before the time when the last three verses were added and the statement made that the tract numbered seventy verses."[105]

The interpolation of the three sutras (LII, LIII and LIV) has been done cleverly to create an impression that Samkhya philosophy is in tune with belief, faith, and Vedic tradition. Sutra LII continues the discussion on bhavas and talks about a twofold creation called *Linga* (the existing body) and bhavas. The sutra says that the Linga cannot function without the bhavas nor the bhavas without the Linga. Therefore, a twofold creation operates.

The content of this sutra is alien to Kapila's thought. The purusha of Kapila exists not because of bhavas or any other factor. If bhavas were that important and decisive in the maintenance of purusha, they would have been included in his principle of 25 tattvas discussed earlier. The different bhavas are only the motivating factors and not essential to the existence of purusha. We may conclude that sutra LII is not a part of the original.

Sutras LIII and LIV talk about three different spheres in the universe and introduce post-Vedic Brahmanic theistic ideas. A division is made between divine *(daiva)*, human, and sub-human bodies and says that the upper sphere, where Brahma resides, is dominated by sattva guna; the middle universe, where human beings reside, is dominated by rajas guna; and in the lower sphere where the sub-humans reside, there is a predominance of tamas guna.

As we have learned, in the whole of Samkhya philosophy there is no talk of spheres. Kapila talks about purusha and prakriti without going into any discussion about the origin of man. The gunas which are constituents of prakriti are not divided into spheres.

Further, we have discussed in chapter one the idea that, during the post-Vedic period, Brahma was added to the list of thirty-three Vedic gods and during the Vedic period they had made a three-fold division of the universe: heaven, atmosphere, and Earth. Each of the spheres had its own gods, which were eleven in number. Keeping this in mind, it is easy to see why the interpolators inserted Brahma and the concept of the three-fold division of the universe in the Samkhya philosophy.

The main purpose of the interpolators was to support the extensive adulteration of the original Gita. Since Kapila is the primary thinker whose

---

[104] Larson, *op. cit.*, p. 193.
[105] A.B. Keith, *op. cit.*, p. 97.

thoughts have permeated all later work on philosophy and Yoga and other branches of Indian cultural life, he was made to appear to be in support of Brahmanic theistic views.

In these interpolated verses, such theological terms as *dan* (donation, charity), *siddhi* (mysterious power), *manusha* (man, instead of purusha of Kapila), *daiva* (divine or gods) and *Brahma* (one of the numerous gods) have been inserted to alter the rationalistic character of Samkhya philosophy. These ideas neither fit into the language nor into the conceptual structure of Samkhya. Hence, they do not belong to the original.

On the basis of evidence cited above, we conclude that the Samkhya Karika has only 60 original verses. Judged on the basis of linguistic and conceptual evidence, the Samkhya philosophy is fully contained in these 60 verses and the remaining 13 verses must be excluded from consideration in order to avoid confusion and distortion.

There is historical evidence of a Samkhya system of 60 verses in *Ahir-budhnya-Samhita* of the Panchratra. Chapter 12 of this Samhita describes five philosophical systems: *Trayi* (the three Vedic lores); the Samkhya; the Yoga; the *Pasupata* (saivism); and the *Sattvata* (Panchratra). It provides a brief description of all these systems.

What is most revealing is that it calls the Samkhya philosophy by the name *Sastitantra*, 'a system of 60 topics'. According to this Samhita, the Sastitantra consists of two mandalas (circles): Prakrita Mandala and Vaikrita Mandala, the former comprised of 32 and the latter having 28 topics.[106] The main contents of these topics are enumerated but not fully explained.[107]

Sutra LXXII says that there are only 60 verses *(Shashti Tantra)* in the Karika of Isvarakrisna when the objections of the opponents are not included. This is a good source of internal evidence that the original Karika indeed contained only 60 verses. If we exclude the interpolated verses from the present text of Samkhya Karika, the number of original verses total only 60 as illustrated below:

Present Samkhya Karika		*Interpolated verses*		*Original*
Number of verses		70, 71, 72, 73	= 4	
in present text	73	46, 47, 48, 49, 50, 51	= 6	
		52, 53, 54	= 3	
Total:	73	Total:	13	Total: 60

[106] When we consider these two terminologies in the context of Samkhya philosophy, it is apparent that Prakrit Mandala refers to aspects of nature; and the Vaikrita-Mandala refers to product of nature. For clarity on these, see Karika, verse 25.

[107] See F. Otto Schrader, *Introduction to the Panchratra and the Ahirbudhnya Samhita* (Madras: The Adyar Library & Research Center, 1916), pp. 110–111. For details on Panchratra, see chapters I and II. For the original *Ahirbudhnya Samhita of the Panchratra*, see Ramanujacharya (edited) (Madras: Adyar Library, 1916) Sanskrit, Dwadas Adhyaya, pp. 106–113.

Chronologically, it is appropriate now to discuss two outstanding Kshatriya thinkers who accepted much of what was taught by Kapila but who made their own distinct contributions in the field of philosophy and affected greatly the mode of life of the people. These thinkers were Buddha and Mahavira. Both were opposed to Brahmanic dominance, Vedic rituals, sacrifices, and exploitation of the people by Brahmanic priests. Though they began their work as reformers, what they preached and practiced emerged as two distinct systems of religion. The most significant aspect of these two systems of religion is that neither of them accepted the concept of an almighty deity.

Gautama Buddha

Gautama Buddha was born in 567 B.C. to a royal Kshatriya family of Kapilavastu (near north Bihar). Though there is a difference of opinion among the historians about the exact date of his birth, 567 B.C. seems to be the date most commonly accepted. Mahajan gives a detailed account of differing views about the dates of birth and death of Buddha, but on the basis of reliable evidence he concludes that Buddha lived for 80 years and his date of birth was 567 B.C. and date of death 487 B.C.[108]

The childhood name of Buddha was Gautama Siddhartha. He was married at the age of 16 to Yasodhara, and at the age of 29 he had a son Rahul. Though Siddhartha was brought up in great luxury, his complacency was shattered when he saw people suffering from sorrow, misery, disease, and death. He wanted to discover the cause and remedy of sorrow.

Concerned with these problems of human life, he left his home and family soon after his son was born and went out in search of truth. He became a wanderer and went from place to place, leading a homeless life. He first tried to learn concentration of mind from Alara and Udraka at Rajagriha (Bihar) but did not find enlightenment. Then one day he took a vow while sitting under a pipal tree near Gaya (Bihar). According to tradition, he vowed to "not leave this place till I attain that peace of mind which I have been trying for all these years".[109]

After years of meditation and great suffering, he achieved enlightenment at the age of 35. After his enlightenment he came to be known as the Buddha or 'The Enlightened One'. He then decided to dedicate his life to the good of the people.

For the remaining 45 years of his life, he went from place to place along with his followers, teaching people how they could overcome sorrow and

[108] Mahajan, *op. cit.*, p. 134.
[109] *Ibid.*, p. 135.

misery. He taught four basic truths of life, the 'Four Noble Truths' in Buddhistic literature:

(i) The first truth is that there is 'existence of sorrow'.
(ii) The second truth is that there is 'cause of sorrow'.
(iii) The third truth is that there is 'remedy for sorrow'.
(iv) The fourth truth is that there is 'a path to attain liberation'.

He explained the steps of the "path" which is known as the Eightfold path:

(i) Right views
(ii) Right thoughts (resolve)
(iii) Right action
(iv) Right speech
(v) Right means of livelihood
(vi) Right effort
(vii) Right mindfulness (remembrance)
(viii) Right meditation

He began his teaching at Sarnath near Banaras and continued delivering his messages by traveling in various parts of the country. He taught through conversation, lectures, and parables. He walked from place to place with as many as twelve hundred followers.[110] Although Buddha did not explain clearly his conception of Nirvana, according to Buddhist literature it signifies a state of happiness, attainable in this life.[111]

He spoke in Pali, the language of the people, and did not use Sanskrit, which the Brahmans used in their Vedic rituals and literature. His emphasis was on self-effort, self-conquest, exertion, and self-improvement. He rejected the caste system, superiority of the Brahmans and meaningless Vedic rituals and ceremonies, and he accepted anyone who came to him as his follower. Though the teachings of Buddha dealt basically with social reform, they gradually took the form of a religious system.[112]

Within a few weeks of Buddha's death, the first Buddhist Council was held at Rajagriha (Bihar) in about 487 B.C. The discourses of Buddha were collated and classified as authoritative canonical texts by an assembly of 500 monks representing various Sanghas (organizational units). The teachings of Buddha were divided into two parts called the *Vinaya Pitaka* and *Dhamma Pitaka*.[113]

The second Council was held in Vaisali (Bihar) in about 387 B.C., one hundred years after the first Council. In this Council certain changes were made to Vinaya Pitaka by the Vaisali monks, those living at Vaisali Unit.

110 *Ibid.*, p. 137.
111 *Ibid.*, p. 140.
112 W. Singh, *op. cit.*, p. 64.
113 Mahajan, *op. cit.*, p. 142.

Thus, some differences grew in the practice of Buddhism.

The third Council was held in 251 B.C. at Patliputra (now called Patna, Bihar), where a third Pitaka was adopted. The fourth Council was held in Kashmir and tried to settle various differences among the followers of Buddhism.[114]

In due time Buddhism established itself as a well-knit organization which facilitated its growth as a religion in India and other countries of Asia. "The religion of the Buddha started in one corner of India and spread not only in India but also made its way to Ceylon (now Sri Lanka), Burma, Tibet, Java, Sumatra, Borneo, Champa, China, Japan, Thailand, and Central Asia."[115]

Buddhism gained popularity and acceptance because of several factors: the simplicity of the teaching, use of the common (vernacular) language of the people, inexpensive practices as opposed to very expensive Vedic and Brahmanical religious practices, setting up of Sanghas (organizational units) and monasteries from which the nuns and monks went out to a particular geographical area and converted people, opening of centers of learning such as Nalanda University in Bihar and, above all, receiving the royal patronage of Asoka, Kanishka, and Harsha.

The most significant aspect of Buddhism is that it did not accept the concept of God. God as an almighty power was never mentioned by Buddha. Nor did he talk about any of the deities of Vedic origin. Further, such other concepts as heaven, hell, soul, and sin were also not recognized. Thus, Buddhism became a religion without God, goddesses, spirits, or any other power beyond man. Buddhism became a religion in the sense that its followers lived the life of religious men, followed the teachings of the master, and continued to serve the people, showing the path of liberation from sorrow. It taught a man to rely on himself in overcoming misery and gaining happiness in life. It considered every man equal and accepted him as such within its fold.

If we compare the teachings of Buddha with that of Kapila, we find that both doctrines of the latter—the theory of proper knowledge and the theory of right action—were accepted by the former. Buddha's teachings of right action and right effort are the same as the Satkaryavada (theory of right action) of Kapila. Similarly, Buddha's teachings of right views and right thoughts are the same as the Samyak Jnana (theory of proper knowledge) of Kapila. It will be seen that Buddha added four steps to Kapila's teachings: right speech, right livelihood, right mindfulness, and right meditation. Thus, from Kapila to Buddha we see a continuity of thought and also an effort to refine and develop existing thought. This process continued, as will be seen when we discuss other thinkers such as Mahavira, Patanjali, and Vyasa.

[114] For details on these Councils, see Mahajan, 'Progress of Buddhism', *op. cit.*, p. 142.
[115] *Ibid.*, p. 143.

Before discussing Mahavira, let it be mentioned here that two important steps of Yoga were already accepted as a part of the teaching of Buddha. These steps were: right mindfulness and right meditation, which became, respectively, *Dharana* and *Dhyana* in Patanjali's Yoga Sutra. This illustrates the gradual development of yogic concepts and practices beginning from Kapila to Vyasa, who composed the original Gita. It will also be seen why and how all these thinkers, from Kapila to Vyasa, became enemies of Brahmanism and why the original Gita was destroyed and replaced by an interpolated version of the original after 800 A.D.

Mahavira

Mahavira was the last *Tirthankara* (prophet) of Jainism. There were, according to sacred books of Jainism, 23 Tirthankaras before him. Therefore, it is essential to say a few words about these early Tirthankaras of Jainism before describing its most widely known figure, Mahavira.

According to the books of Jainism, Rishabha was the founder. Though not much is known about Rishabha and his 21 successors, there is a historical account available about the twenty-third Tirthankara, Parsvanath. The most significant aspect of Jainism is that all the Tirthankaras, beginning with Rishabha to Mahvira, were Kshatriya, most of them born in royal Kshatriya families.

Parsvanath was the son of Asvasena, King of Banaras. He was married to Prabhavati, daughter of the king of Naravarman. He remained a householder up to the age of 30 and then became an ascetic after renouncing the worldly life of palatial luxury. "After deep meditation for 83 days, he attained the highest knowledge called Kevalam. He had 164,000 men and 327,000 women as his followers. He is believed to have lived about 800 B.C. and his death took place 250 years before the death of Mahavira."[116] He taught four vows: (i) not to injure life, (ii) not to lie, (iii) not to steal, and (iv) not to possess any property. Mahavira added the fifth vow to this list, chastity.

Mahavira was born in a Kshatriya family of Vaisali (Bihar) and the name of his father was Siddhartha. The original name of Mahavira was Vardhamana. Though there is some difference of opinion about when he lived, the most accepted is 540 B.C. as the date of birth and 468 B.C. as the date of death. He was a contemporary of Buddha.

Vardhamana was married to Yashoda and he had a daughter. When his parents died, he became an ascetic with the permission of his elder

[116] *Ibid.*, p. 124.

brother. He wandered around from place to place, homeless, and naked for twelve years. People struck, abused, and mocked him, but he remained unconcerned and kept on meditating. According to Mahajan, "In Ladha, the inhabitants persecuted him and set dogs on him. They beat him with sticks and with their feet, and threw fruit, clods of earth and potsherds at him. They disturbed him in his meditations by all sorts of torments."[117] He reached Nirvana (supreme knowledge) in the thirteenth year of his wandering, under the sal tree at the age of 42. He was from then on called Mahavira, which means 'the conqueror'. After achieving Nirvana, he carried on his teachings by going from place to place for 30 years until he died at the age of 72.[118]

Like Kapila and Buddha, he was concerned with how one can achieve the good life. His teachings for achieving the good life are called three Jewels or Ratnas. They are:

(i) Right faith
(ii) Right knowledge
(iii) Right action

He put great emphasis on *Ahimsa* (non-injury) and taught his followers to live a life of virtue and morality. According to Jain religion, even stones, wind, fire, and plants are endowed with life and possess certain degrees of consciousness. He accepted the practice of Yoga, Meditation (Dhyana), and Deep Meditation *(Samadhi)*. In him we find a greater acceptance of Yoga (both Hatha Yoga and Raja Yoga), which was later systematized by Patanjali.

Mahavira did not believe in the existence of God. He did not believe that God created and controlled the whole universe.[119] He considered the recital of Mantras as a waste of time and rejected the sacrificial ceremonies. In Jainism, there is no worship of gods, goddesses, or spirits. The images of the Tirthankaras are worshipped in their temples.

Like Buddhism, Jainism does not accept the authority of the Vedas and condemns the Brahmanic practices of rituals, ceremonies, and sacrifices. Jainism opposes the Brahmanic monopoly of religion and rejects the caste system. Equality of man is accepted without any discrimination.

"Jainism spread in all parts of India, but, after some time, it began to decline. The Jains attribute the first destruction of their temples to the hostility of the Brahmans, especially under Ajayapala in 1174 to 1176 A.D."[120]

Two hundred years after the death of Mahavira, a Jain Council was held at Patliputra (Patna) which decided upon the canon *(Siddhanta)* or

[117] *Ibid.*, p. 125.
[118] W. Singh, *op. cit.*, p. 60.
[119] *Ibid.*, p. 126.
[120] Mahajan, *op. cit.*, p. 128.

principles of sacred literature, though these were not accepted by all the Jains. The second Council was held at Vallabhi in Gujrat in the fifth century A.D., at which time "the Jain canon was given a definite shape in which it is to be found today."[121]

Unlike Buddhism, Jainism did not advocate conversion to its religion and it did not spread outside the country. "While Buddhism has almost disappeared from India, Jainism still flourishes in several parts of the country. All parts of India contain followers of Jainism, but the chief centers of this faith today are Malwa, Gujrat, and Rajputana."[122]

In comparing the main teachings of Mahavira with that of Kapila, one notices that the former has accepted the doctrines of the latter. The right knowledge of Mahavira is the same as the theory of proper knowledge of Kapila. Similarly, the right action of Mahavira is the same as Satkaryavada (right actionism) of Kapila.

We will also see how the rationalistic thoughts of Kapila, Buddha, and Mahavira have been carried on in the Yoga system of Patanjali.

Patanjali

We do not have satisfactory informtion about the place and date of birth of Patanjali. A great majority of Indian scholars who have studied Patanjali seem to accept 300 B.C. as his period.[123] S.N. Dasgupta, a recognized scholar on Patanjali, gives a detailed account of varied opinions of both Indian and Western scholars who have tried to fix the date of Patanjali and concludes, "I am disposed to think that the date of the first three chapters of the Yoga Sutra must be placed somewhere between the fourth century B.C. and the second century B.C."[124] In my own study I have come to the conclusion that Patanjali wrote his Yoga Sutra about 400 B.C.

This is not to say that Yoga as a system begins with the writings of Patanjali. I have mentioned earlier that Yoga was practiced during the period of the Harappa-Mohenjodaro civilization in 3000 B.C. I have also noted in the preceding pages that Yoga was practiced by Mahavira, the twenty-fourth Tirthankara of Jainism, and also by Buddha, the founder of Buddhism (600–500 B.C.). The practice of meditation and Yoga was recommended as the way to obtain true knowledge in the Nyaya philosophy of Gautama. Such evidence proves the continuity of Yoga practices

[121] Ibid., p. 128–129.
[122] W. Singh, op. cit., p. 62.
[123] Ernest E. Wood, Practical Yoga: Ancient and Modern (New York: E. P. Dutton and Co., 1948), p. 25. See also K.P. Bahadur, The Wisdom of Yoga (New Delhi: Sterling Publishers Pvt. Ltd., 1977), p. 10.
[124] S.N. Dasgupta, Yoga Philosophy (Delhi: Motilal Banarsidass, 1974), p. 69. See also ch. II, pp. 42–69.

in Indian civilization from its earliest times to the days of Patanjali, who systematized and presented it in written form.

As already noted, the writings of the Harappa-Mohenjodaro period have not yet been fully deciphered. Thus, we cannot say whether there were writings on Yoga during that period. The first systematic presentation of Yoga known to us is the Yoga Sutra of Patanjali.

Patanjali accepted the basic tenets of Samkhya Darshan of Kapila and presented it in a way that made Yoga a system comprised of philosophy and practice. Though Patanjali incorporated the fundamentals of Samkhya Darshan, he added much of his own as if to make it appear an improved version of Kapila's major theme of how to remove sorrow and achieve happiness in life.

S.N. Dasgupta sums up this view well: "Patanjali was probably the most notable representative of the Samkhya school of yoga... Patanjali not only collected the different forms of yoga practices, and gleaned the diverse ideas which were or could be associated with the yoga, but grafted them all on the Samkhya metaphysics, and gave them the form in which they have been handed down to us."[125] Macdonell cites historic evidence of close connection between Yoga and Samkhya and points out that, "In the *Mahabharata* the two systems are actually spoken of as one and the same."[126]

It has been stated earlier that in the teaching of Kapila, Buddha, and Mahavira the emphasis was on acquiring proper knowledge (Samyaka Jnana) of things and acting in accordance with the principles of right action (Satkaryavada) in order to eradicate sorrow and achieve happiness. To Patanjali something more was needed to achieve happiness.

It seems as if Patanjali is telling Kapila that dukha (sorrow) could be due not only to lack of proper knowledge and improper action but also to physical and mental ailments. Pain could result from sickness, and disorders might arise from bodily malfunction as well as from mental disharmony. Thus, to Patanjali the purusha needed to know and practice Yoga, a combined system of acquiring knowledge, developing control and discipline, and mastering practices on both the physical and mental level. A man could then be free from sickness and disorders and would be able to achieve happiness in life. These aspects are explained in the Yoga Sutra.

Yoga Sutra

The present Yoga Sutra has a total of 195 sutras (verses or aphorisms) and contains four chapters. Chapter I is named Samadhi Pada and has 51 verses. It explains certain aspects of Yoga.

[125] S.N. Dasgupta, *op. cit.*, p. 51.
[126] A.A. Macdonell, *op. cit.*, p. 396.

Chapter II, entitled Sadhana Pada, explains yoganga (limbs of yoga) and describes the techniques of their practice and mastery. It has 55 verses and covers yama, niyama, asana, pranayama, and pratyahara.

Chapter III is entitled Vibhuti Pada and explains samyama, the method of practicing dharana, dhyana, and samadhi. It has 55 verses and describes various kinds of power one acquires through the practice of samyama.[127]

Chapter IV, called Kaivalya Pada, describes various types of realization one achieves through yogic practices. It has only 34 verses.

The Yoga system as presented by Patanjali consists of eight limbs, which might be considered steps or parts. These are: *yama, niyama, asana, pranayama, pratyahara, dharana, dhyana* and *samadhi*. Patanjali explains each of these steps very clearly but briefly and describes the results of their practice. For the purpose of a better understanding of the Yoga system, let me mention what these limbs are and how they are practiced.

Yama means the observance of five forms of self-restraint or discipline: (i) non-violence, the commitment to do no harm *(ahimsa)*; (ii) truthfulness *(satya)*; (iii) honesty *(asteya)*; (iv) continence *(brahmacharya)*; (v) freedom from greed and covetousness *(aparigraha)*. According to Patanjali, these vows of yama must be practiced by the Yoga practitioner everywhere regardless of place, time, and circumstances. The results of observing these principles are explained in five verses (Ch.II, 35–39):

By observing the principle of non-violence (ahimsa) in one's life and surroundings, hostility *(vaira)* does not occur. When firmly established in truthfulness (satya), the fruit of action rests on the action of the practitioner. When an individual practices honesty (asteya), all kinds of benefits are enjoyed. By firmly observing sexual abstinence (brahmacharya), one gains energy and vigor. By steadily refraining from greed, one gains knowledge of all aspects of life.

Niyama involves developing or mastering the five qualities of: (i) cleanliness, purity *(shaucha)*; (ii) contentment *(santosha)*; (iii) austerity, dedicated practice *(tapa)*; (iv) self-study *(swadhyaya)*; (v) self-mastery, self-perfection *(pranidhanani)*.[128]

Patanjali explains the process of achieving these qualities in six verses (Ch. II, 40–45) and points out their respective results. By observing physical cleanliness or purity (shaucha), he says, one develops a disinclination to come into physical contact with others. By observing mental cleanliness (purity) through the process of nurturing the quality of sattva guna, one achieves cheerfulness and the condition of one-pointedness of the mind, control of the senses, knowledge of the self (purusha), and proper fitness.

---

[127] Some books on Patanjali mention 56 verses in Ch. III. The verse no. 22 is omitted in books showing only 55 verses.

[128] The extant texts on Yoga Sutra mention isvara-pranidhanani. The word isvara was interpolated in Yoga Sutra during the period when the original Gita was altered to promote monotheistic doctrine. Therefore, the prefix isvara is excluded here. For detail on interpolations in Yoga Sutra, see the later part of this section.

By observing contentment (santosha), one gains unsurpassed happiness. Through dedicated practice (tapa), impurities are destroyed and perfection of the body and sense organs realized. Through self-study (swadhyaya), one gains one's true goals. By self-endeavor and self-mastery (pranidhanani), one achieves perfection in Samadhi (deep meditation).

Patanjali provides general guidelines for removing obstacles to observing principles of Yama and Niyama, saying that when the mind is disturbed by an improper thought, the remedy is to contemplate its opposite. He goes on to explain (Ch. II, 34) that the need to contemplate the opposite arises because an individual might indulge in improper thoughts related to violence, greed, delusion, or anger. Or he might approve of such thoughts or deeds in others. As a result, the individual will endlessly suffer pain, sorrow, and ignorance.

Asana is body-posture to be practiced with comfort and in a steady way. Patanjali explains the fundamental principle of practicing asanas (postures) in Ch. II 47–48, saying that when the principle of motion (effort) and motionlessness (relaxation) is applied endlessly there is no ill result due to the application of this pair of opposite principles.

It needs to be noted here that, although Patanjali does not name the asanas (which are generally counted as 84 in number and now practiced all over the world in varied forms), he gives the basic rationale for practicing them. Unfortunately, most of the teachers of Yoga do not follow this basic principle of motion-motionlessness in their own practice or in teaching, and, as a result, they suffer from various ill effects.[129] The beneficial result of practicing asanas comes from proper application of the principle of motion-motionlessness.

Pranayama is control of breath by interruption in the flow of inhalation and exhalation. It can be regarded as a form of breathing exercise. There are about eight most popular forms. Patanjali mentions only four kinds of pranayama, which are practiced by controlling the breath externally, internally, and with total restraint. According to Patanjali, through the practice of pranayama, one becomes fit for the practice of *dharana* (concentration).

Pratyahara is not very clearly explained (Ch. II, 54–55), but from what is said by Patanjali we can derive its actual meaning. The word pratyahara is comprised of two sanskrit words, *prati* and *ahara*. Prati means opposite and ahara means food. Pratyahara can be understood when we examine its meaning in the light of Ch. II, 33, where Patanjali has stated that when the mind is disturbed by improper thoughts the remedy is to contemplate the opposite.

Once the senses (*indriyas,* or sense organs) are involved in external or internal objects, activities of the bodily limbs begin to operate in accordance

[129] For a comprehensive discussion of this principle, see Phulgenda Sinha, *Yoga: Meaning, Values and Practice* (Patna: Indian Institute of Yoga, 1970), pp. 5–6.

with that involvement. When the mind holds on to something (a concept, event, object, desire, and so on), a picture-like visualization of the thing so held takes place in the mind. This visualization automatically triggers activation of action organs and all concerned bodily limbs and organs. Thus, we can say that action is the resultant state of mental involvement.

Unless there is proper and desirable involvement of the senses in the object or goal, proper action will not result. Since the fruit of action depends upon the action (as explained in Ch. II, 36), it is imperative that the sense organs involve themselves in desirable objects or the goal. Thus, according to pratyahara, there should be withdrawal of senses from the undesirable and involvement of them with the desirable opposite, so that the fruit of action will be satisfactory. As Patanjali has explained in Ch. II, 55, only then would there be the highest mastery over the senses. For example, if the object is to be healthy, then the involvement of mind and the senses should be to see what good health would look like, what the appearance of the body, face, limbs, and so on would be. The projection of the mind should be to all those aspects which a healthy body would entail. Since the mind has a tendency to fly off and see a variety of things, it should be withdrawn from seeing the opposite of the healthy condition (sickness, weakened limbs and organs, and disease). Thus by using pratyahara, one would achieve the desired health and would eliminate the unwanted opposite.

Dharana means concentration. It is practiced by concentrating or fixing the mind on an object, spot, or place within a limited area. According to Patanjali, when the mind achieves a condition of one-pointedness towards the object being observed, there is dharana. Patanjali explains it in a single verse (Ch. III, I) and then goes on to explain the next limb or step.

Dhyana is uninterrupted attachment or flow of the mind towards the object of observation. When the mind continues to consider or observe the object of attachment with unbroken flow, that is dhyana, which means meditation. Again, Patanjali explains it in a single verse (Ch. III, 2) and goes on to explain the next step.

Samadhi is when the mind continues to consider the same object of attachment in its true form without any distraction or consciousness of self. Samadhi is translated as contemplation or deep meditation.

It can be seen that the practices of dharana, dhyana, and samadhi are linked to one another and are not isolated. Patanjali, therefore, considers them together and calls the combined practice of these three steps samyama (Ch. III, 4). It is practiced in stages and is internal in nature as compared to the external practices of asanas, pranayama, and pratyahara.

Patanjali describes various types of benefits obtained from practicing samyama. He devotes a major part of Chapter III to describing these benefits and covers the core points of Samkhya philosophy and the results

of Yoga practice in the remaining section. Since these aspects are inter-
spersed, I am covering them under two sub-headings.

Samyama and its Results

Samyama, again, is a combined form of concentration, meditation, and
deep meditation. The practitioner goes from one stage of mental involvement to another in succession. It is inclusive of all the steps related to mind:
its power, its functions, and its achievements. With this understanding, let
us now see how it is practiced and what are the results.

Patanjali talks about three types of results due to the practice of samyama: (i) *nirodha parinama* (outcome of control), (ii) *samadhi parinama*
(outcome of deep meditation), and (iii) *ekagrata parinama* (outcome of
concentration). These results are explained briefly below:

When the outgoing impression of the mind is controlled, at that moment
the mind is permeated with an impression called nirodha parinama (the
result of control).

When the many-pointedness condition of the mind dissolves and one-
pointedness arises, that is called samadhi parinama (the result of deep
meditation).

When one achieves the condition of the mind in which the object (seen
by the outer eyes) subsides and a shape similar in proportion arises (before
the inner eye), that is ekagrata parinama (the result of concentration).

By practicing samyama on the aforesaid three transformations (nirodha,
samadhi, and ekagrata), the state of confusion of the mind is resolved and
knowledge of the ideas or the contents of the mind is gained (Ch. III,
16–17).

By performing samyama on the image of friendliness, one acquires the
power of friendliness. By focusing on strength, one becomes strong. By
projecting the light of the mind on the desired object, the knowledge of the
subtle (minute), the hidden, and the distant is gained (Ch. III, 26).

Patanjali claimed that by practicing samyama on certain parts of one's
own body, various kinds of results are obtained (Ch. III, 30–35). By practicing samyama on the navel *(nabhi chakra)*, knowledge of the arrangement
of the body arises. By practicing samyama on the pit of the throat *(kantha-
koop)*, there is a cessation of hunger and thirst. By practicing samyama
on the nerve center below the throat-pit *(kurma nadi)*, one gains stability
and steadiness. By practicing samyama on the dormant light under the
crown of the head, which he calls *murdhajyoti*, the practitioner achieves
the vision of self-perfection or the vision of perfected ones. By practicing
samyama on the luminous image of the mind *(pratibha)*, one gains knowledge of everything held in the mind. And by practicing samyama on the
heart *(hridaya)*, knowledge about the nature and functioning of the mind
is acquired.

While describing numerous results of samyama, Patanjali mentions certain key concepts of Samkhya philosophy and points out the benefits of practicing Yoga. These are noted below.

Samkhya, Yoga, and Results

Patanjali points out some of the fundamentals of Samkhya philosophy in several verses of Ch. II and Ch. III. The key concepts of Kapila covered by Patanjali are: purusha, prakriti (pradhana), jnana, gunas, dukha, sukha, action and its result (fruit of action), self-interest, enjoyment, and kaivalya. Since patanjali's main purpose is to describe the process of practicing various steps of Yoga and to point out their results, he does not go into a detailed discussion of the conceptual, theoretical, and philosophic aspects of Samkhya. He merely refers to them, as if assuming that his readers are familiar with the terminology.

Patanjali accepts both theories of Kapila: theory of proper knowledge (jnana) and theory of right action (satkarya). In Ch. III, 15, he says that the difference in the result (parinama) is due to the variation or difference in the cause (hetu). In this statement, it can be seen that Patanjali accepts the basic tenet of Kapila's theory that the 'effect subsists in the cause'. Further, in Ch. II, 36, while discussing the principles of yama, Patanjali makes a categorical statement that the fruit of action (kriyaphal) rests solely on the action of the doer (practitioner). If we look into Patanjali's description of samyama and its results (Ch. III), it is apparent that the theory of right action is strongly emphasized.

Likewise Kapila's theory of proper knowledge (samyaka jnana) is comprehensively covered by Patanjali. This is evident when we consider what Patanjali has said while discussing yama and niyama and the results of samyama, and when talking about purusha, gunas, prakriti, and kaivalya. Let me mention a few examples:

In Ch. II, 44, Patanjali says that one gains the knowledge of what is aimed at by self-study (swadhyaya). In Ch. III, 16, he says that by practicing samyama on the three kinds of results (parinama) one gains knowledge of the past and future, and he talks about various kinds of knowledge (jnana) acquired through different samyama.

In Ch. III, 36, Patanjali says that purusha and sattva (one of the three gunas) are absolutely distinct and quite separate. The knowledge of the purusha and his enjoyment (bhoga) result from performing samyama in self-interest (swartha) and not in the interest of another person (parartha). He goes on to say that, from this experience of the practice, one acquires the discriminative knowledge of hearing, touch, sight, taste, and smell. With the knowledge of the distinction between purusha and sattva (guna), one achieves supremacy over all states and forms of existence and gains the knowledge of everything (Ch. III, 50). By mastering this knowledge, the seed of defect is destroyed and one gains *kaivalya* (liberation from sorrow) (Ch. III, 51).

How the purusha comes to know prakriti (nature) is explained by Patanjali in Ch. III, 48–49. He says that by performing samyama upon the process of apprehension (cognition), imaging *(swaroop)*, self-consciousness, and purposiveness, one gains mastery over the sense organs. As a result of this mastery, there is instantaneous perception of the object concerned, with speed like that of the mind and without the use of any vehicle, and one gains complete mastery over pradhana (nature).

Though the results of practicing various steps of Yoga have already been pointed out, Patanjali describes five kinds of benefits (results) due to the practice and observance of the system as a whole. These unique benefits are the result of practicing Yoga in its totality. The five results are: (i) beauty *(rupa)*, (ii) fine complexion *(lavanya)*, (iii) strength, power *(bala)*, (iv) adamantine endurance *(bajra-sahanan-twani)*, and (v) wealth in the form of health and perfect body *(kaya-sampata)* (Ch. III, 47).

Patanjali advises that one should avoid the feeling of vanity and boasting when certain power is achieved because there is the possibility of the revival of evil or experiencing undesirable recurrence (Ch. III, 52).

Patanjali sums up his discussion (Ch. III, 53–55) by explaining that through the practice of samyama on time and its process of succession (kshanna-tat-kramayoh), one acquires knowledge of reality. One may acquire this knowledge through a heightened experience of time, experienced as a succession of the smallest perceptible intervals. With this knowledge, one can see differences among entities which might otherwise appear superficially alike. The knowledge so acquired is transcendent, apprehends all objects simultaneously and transcends the world process which produces time.

In his description of the steps of Yoga we notice that Patanjali is very clear, logical, and rational in his approach. There is no sign of mysticism, religious motivation, or spiritualism in his presentation of Yoga as a system which can be practiced universally.

Unfortunately, Patanjali's writings have been subject to misinterpretations as well as interpolations, which together have distorted the image of Yoga as a rational system. The misinterpretations have been by those commentators—both Indian and non-Indian—who have been religiously motivated and have tried to see Patanjali as a theist. There are other scholars who have accepted these misreadings without question, due partly to the absence of any objective studies of Patanjali. I hope there will be some effort by both Indian and Western scholars to conduct further research on Patanjali and present him in an authentic way.

As regards detecting interpolations in the Yoga Sutra, there has been good work by both Indian and Western scholars, who have pointed out those verses which were added later.

Interpolations in Yoga Sutra

According to S.N. Dasgupta, the whole of Ch. IV is interpolated into the main text of Yoga Sutra.[130] Dasgupta points out that Patanjali had put "*iti*", which denotes conclusion, at the end of the third chapter but there is another "iti" at the end of the fourth chapter. Further, "the Sutras 30–34 of the last chapter seem to repeat what has already been said in the second chapter."

According to Dasgupta, the last chapter is disproportionately small, as it has only 34 sutras (verses), whereas the number of sutras in other chapters are 51 to 55. On the basis of this evidence, Dasgupta concludes: "The last chapter is a subsequent addition by a hand other than that of Patanjali who was anxious to supply new arguments which were felt to be necessary for strengthening of the yoga position from an internal point of view, as well as for securing the strength of the yoga from the supposed attacks of Buddhist metaphysics."

Dasgupta further observes, "There is also a marked change (due either to its supplementary character or to the manipulation of a foreign hand) in the style of the last chapter as compared with the style of the other three."[131]

A detailed account of interpolation to the main text of Yoga Sutra is provided by J.W. Hauer, a noted German scholar on Patanjali. Hauer in his book *Der Yoga* points out that the oldest portion of Yoga Sutra is the Yoganga section (Ch. III, 28–Ch. III, 55), which may go back to the second century B.C. The kriyayoga section (Ch. II, 1–27) and isvara-pranidhana-section (Ch. I, 23–51 are the next oldest. The latest portion of the text is the nirodha-section (Ch. I, 1–22). The last section (Ch. IV, 2–34) was added just before the final redaction and represents a reaction against both the yogacara school of Buddhism and the Samkhya. The final redaction of Yoga Sutra, according to Hauer, was done probably in the fourth century A.D. [132]

On the basis of the findings of S.N. Dasgupta and J.W. Hauer, the original writing of Patanjali can be separated from the interpolated verses. When we separate the original from the later additions, the contents of the present text of Yoga Sutra consist of 83 original verses (Ch. II, 28–55 plus

130 S.N. Dasgupta, *A History of Indian Philosophy, Vol. I* (Cambridge: The University Press, 1932), pp. 229–230. See also his *Yoga Philosophy, op. cit.*, pp. 51–53.

131 *Ibid*, p. 230.

132English translation quoted from G.J. Larson, *Classical Samkhya, op. cit.*, p. 150. For the original in German see J.W. Hauer, *Der Yoga* (Stuttgart: W. Kohlhammer Verlag, 1958), pp. 238–239 and 221–239.

Ch. III, 1–55) and 112 interpolated verses (whole of Ch. IV, 1–34; whole of Ch. I, 1–51; 1–27 in Ch. II; and Ch. III, 56.)

A close reading of Ch. I and part of Ch. II (1–27) gives us the impression that all that has been discussed in these verses is either repetition, commentary, or unrelated additions and at some places is even contradictory to what Patanjali has said in the basic text on Yoganga (II, 28–55 and III, 1–55). Garbe expresses the same view: "we can say that the yogasutra I. 23–27, II. 1, 45, which treat of the person of God, are unconnected with the other parts of the text-book, nay, even contradict the foundations of the system."[133]

Macdonell expresses a similar view, saying: "Indeed the parts of the Sutras dealing with the person of God are not only unconnected with the other parts of the treatise, but even contradict the foundations of the system."[134]

Let me point out a few inconsistencies. In Ch. I, 2, Yoga is defined as "controlling the senses or controlling the fluctuations of mind". This definition of Yoga is not appropriate when we consider the Yoganga view of Yoga presented by Patanjali in Ch. II, 28. There, Patanjali describes how by practicing all the limbs of Yoga (Yoganga) in a combined way, the impurities are destroyed, knowledge radiates, and wisdom arises. Thus, to Patanjali it is not only controlling the fluctuations of mind but the total result of practicing yama, niyama, asana, pranayama, pratyahara, and the samyama (dharana, dhyana, and samadhi) that one achieves the benefits of Yoga.

Further, Ch. I has been named Samadhi Pada. If we consider what Patanjali said in Ch. III about dharana, dhyana, and samadhi, the name of the first chapter should have been Samyama Pada and not Samadhi Pada. The practice of all the steps in sequence produces the unique result to the practitioner, not the practice of samadhi alone.

One most irrelevant and contradictory concept introduced in Ch. I and mentioned in Ch. II also is that of *isvara*. Isvara is mentioned in Ch. I, 23. The next verse explains that the individual possessing certain qualities is isvara (purusa visesa isvarah). This has been interpreted by a majority of both Indian and foreign scholars to denote the concept of God. Only a few scholars have rejected the misinterpretation. P. Chakravarti in his book *Origin and Development of the Samkhya System of Thought* argues that, "Indeed, there is not a single couplet anywhere in the exposition of the Samkhya and Yoga in the Mbh., which speaks of isvara as the supreme being from whom proceeds creation and destruction."[135]

[133] Richard Garbe, *The Philosophy of Ancient India* (Chicago: Open Court Publishing Company, 1897), p. 15.

[134] Macdonell, *op.cit.*, p. 397.

[135] Pulinbihari Chakravarti, *Origin and Development of the Samkhya System of Thought* (New Delhi: Oriental Books Reprint Corp., 1975), p. 66.

It should be noted here that the concept of God entered into Indian literature at the time of the revival of Brahmanism around 800 A.D. In our present study it has been shown that from the earliest time to the time of Patanjali, there is no mention of isvara as god in any Indian literature. How then could Patanjali talk of isvara, when the very concept was unknown to Indian civilization during and before his time?

It appears quite clear to me that the concept of isvara as god was introduced in the name of Patanjali at the time when the interpolators changed the original Gita during the eighth or early ninth century A.D. They made these changes in the writings of Patanjali to substantiate their own religious views, the details of which will be revealed in the next chapter. For the interpolators, it would have been impossible to change the original Gita (which is basically a book on Yoga) without making changes in the foundational book on Yoga—the Yoga Sutra.

Further, even when we accept the concept of isvara as nothing more than purusha (man), the question is: Was Patanjali interested in bestowing any honor or special name to anyone possessing certain qualities? In the discussion of Yoganga, Patanjali does not indicate this idea where he specifically describes the various kinds of power and qualities one acquires by the practices of samyama. To Patanjali the achievements from the practices of Yoga are open to all universally. He does not differentiate one purusha from another. How then could Patanjali write "purusa visesa isvarah"? Thus, even if we consider isvara as nothing more than purusha, this is not Patanjali's usage but the interpolator's. I hope the subsequent chapters will throw more light on the causes of redaction and also the motive behind those changers.

An Appraisal of Patanjali

Before summing up, I must make a few observations on Patanjali's writings. These observations are implied in his presentation of Yoga as a system requiring certain knowledge as well as practices. The most noteworthy fact obvious in his writing is that men are equal, physically and mentally. Patanjali does not differentiate one purusha from another on any basis, be it of birth, race, caste, class, color, or creed. Any person practicing Yoganga (the steps of Yoga) derives the same benefits, acquires the same power, and is able to lead a joyful and happy life. He does not need the favor of any other power, be it worldly or heavenly. Humans possess power, physical and mental, which they can develop properly and use to achieve what they desire and to find solutions to problems facing them. Patanjali's purusha trained in Yoga discipline and practices, is better equipped and more capable than the purusha of Kapila to overcome misery and sorrow and lead a joyful life.

Furthermore, Patanjali does not advise an escape from social responsibility or worldly life to achieve happiness. On the contrary, Yoga can be practiced by any person involved in any profession and at any place in the world. For practicing Yoga, one does not need to wear a particular kind of garment, eat any special food, or live in any special style. Yoga is suited to man living in society, to a man with a family, with household or career responsibilities, and at any age.

   If we consider the thinkers of the Age of Indian Philosophy, we note that beginning with Kapila there is an effort to improve, refine, and enlarge the philosophic and theoretical presentations and make them more and more adaptable by the common man. The major concern of all the thinkers of this period—Kapila, Buddha, Mahavira, Patanjali, and Vyasa—had been to find a remedy for sorrow and to point out the way to achieve happiness. These thinkers tried to add to what was taught by the preceding thinkers. We find the culmination of this trend in the writings of Vyasa, who wrote the original Gita.

2
THE ORIGINAL GITA

When learning about the original Gita, a reader may wish to know: (i) who wrote it and when? (ii) what was the content of the original? (iii) why, when, and by whom was the original changed into the present Bhagavadgita? And (iv), what have been the consequences of this change on Indian society and culture as a whole? These pertinent questions must be answered in order to acquire a comprehensive view of this change and its subsequent repercussions. A few of these questions are answered in this section and the remaining are dealt with in subsequent sections.

The import of these questions can be assessed from the fact that more than 2,000 versions of the Bhagavadgita have been published since 1785, when the first European edition was printed in London. The compiler of an international bibliography of the Bhagavadgita, Jagdish Chander Kapoor, writes that he collected 6,000 citations, out of which he selected 2,795 entries in 50 different languages.

According to Kapoor, the Sanskrit text of the Bhagavadgita is "extensively translated into every major language of the world and variedly interpreted by Western scholars." And he goes on to say: "Hundreds of scholarly publications by Christian missionaries and Orientalists have perpetuated the debate over its dialectical dictums. It was Shankaracharya, the illustrious Sanskrit scholar, who started this debate by writing the first commentary on the Bhagavadgita in 750 A.D.[1] Later, intellectuals such as Gandhi, Aurobindo Ghose, Hartmann, Hegel, Humboldt, Huxley, Isherwood, Jnandeva, Ramanuja, Schlegel, Schroder, Steiner, Tagore, and Tilak followed suit."[2]

The worldwide interest in the Bhagavadgita was noted by Nicol Macnicol in his book *Indian Theism*. According to Macnicol, "in its intellectual seriousness, its ethical nobility, and its religious fervour, the Bhagavadgita presents to us a combination that is unique in Indian religion, and that explains the remarkable influence the poem still exercises over many types of the Indian mind. It is one of the three authoritative scriptures upon

---

[1] The dates for Shankaracharya are 788 A.D. to 820 A.D. For more on Shankaracharya, see Chapter 3.

[2] Jagdish Chander Kapoor, *Bhagavad-Gita: An International Bibliography of 1785–1979 Imprints* (New York: Garland Publishing, Inc. 1983), pp. XIII–XIV.

which each of the Vedantic systems of philosophy—Advaita, Visistadvaita, Dvaita and Suddhadvaita—claims to be based."[3]

Another scholar, R.C. Zaehner, expresses a similar view by saying, "In actual fact it is not only the most popular but the most commented on of all the sacred texts of Hinduism. There is scarcely a sage or saint in India who has not commented on this most influential of all Hindu religious texts, from the time of Sankara in the ninth century to Vinoba Bhave of our own day."[4]

In fact, the popularity of the Bhagavadgita is not due solely to its religious content. Its place of prominence among the contemplative canons of world literature can be attributed to the fact that it addresses enduring human concerns in language of great lyricism. This is why William von Humboldt once referred to the Bhagavadgita as the most beautiful philosophical song.[5]

The philosophical value of the Bhagavadgita was noted by Radhakrishnan when he observed, "It is a book conveying lessons of philosophy, religion and ethics. It is not looked upon as a Sruti, or a revealed scripture, but is regarded as Smriti, or a tradition. Yet if the hold which the work has on the mind of man is any clue to its importance, then the Gita is the most influential work in Indian thought."[6]

It must be admitted that any critical inquiry related to any facet of the Gita is bound to stir up controversy. Indeed, the controversy has been going on for centuries. And it has not varied much within the last hundred years. This is evident when we consider what has been debated among the various scholars who have examined the Gita's history.

Among the earliest investigative works, the most noteworthy is the book by K.T. Telang, published in 1882. In his introductory section he observes, "There is no exaggeration in saying, that it is almost impossible to lay down even a single proposition respecting any important matter connected with the Bhagavadgita, about which any such consensus can be said to exist."[7]

Half a century later, the same difficulty was expressed by another scholar, S.C. Roy: "Modern scholars are still groping in the dark as to the question of the integrity of the Gita in its present form, for some of them hold it to be a genuine product of its original author, while others suspect that the text has passed through various stages of systematic interpolation."[8]

Even now, decades after Roy, the situation is not much changed. Instead of diminishing, the controversy continues to escalate. The unresolved nature of this argument is well expressed by G.S. Khair in his investigative

[3] Nicol Macnicol, *Indian Theism* (Delhi: Munshiram Manoharlal,1968), p. 75.
[4] R.C. Zaehner, *Hindu Scriptures* (London: J.M. Dent and Sons Ltd., 1966), p. XV.
[5] See Radhakrishnan, *Indian Philosophy*, p. 519.
[6] *Ibid.*
[7] Kashinath Trimbak Telang, *The Bhagavadgita* (Oxford: The Clarendon Press, 1882), p. 1.
[8] S.C. Roy, *The Bhagavadgita And Modern Scholarship* (London: Luzac & Co., 1941), p. 6.

work, *Quest for the Original Gita*. According to Khair, "Indian and Western scholars are still confused and divided among themselves on the questions of the authorship, the ultimate message and the date of the poem. The great divergence that exists in the views of scholars who have deeply studied this book testifies at once to the popularity and the very controversial nature of the poem."[9]

Most recently, an American scholar, R.N. Minor, who has made an exhaustive study of all the prominent scholarly works on the Bhagavadgita by both Western and Indian writers, observes that the issues of authorship and date are still unresolved and concludes that "there appears to be little hope of evidence coming to light which will improve this situation."[10]

This is an unduly pessimistic view, as the present work will attempt to demonstrate. But before proceeding to untangle the issue of the original authorship, let us briefly survey what other scholars have had to say on the matter.

The Matter of Scholarly Thought

Among the serious attempts by scholars to identify the original version and establish its date, the most noteworthy is the work of the German scholar, Richard Garbe. According to Garbe, "the original Gita has its origin in the first half of the Second Century B.C. and the Recension of the Poem in Second Century A.D."[11]

"The re-edited form of the poem which lies before us belongs to the period in which Krishna began to be identified with *brahman* and when Krishna-ism as a whole began to be vedanticized." Explaining the difference between the original and the rewritten versions, Garbe points out that "in the old poem Krishnaism philosophically based on the Samkhya-Yoga is proclaimed; in the additions made in the recension, the Vedanta philosophy is taught."[12]

Another noteworthy German scholar, Rudolf Otto, in his book *The Original Gita*, observes, "The chronology of The Original Gita depends on that of the 'Krishnaized' Epic, but is independent of the chronology of the interpolated Doctrinal Treaties. The Third Century B.C., therefore, is perhaps too low a limit for *The Original Gita* itself, while the insertion of

---

[9] G.S. Khair, *Quest For The Original Gita* (Bombay: Somaiya Publications Pvt. Ltd., 1969), p. 7.

[10] Robert N. Minor, *Bhagavad-Gita* (New Delhi: Heritage Publishers, 1982), p. XXXIII.

[11] Richard Garbe, *The Bhagavadgita*, translated by Rev. D. Mackinchan (Bombay: The University of Bombay, 1918), p. 50.

[12] *Ibid.*, pp. 7–8.

the individual treaties may have been effected very much later, and was presumably a rather prolonged process."[13]

While talking about the date and authorship, Eliot Deutsch in his book *The Bhagavadgita* says: "The Gita was definitely composed later than the (early) Upanishads . . . the period of the Gita's composition would fall somewhere between the fifth century B.C. and the second century B.C. The final recension of the work was made sometime in the Gupta period (fourth to seventh centuries A.D.), and the earliest manuscript source dates back to Shankara's commentary in the ninth century."[14]

Likewise, some highly respected Indian public figures and scholars have expressed doubts about the authenticity and integrity of the Bhagavadgita. Prominent among these are Mahatma Gandhi, Swami Vivekananda, G.S. Khair, R.V. Vaidya, T.G. Mainkar, and S.D. Pendse. They have all held the view that the present Bhagavadgita is an interpolated version and not the original. [15]

Swami Vivekananda strongly doubted the authenticity of the Bhagavadgita and went all around India in search of the original, but could not find it. He expressed his hope that, in the future, some serious effort would be made to locate the ur-text. While talking about the authorship of the present Bhagavadgita, Vivekananda says, "some infer that Shankaracharya was the author of the Gita, and that it was he who foisted it into the body of the Mahabharata." And he goes on to mention that, "In ancient times there was very little tendency in our country to find out truths by historical research."[16]

Emphasizing the importance of historical investigation for the study of ancient works, Vivekananda says, "it has its use, because we have to get at the truth; it will not do for us to remain bound by wrong ideas born of ignorance. In this country people think very little of the importance of such inquiries. Many of the sects believe that in order to preach a good thing which may be beneficial to many, there is no harm in telling an untruth, if that helps such preaching, or in other words, the end justifies the means . . . But our duty should be to convince ourselves to the truth, to believe in truth only."[17]

Since Gandhi considered himself a devout follower of the Gita and called it 'My Mother', his observations about it are very significant. Gandhi said, "there are many things in that poem that my poor understanding cannot

---

[13] Rudolf Otto, *The Original Gita*, translated by J.E. Turner (London: George Allen & Unwin Ltd., 1939), p. 14.

[14] Eliot Deutsch, *The Bhagavadgita* (U.S.A.: University Press of America, 1968), pp. 3–4.

[15] For a comprehensive view of Indian scholars, see Prem Nath Bazaz, *The Role of Bhagavadgita in Indian History* (New Delhi: Sterling Publishers Pvt. Ltd., 1975), pp. 164–169 and Ch. 10; R.V. Vaidya, *A Study of Mahabharata* (Poona: A.V.G. Prakasha, 1967), pp. 1–46.

[16] Swami Vivekananda, *Thoughts on the Gita* (Calcutta: Advaita Ashrama, 1967), pp. 1–8; and also see *The Complete Works of Swami Vivekananda*, Vol. IV (Calcutta: Advaita Ashrama, 1978), p. 103.

[17] *Ibid.*, (The Complete Works), pp. 105–106. For more about his views, see the section "Thoughts on the Gita", pp. 102–110.

fathom. There are in it many things which are obvious interpolations. It is not a treasure chest. It is a mine which needs to be explored, which needs to be dug deep and from which diamonds have to be extracted after removing much foreign matter."[18]

In stark opposition to the aforesaid views, which this author shares, several noted Indian scholars such as Bal Gangadhar Tilak, Radhakrishnan, K.T. Telang, and Kashi Nath Upadhyaya have expressed the view that the Bhagavadgita as we know it today has come down to us basically unchanged in its fundamental doctrines, though it might have been expanded. About the date, all but Telang hold the view that it was written in 500 B.C. or even earlier. Telang's view is that it was composed in 300 B.C. or earlier. Thus, beginning with Telang, these scholars put the date of the Bhagavadgita somewhere between 300 B.C. and 500 B.C.[19]

The views of Indian scholars of this persuasion are summed up by S.C. Roy when he says: "Apart from such inevitable changes and some isolated cases of interpolation, our poem seems to have retained essentially the same form and content as it had in the original."[20]

The traditionalist defense of the textual integrity of the present-day Bhagavadgita has struck at least one Western academic as evidence of serious scholarly deficiency. John Davies questioned whether certain Indian writers held to those standards of intellectual independence so long established in the West. And he observed, "I, too, have consulted Hindu commentators largely, but have found them deficient in critical insight, and more intent on finding or forming Vedantist doctrines in every part than in giving the true sense of the author. I have examined their explanations with the freedom of inquiry that is common to Western habits of thought, and thus, while I have sometimes followed their guidance, I have been obliged to reject their comments as misrepresenting the doctrines of the author."[21]

Note, however, that the traditionalist view does find an occasional adherent in the West. Among those Western scholars defending the textual integrity of the present-day version, the most prominant are Étiene Lamotte, Emile Senart, Franklin Edgerton, Rudolf Steiner, and Robert N. Minor.[22] Edgerton may be said to represent this viewpoint when he con-

---

[18] M.K. Gandhi, *The Teaching of the Gita* (Bombay: Bhartiya Vidya Bhavan, 1962), p. 6. The original appears in *Young India*: May 21, 1928 under the heading "Neither Fiction nor History."

[19] See B.G. Tilak, *Bhagavadgita Rahasya*, Vol. I and Vol. II (Poona: Lokamanya Tilak Mandir, 1935), p. 800. For his view on the date and contents of the Poem, see pp. 785–831; Radhakrishnan, *Indian Philosophy*, p. 524; K.T. Telang, *The Bhagavadgita*, p. 34; K.N. Upadhyaya, *Early Buddhism And The Bhagavadgita* (Delhi: Motilal Banarsidass, 1971), pp. 16–29.

[20] S.C. Roy, *op. cit.*, p. 9.

[21] John Davies, *The Bhagavadgita* (London: Trubner and Co., 1882), p. 207.

[22] See Étiene Lamotte, *Notes Sur La Bhagavadgita* (Paris: Librairie Orientaliste Paul Geuthner, 1929), pp. 1–9 and 127–137; Emile Senart, *La Bhagavadgita* (Paris: Societe Dedition, 1967), pp. III–XVIII; Franklin Edgerton, *The Bhagavadgita* (Massachusetts: Harvard University Press, 1972), p. XIV; Rudolf Steiner, *The Bhagavadgita And The Epistles of Paul* (New York: Anthroposophic Press, INC., 1971), pp. 16–36; R.N. Minor, *op.cit.*, p. XLIII.

cludes that "there is absolutely no documentary evidence that any other form of the Gita than that which we have was ever known in India."[23]

To gain a clear picture of what is involved in this debate, let me quote the judgment of John Davies, who reached some very significant conclusions about the Bhagavadgita. In a historical comparison of Indian philosophical and religious thought, John Davies observes:

"It may be certainly affirmed that if any one, after reading the Puranas or other popular religious books of the Hindus, should then turn for the first time to the study of the Bhagavadgita, he must be conscious of having come to a new country where nearly everything is changed. The thoughts, the sentiments, and the methods of expression have another stamp."[24]

Davies examines at great length the question of the date and authorship of the Bhagavadgita and concludes: "From a long study of the work, I infer that its author lived at or near the time of Kalidasa."[25]

According to Davies, the author of the Bhagavadgita was a Brahman.[26] Holtzmann also expresses the same view by arguing that the "original Mahabharata was turned into a Dharma-Sastra by the Brahmans after 900 A.D."[27] It was Rudolf Otto's opinion that the Brahmanizing of the Bhagavadgita is proven by Brahmanization of *The Anugita*. In Otto's own words, "It will therefore be no error to assume that they constituted the initial attempts to immunize *The Gita*, in the sense of the same 'Brahmanizing' direction."[28]

Davies provides a historical argument concerning the possible, even probable, influence of Christian doctrines on Brahmanism, saying: "We have positive evidence that a knowledge of Christianity existed there before the third century A.D." By the third and fourth centuries A.D., St. Thomas's Church was established at Malipur, and Pantaenus was sent by the bishop of Alexandria to instruct the Brahmans on the Christian faith.[29]

One most important contribution of Davies is the tracing of the lineage of Vyasa. He provides the dynastic line of descent of Chandra-Vansa (Lunar Dynasty), which shows that Vyasa was a Kshatriya, the grandfather of the Pandava brothers. Vyasa was the son of Rishi Parasara.[30]

---

[24] Davies, *op.cit.*, p. 188.

[25] Kalidasa is regarded as the greatest of Indian poets and some refer to him as the Indian Shakespeare. Though the dates for Kalidasa are not conclusively settled, both Telang and Macdonell hold the view that he lived between the fifth and sixth centuries A.D., during the period of the Gupta ruler, Vikramaditya. See Macdonell, *A History of Sanskrit Literature* (New York: Haskell House Publishers, 1968), p. 318; Telang, *op. cit.*, 28; Davies, *op. cit.*, pp. 190 and 200. For more on Kalidasa's life, see A.B. Keith, *A History of Sanskrit Literature* (Oxford: The Clarendon Press, 1928), pp. 78–108.

[26] Davies, *op.cit.*, p. 187.

[27] Holtzmann, *Das Mahabharata*, pp. 163–164.

[28] Otto, *op. cit.*, p. 15.

[29] Davies, *op. cit.*, pp. 186–200.

[30] *Ibid.* See "The Traditionary Line of Descent of The Lunar Dynasty", p. 202. This line of dynasty is given by Professor Dowson in "Classical Dictionary of Hindu Mythology." Also, see the Appendix of this book.

From the evidence compiled by Davies, it is reasonable to conclude that Vyasa is the author, not of the Bhagavadgita (as many claim), but of the original Gita. As Davies characterizes the authorial hand which produced the present-day version of the Bhagavadgita: "The author was a Brahman, and he retained a degree of respect, or rather toleration, for the Vedic doctrines and ritual, but he subordinates them entirely to the duty and happiness of pious meditation. They were of no efficacy to the perfect Yogin."[31]

Chronological Accounts of the Original Gita

The original name of the poem was simply Gita. In order to distinguish it from the later Bhagavadgita, I will refer to it as the original Gita. The original was variously known in Indian antiquity as Gita, Gita-Shastra, and Smriti.

Gita means a composition in metrical form which can be sung or chanted.

Gita-Shastra means a tutorial document which presents the teachings of an acclaimed authority. Since the teaching of the Gita contains the Samkhya Yoga philosophy, it has rightly been referred to as a Shastra.

Smriti refers to a work which is remembered. Since the Gita was chanted and sung, it was remembered and memorized, long before writing developed. The Gita predates the widespread practice of writing and was thus a part of the oral tradition of ancient India.

With these explanations of the alternate names of the Gita, let me now present evidence to show where these names appear in the historical record. The most important ancient Indian document mentioning the Gita by name is the epic Mahabharata. Therefore, let us consider it first.

Evidence in the Mahabharata

The Mahabharata, in four separate places, refers to the Gitapriya, Gita Vadanakapriya, Gita Vaditracalin, and Gita Vaditra tattvajna.[32] It also refers to the Bhagavadgita in two places (outside the Bhagavadgita Parvan).[33]

The appearance of the name Bhagavadgita presents no problem for the argument advanced in this book because the epic Mahabharata has also

---

[31] *Ibid.*, p. 187.

[32] See S. Sorensen, *Index to The Names in The Mahabharata* (London: Williams & Norgate, 1904), p. 309.

[33] *Ibid.*, p. 114.

undergone modifications on at least three different occasions.[34] One of these revisions incorporated the altered form of the Gita in a section titled "the Bhagavadgita parvan" (section on the song of the exalted one) and references to this version were then interpolated elsewhere in the epic. Fortunately, those responsible for rewriting the epic left intact and uncorrupted the original references in the text. The modifications were simply accredited to the ancient 'core' documents. (For a further discussion, see Chapter V.)

Evidence in Alberuni's Work

Another piece of evidence that the name Gita was current in ancient India is found in the writings of the famous Arab Muslim scholar Alberuni, who lived in India from 1017 to 1031 A.D. Alberuni wrote *Kitabul Hind*, translated into English as *Alberuni's Indica*.[35]

In his writings, Alberuni gives a comprehensive description of Samkhya philosophy, Yoga, and the Gita together with a full account of the Hindu religion. He mentions the Gita 14 times in various contexts. Not once did he mention the Bhagavadgita. Furthermore, Professor Dani, the translator of *Kitabul Hind*, has specifically pointed out that the Gita referred to by Alberuni is not the Bhagavadgita.[36]

Since Alberuni knew Sanskrit and was an assiduous cataloguer of Indian intellectual culture, it seems unlikely that he would have omitted any reference to the Bhagavadgita if it were widely known at that time. Thus, we may argue that the Gita, and not the Bhagavadgita, was the common cultural property of the Indian people up to the early eleventh century A.D.

Furthermore, Alberuni's silence indicates that the vulgate text of the Bhagavadgita, even if it might have been composed during the time of Shankaracharya, must have been known only to a small circle during this period. This inference is supported by the fact that Alberuni does not discuss Vedanta or the Advaita-Vedanta philosophy of Shankaracharya, even where he talks at great length about Hindu religion and the concept of Brahmanda.[37]

Evidence in the Bhagavadgita Bhashaya

References to the Gita-Shastra are found in the commentary of Shankaracharya. In his introductory note on the *Bhagavadgita Bhashyam*

---

[34] See S.P. Gupta (ed.) *Mahabharata: Myth and Reality* (Delhi: Agam Prakashan, 1976), pp. 3–4. For the views of Western scholars see, Belvalkar, *History of Indian Philosophy* (New Delhi: Oriental Books Reprint Corp., 1967), pp. 421–426.

[35] *Alberuni's Indica*, translated by Professor Ahmad Hasan Dani (Pakistan: University of Islamabad, 1973).

[36] *Ibid.*, p. 64. For details on the Gita, see pp. 64–102.

[37] *Ibid.*, p. 210–224.

(Commentary on the Bhagavadgita), Shankaracharya mentions that Veda-Vyasa composed the book entitled Gita (Gitanamaka), which was explicated by various commentators who often opposed one another.[38]

According to his own account, the commentators on the Gitashastra had discussed *Jnana-nishtha* and *Karma-nishtha* (knowledge and action based doctrines), derivatives of Samkhya and Yoga. Shankaracharya pointed out that these doctrines of Jnana-nishtha and Karma-nishtha were inadequate for achieving Kaivalya (salvation). He emphasized that *moksha* (salvation) can be achieved by a dharma based on renunciation of all actions and by acquiring self-knowledge. He advanced these arguments to justify the need for writing his commentary.[39]

Evidence in the Brahma-Sutras

References to the Gita as Smriti are found in the *Brahma-Sutras* 2.3.45 and 4.2.21. This claim is validated by the subsequent commentaries of Shankaracharya, Ramanuja, and others, all of whom have accepted these as references to the Gita.

According to an investigative work of P.M. Modi, the Brahma-Sutras mention Smriti in contexts which can refer only to "a work like the Gita or the Mahabharata".[40] Further, verse 4.2.21 clearly states that the Smriti (Gita) contains the doctrines and teachings of Samkhya and Yoga, whose adherents practice as *sadhana* (discipline).[41] Here we have a very clear reference to the Gita not only by name but also by its subject-matter. Significantly, the Sutras make no mention of the Bhagavadgita.

From the foregoing accounts, it seems that there is substantial historical evidence to support the existence and popularity of the original Gita in India prior to the eleventh century A.D. Though it might appear shocking to some, there is no historical evidence of the Bhagavadgita's existence in India prior to Shankaracharya. This suggests that the Bhagavadgita did not exist prior to the ninth century A.D. A detailed defense of this hypothesis will be given shortly.

One of those who would have been shocked by the claim put forth in this book is K.T. Telang, whose early and influential work on the Bhagavadgita is frequently cited by both Indian and Western scholars. In his book *Bhagavadgita*, K.T. Telang mentions external evidence to establish the age of the Bhagavadgita. As testimony, he cites the *Kadambari* of Banabhatta (seventh century A.D.).

---

[38] *Shrimad-Bhagavadgita: Shankar Bhashya*, Hindi, (Gorakhpur, India: Gita Press, 1967), p. 14.

[39] *Ibid.*, pp. 15–27.

[40] P.M. Modi, "Meaning of Smriti in the Brahma-Sutras", *Indian Historical Quarterly*, Vol. XII, Dec. 1936, pp. 714–19.

[41] *Brahma-Sutras*, 4.2.21. See Swami Vireswarananda, *Brahma-Sutras* translation (Calcutta: Advaita Ashrama, 1965), p. 437.

External Evidence

The Kadambari compares a palace scene with a scene of the Mahabharata: *Ananta gita Karnan ananditanaram* (translation: in which the people were delighted by hearing innumerable songs). When considered in the context of the Mahabharata, the above quotation probably refers to the Gita. It implies that as Arjuna was delighted by hearing the Gita (song), so the people of the palace were also delighted. This reference to the Gita is assumed by Telang to mean the Bhagavadgita.[42]

Let us consider another claim by Telang. He cites the works of Kalidasa to prove the age of the Bhagavadgita. There is a passage in *Raghuvansa* of Kalidasa, canto X, stanza 67, in which the gods addressing Vishnu say: "There is nothing for you to acquire which has not been acquired. The one motive in your birth and work is the good of the worlds."

This verse of Raghuvansa appears in the original Gita verses 67 and 68.[43] The idea of the good of the worlds is expressed in several verses of the original Gita, such as 67, 68, 69, and 70.

Likewise, Kalidasa in his other work, *Kumarasambhava*, canto VI, stanza 67, refers to the concept of "firmly fixed". This expression certainly refers to the Gita as verses 44 and 45 explain.[44]

Based on such historical evidence, Telang tried to prove the existence of the Bhagavadgita prior to the time of Kalidasa and also Banabhata. But this argument carries little weight if we posit the existence of an ur-text Gita which survived in the time of Shankaracharya.

In order to differentiate this Gita from the vulgate text of the Bhagavadgita, let us trace the historical records of the latter.

Chronological Accounts of the Bhagavadgita

A revealing fact about the Bhagavadgita (Song of the Supreme) is that there is no historical evidence of its existence in India prior to the time of Shankaracharya (788–820 A.D.). This implies that the Bhagavadgita as we know it today could have come into existence during the ninth century A.D. or possibly some time later.[45] It is true that the epic Mahabharata refers twice to the Bhagavadgita and has a section called Bhagavadgita Parvan (chapters 25–42 of the Bhishma Parva). But all these are interpolated sections of the epic.

[42] For the interpretation of Telang, see *op. cit.*, pp. 27–29.
[43] For the original, see the Text of the Original Gita in Part Two of this book.
[44] *Ibid.*
[45] We will examine this aspect in Chapter 3.

It is accepted by most Indian and Western scholars that the present text of the epic is not the original. Belvalkar in his *History of Indian Philosophy* states emphatically that "some of the additions and interpolations in the present form of the Mahabharata are so very obvious that it would be absurd to refuse to recognize them as such."[46]

In his recent work, *A History of Sanskrit Literature*, Macdonell proposes that "The epic underwent three stages of development from the time it first assumed definite shape; and this conclusion is corroborated by various internal and external arguments."[47]

None of the texts to which Shankaracharya makes reference in his Bhagavadgita-Bhashyam have survived. This point is clarified by the Hindi translator of the Bhagavadgita-Bhashyam who states: "It is proven by the saying of the Acharya (Shankaracharya) that at the time of his commentary, there were many commentaries on the Bhagavadgita popularly known *(prachalita)* to the people. But, sorry to say, not any of them is now available."[48]

What is most dubious about this commentary is that 57 verses of the present Bhagavadgita are completely omitted by Shankaracharya. All the 47 verses of Chapter One and verses 1 to 10 of Chapter Two are not commented upon. He begins his commentary with verse number 11 of Chapter Two.

This inconsistency of Shankara's Bhashya has been thoroughly investigated by J.A.B. Van Buitenen. In an article entitled *The Critical Edition of the Bhagavadgita*, Van Buitenen points out, "The earliest testimony concerning the Gita is that of Sankara, and the Gita text adopted by the Editor is really Sankara's text with but 14 highly insignificant variants."[49]

Van Buitenen further observes, "It should, however be noted that Sankara does not comment on the first 57 stanzas of the Gita, which include the entire first chapter. Sankara therefore holds no authority for the present reading."[50]

Van Buitenen provides a comprehensive account of these shortcomings and writes: "This should prove that very close to Sankara's date there existed two variant texts that were equally authoritative. Therefore, the question of the 'critical edition' of the Bhagavadgita can again be raised legitimately."[51]

Van Buitenen offers a comparative study of the commentaries of Bhaskara and Shankaracharya. The commentary of Bhaskara is entitled

---

[46] Belvalkar, *op.cit*, p. 426 and pp. 421–426. For scholarly views on interpolations in the *Mahabharata*, see S.P. Gupta (ed.), *op. cit.*, p. 255; R.V. Vaidya, *op. cit.*, pp. 33–46; and Holtzmann, *op. cit.*, p. 194.

[47] A.A. Macdonell, *op. cit.*, p. 284.

[48] Harikrishnadas Goenka, *Shankar Bhashya, op. cit.*, p. 9.

[49] Van Buitenen, *Journal of the American Oriental Society*. Vol. 85, March 1965, pp. 99–109.

[50] *Ibid.*, p. 102

[51] *Ibid.*, p. 104.

Bhagavadanusa Yanusarana and consists of two manuscripts: one written in Kashmiri script and the other in Devanagri script. According to Van Buitenen, "The significance of Bhaskara's text thus is that it proves the existence of a generally accepted Gita text well before both him and Sankara."[52]

Based on his comparative study of Bhaskara and Shankara, Van Buitenen concludes: "I believe that the conclusion is unavoidable that in the ninth century there existed a text of the Bhagavadgita which had equal authority with that used by Sankara; that it existed outside Kashmir; and that it is the prototype of the so-called Kashmir version. The consequence of this conclusion is that the Kashmir version is late and secondary, not to the Vulgate, but to Bhaskara's text."[53]

Furthermore, the Bhagavadgita itself provides some internal evidence of its late composition. For example, verse XV, 15 mentions *Vedantakrita* (author of the Vedanta). This verse is a clue that the composition of the vulgate text took place when the doctrine of Vedanta came into prominence. Since the promulgation of Vedanta is closely linked to Shankara, it is evident that the Bhagavadgita has its origin in the same period.

Likewise, verse X, 23 compares the Vedic god Rudra with Shankara. The more apt comparison would have been to Shiva, as is apparent when we examine their common characteristics. Rudra has been characterized as fierce, destructive, unsurpassed in might, and malevolent. But he is also bountiful, a bestower of blessings, whose favor is easily invoked. These characteristics are also those of Shiva, a post-Vedic god who became a successor of Rudra.[54] The comparison of Rudra with Shankara instead of Shiva provides an additional clue to the dating of the Bhagavadgita.

To give one more instance, in verse IV, 2 Krishna is telling Arjuna that the Yoga of the Kshatriya tradition, handed down in regular succession by Rajarshi—who were both *Raja* (king) and *Rishi* (sage)—had been destroyed *(yogo nashtah)*. The question is: when and by whom was this Yoga destroyed? When we critically examine this question in the context of the religious and philosophic history of India, it becomes apparent that this occurred around 800 A.D. and shortly thereafter.[55] From this verse also, it is not difficult to deduce the period when the vulgate text came into being.

From the foregoing, it can be persuasively argued that the date of the Bhagavadgita does not extend prior to the date of Shankaracharya. What existed before this time was a text likely to have been written by Vyasa, a text known throughout ancient Indian culture as the Gita.

---

[52] *Ibid.*, p. 109. For details of Bhaskara's commentary see pp. 106–109. The date of Bhaskara, according to Van Buitenen, is a century after Shankara. See p. 105.

[53] *Ibid.*, p. 105.

[54] Macdonell, *A Vedic Reader, op. cit.*, pp. 56–57.

[55] For comprehensive coverage, see Ch. 3.

The Author of the Gita

Historical evidence and Indian tradition agree in attributing the authorship of the original Gita to Vyasa. One reason for some past confusion in establishing his authorship is that he was also known as Veda-Vyasa (the compiler of the Vedas) and as the compiler of the epic Mahabharata. Since his name is attached to three most important literary texts of ancient India, each of which dates from a different time, it is not surprising that recognition of Vyasa's authorship has been slow in coming.

What has added to this uncertainty is that during the course of history, his name began to be used as a title. Since Vyasa came to connote great learning and wisdom, people began using the name as title for those who could recite ancient scriptural texts or conduct ceremonial rituals. With the passage of time, the name as signifier of a distinct historical figure became blurred.

In order to clarify this situation, we must examine the historical records of India to determine: (i) Who was Vyasa? (ii) What evidence is there to support the contention that Vyasa composed the original Gita? (iii) Was Vyasa also a compiler of the Vedas and the Mahabharata? Let us now examine each of these questions.

Vyasa

Vyasa was a kshatriya rishi (sage) and belonged to the Chandra-Vansi (Lunar) dynasty. He was the grandfather of Arjuna and the Pandava brothers. The name of his father was rishi (sage) Parasara, and his mother's name was Satyavati.[56] The great grandfather of Vyasa was Bharata, whose descendents were known as Kurus. They had built their kingdom at Hastinapur. Since the great war (recounted in the Mahabharata) involved the descendents of this dynasty of Bharata, who then ruled over a greater part of India, this kingdom began to be referred to as Bharata-Varsha (the present-day name of India).

Considering the lineage of Vyasa and the role the members of his family played in the Mahabharata, it is plausible that this learned rishi composed the philosophic song—the Gita, depicting the ethical dilemma faced by some of the leading figures involved in this war. And it is also reasonable to believe that he composed a historical account of the war and called it *Jaya* (Victory), which was in fact the original name of the Mahabharata.

---

[56] For details about the lineage of Vyasa, see John Davies, *The Bhagavadgita* (London: Trubner & Co. 1882), pp. 202–203.

Historical evidence of Vyasa is cited in the Mahabharata itself. The epic specifically refers to him as Vyasa, as compiler of the Mahabharata, as Veda-Vyasa, and describes his lineage.[57]

Evidence of Vyasa being the author of the Gita is found in several ancient literary texts. The most solid evidence is in the *Bhagavadgita-Bhashya* of Shankara. In his commentary Shankaracharya writes that the Gita was composed by Veda-Vyasa.[58]

Another clear account of Vyasa's authorship is found in *Alberuni's Indica*. Alberuni talks at great length about the Gita and at several places refers to Vyasa, the son of Parasara, as its author.[59]

Besides these, there is internal evidence in the Bhagavadgita itself, which clearly states that Vyasa is the author of the Gita. Verse XVIII, 75 says that the composition of the Bhagavadgita has been due to Vyasa (Vyas-aprasada). Though this section is interpolated, it does reveal who the actual author of the original was.

We find one indirect reference to Vyasa's authorship in the work of Madhava Acharya, who lived in the fourteenth century. In his *Vedartha-prakasha*, Madhava Acharya attributes the actual composition of the Mahabharata to the sage Vyasa.[60] Since it is established that the author of the original Mahabharata was the same person as the author of the Gita, it can be deduced that Vyasa was the author of the Gita.

We now need to determine if Vyasa (putative author of the Gita); Veda-Vyasa (compiler of the Vedas); and Vyasa (compiler of the Mahabharata) were the same person.

We know that the Vedas are called *Sruti*, or revealed scripture. The hymns of the Veda were composed by different families and were committed to memory. They were handed down orally from one generation to the next. Thus, for centuries they remained unwritten and also uncollected.[61]

When the time finally came to put the Vedic hymns in a more permanent form, the task would naturally fall to someone renowned for his poetic skill and mastery of the scriptures. Furthermore, the individual must have had to be able to command the resources of the royal court, for this was a prolonged and costly project. Vyasa was clearly such an individual.[62]

The identification of Vyasa as a compiler of the Mahabharata is supported by recent scholarly findings. It is now well established that the epic, in its earliest form, contained only 8,800 verses and that its name was

[57] For details on all these references, see S. Sorensen, *op. cit.*, pp. 758–760.

[58] *Bhagavadgita-Bhashya, op. cit*, p. 14.

[59] See *Alberuni's Indica, op. cit.*, pp. 62, 73.

[60] See Monier-Williams, *Indian Wisdom* (Varanasi: Chowkhambha Sanskrit Series Office, 1963), p. 373.

[61] For a clear account of the origin, growth and earliest collected form of the Rig Veda, see A.A. Macdonell, *A Vedic Reader, op. cit.*, pp. XII–XVI.

[62] See Monier-Williams, *op. cit.*, p. 111, 372–373.

Jaya (Victory).[63] Considering the original form of the epic and the author's family background and scholarly ability, it is quite reasonable to surmise that it was Vyasa who presented a historical account of this great war in a poetic form.

A historical account of Vyasa as compiler of the Mahabharata is also found in a traditional story. It is recounted that Vyasa dictated the Mahabharata to Ganesha, who put them in a written form.[64] According to this story, Vyasa is not the actual writer but only a compiler of the epic. Considering the period of Vyasa when literatures were still composed in oral form and memorized, it is not surprising that we find the Mahabharata referred to as a smriti.

Neither the Mahabharata nor the Gita, in their original forms, were works of great length. The epic contained no more than 8,800 verses, and the Gita (as we shall see) contained only 84. Both could easily have been the products of one man and might, in fact, have been composed as a single work.

There is thus no reason to dismiss the traditional attribution of the Gita, the Vedas, and the Mahabharata to the same person. Monier Williams reached the same conclusion when he observed: "It may seem strange that the compilation of wholly different works composed at very different epochs, such as the Vedas, Maha-bharata, and Puranas, undoubtedly were, should be attributed to the same person; but the close relationship supposed by learned natives to subsist between these productions, will account for a desire to call in the aid of the same great sage in their construction."[65]

Date of the Original Gita

We now attempt to determine the date of the Gita, even though we do not know the exact date of Vyasa. A clue is provided by the fact that both the Gita and the Mahabharata were known as Smriti, meaning that the compositions were orally transmitted. We can thus broadly pinpoint the date of Vyasa by knowing the date of the Mahabharata. And we can determine the date of the Gita in its written form by knowing when writing began in India. Let us first consider the date of the Mahabharata.

According to recent studies of S.P. Gupta, there is no reference to the Mahabharata in the Vedic literature, and no Indian literature mentions it until the fourth century B.C.[66] This fact indicates that the great war

---

[63] For details, see R.V. Vaidya, *op. cit.*, p. 11; and S.P. Gupta, *op. cit.*, pp. 3–4.
[64] This account is fully described by S. Sorensen, *op. cit.*, p. 758.
[65] Monier-Williams, *op. cit.*, pp. 372–373.
[66] S.P. Gupta, *op. cit.*, pp. 3–51.

occurred during the fourth century B.C. and therefore the period of Vyasa is the same. From this reasoning, we have historic ground for concluding that the Gita in its original form was also composed during the fourth century B.C. Since writing was not yet common, the composition remained in the possession of a few scholar-scribes.

According to the findings of Macdonell, the use of ink *(mashi)* and pen *(kalama)* was prevalent in India during the fourth century B.C. Palm leaf writing became common by the first century A.D.[67] This indicates that during the time of Vyasa writing was known, though not widely practiced. Since Vyasa was a rishi of a royal family, we can assume that he not only knew how to write but that he composed his poems in written form. Not many copies could have been made, of course, and as a result, most people still had to learn these poems by memorization. Thus, the work of Vyasa could be included among those which were orally transmitted (Smriti), even though they existed in written form.

Glimpses of the Original Gita

Before mentioning its salient features, let me point out why it was used as a title. As noted earlier, the word 'Gita' means song. It is very commonly used in India even now. The word might be spelled in English either geeta or gita.

Vyasa used the word Gita as a title of his work because he composed it in a form which could be sung and easily remembered even by the illiterate masses of his time. By composing the verses in song form, he not only simplified the abstract, dry, and complex philosophy of Samkhya Yoga but also made it accessible to the man on the street. For this reason the original Gita of Vyasa became very popular amongst the masses of that period. It was this popularity of the book which motivated its alteration, making it a vehicle of religious expression.

We can comprehend the contents of the original by way of posing a question: What was its purpose? The need for it arose because neither Kapila nor Patanjali had provided solutions to all forms of sorrow. To Vyasa, the answer to the question raised by Kapila in the very beginning of his treatise Samkhya Darshan was only partially answered.

Kapila had raised a basic question: What causes sorrow (dukha) and what is the remedy? In answering this question, he pointed out that lack of proper knowledge of things and incorrect action cause sorrow (dukha). As a remedy, he provided two theories: (i) the theory of Samayak Jnana

---

[67] Macdonell, *A History of Sanskrit Literature*, pp. 18–19.

(proper knowledge), and (ii) the theory of Satkaryavada (right action). To Kapila, a person equipped with the knowledge of these theories would eliminate sorrow and live a happy and prosperous life on his own *purusartha* (self-endeavor).

Patanjali tried to make these concepts more comprehensive by integrating them with his own system of Yoganga (the eight steps of Yoga). To Patanjali, a man who acquired health by practicing asana and pranayama, mastered the techniques of concentration and meditation, acquired self-perfection in the practices of Samyama, and acted in accordance with the concept of pratyahara would be better able to eradicate and prevent sorrow and live a happy life than by merely knowing and acting in accordance with Samkhya philosophy. By adding to what was taught by Kapila, Patanjali improved and expanded the applicability of the whole combined system, called Samkyha Yoga. On the whole, it appeared as if the answer was now complete. By knowing and practicing Samkhya Yoga, no one would suffer from sorrow or agony any more and no one would be deprived of a happy and healthy life.

At this point comes Vyasa. To him the method for eradicating sorrow and providing a healthy and happy life was not yet complete. The unanswered question, as it appeared to Vyasa, can be put in this way:

Sometimes a man is faced with a situation in which it is very difficult to decide what to do. If he acts one way, it will be bad; if he acts another way, it will be worse. What should he do in that condition? This condition of indecisiveness might be very tortuous, painful, and disturbing. The remedy for sorrow resulting from such a situation was not provided by Kapila or by Patanjali. Thus, Vyasa felt that unless an answer to this type of sorrow were provided, man would still not be free from sorrow and would not enjoy a healthy and happy life.

Vyasa cites the case of Arjuna, a Kshatriya warrior king, to illustrate his point. Arjuna is faced with a similar situation in a war against his own relations, who had unjustly usurped his kingdom and throne. Being a great warrior and confident of his own indestructible power and skill, and assured of his victory over the enemy, he still was in great sorrow and agony. He felt that he would have to kill his own kith and kin. As a result, many young women would become widows, young offspring would become orphans, and much of the family and its wealth would be destroyed. The problem of whether to gain such a victory or not caused Arjuna much anguish.

Though Arjuna was a learned man, familiar with the Samkhya Yoga philosophy and its theories, he could not find answers for his type of problem. The situation he was faced with caused him to perspire and tremble, and he was in a terrible state. The remedy for the type of sorrow faced by Arjuna needed to be provided in order to make the teaching of Samkhya Yoga more complete and all-inclusive. The answer to Arjuna's problem was provided by Vyasa in the original Gita, in the form of a dialogue between Arjuna and his counsellor-charioteer, Krishna.

Since Vyasa accepted the basic philosophy of Kapila and the practices of Yoga and presented them in a lucid, easy to sing and remember form, the song became very popular. With the inclusion of all the rational, humane thoughts and practices of its time, the Gita in its original form became a precious jewel of Indian culture, highly treasured by the masses.

As I will argue below, this Gita remained intact up to 800 A.D. It was available in handwritten book form on palm leaves. Since printing had not yet been invented, and paper was not introduced until the Muhammadan conquest, copies of the Gita must have been few in number.[68]

When the original was changed, the interpolators made those changes in the name of Yoga. They did not remove what was already there but added to it a new religious philosophy. The eighteen chapters of the present Bhagavadgita, have been named after some forms of Yoga. The interpolators did this to make people believe that the Bhagavadgita was a work of Yoga philosophy and that it contained all with which people were already familiar. By not destroying the original and by declaring the amended Bhagavadgita to be the original, the leaders of the Brahmanical revival movement were successful in establishing it as a genuine work of Indian culture. Though full of contradictions, and opposing thoughts, it continued to be supported by some Indian and Western scholars and remained unchallenged until the twentieth century. Expressing his views on how the interpolations in the original Gita were made, Garbe writes:

> Since the interpolations are distributed very unevenly over the 18 hymns, it is natural to suppose that the Original Gita consisted of a smaller number of hymns. The division into 18 adhyayas (chapters) is probably an imitation of the division of the *Mahabharata* into 18 parvas; perhaps at that time also the 18 puranas were known.[69]

Contents of the Bhagavadgita

The present Bhagavadgita has 18 chapters, all named after some form of Yoga. The names of the chapters, along with their English translation and the number of verses in each of them, are noted below:

Chapter	Name	Verses
I.	Arjuna-Visada Yoga (Yoga of Dejection of Arjuna)	47

---

[68] *Ibid.*

[69] Richard Garbe, *The Bhagavadgita*, translated by D. Mackichan (Bombay: The University of Bombay, 1918), p. 10.

II.	Samkhya Yoga (Yoga of Samkhya System)	72
III.	Karma Yoga (Yoga of Right Action)	43
IV.	Jnana-Karma-Sanyasa Yoga (Yoga of Knowledge, Action and Renunciation)	42
V.	Karma-Sanyasa Yoga (Yoga of Action and Renunciation)	29
VI.	Dhyana Yoga (Yoga of Meditation)	47
VII.	Jnana-Vijnana Yoga (Yoga of Knowledge & Science)	30
VIII.	Aksara-Brahma Yoga (Yoga of the Word BRAHMA)	28
IX.	Raja-Vidya-Raja-Guhya Yoga (Yoga of Kingship and its Insights)	34
X.	Vibhuti Yoga (Yoga of Manifestations)	42
XI.	Visva-Rupa-Darshana Yoga (Yoga of Seeing the Universal Form or Cosmic Form)	55
XII.	Bhakti Yoga (Yoga of Devotion)	20
XIII.	Ksetra-Ksetrajna-Vibhaga Yoga (Yoga of Field or Division and the Knower of the Field)	34
XIV.	Gunatraya-Vibhaga Yoga (Yoga of Three Gunas Constituents)	27
XV.	Purusottama Yoga (Yoga of the Highest Purusa)	20
XVI.	Daivasura-Sampat-Vibhaga Yoga (Yoga of Distinction Between Devil and Godly)	24
XVII.	Sradha-Traya-Vibhaga Yoga (Yoga of the Distinction of Three Kinds of Faith/Worship)	28
XVIII.	Moksha-Sanyasa Yoga (Yoga of Liberation and Renunciation)	78
	Total Number of Verses	700

Evidence Showing the Continuity of the Original Gita up to 800 A.D.

For a clear image of Indian conditions up to 800 A.D. we have to look into several historic records. We find some good descriptions in the writings of three Chinese travelers who visited India before 800 A.D. and in the writings of Alberuni, who visited India from 1017 to 1031 A.D. Other historical accounts of India come from the time of King Asoka (269 B.C.) up to the time of the Gupta period (700 A.D.) and the century following.

In order to comprehend the continuity of rational thought and practices prior to 800 A.D., we have to keep in mind several facts: (i) Buddhism as a religion represented all that was the essence of the thought of Kapila; (ii) the philosophic assertions of Samkhya Yoga were incorporated in Buddhistic teachings; (iii) the original Gita of Vyasa was an expansion of the basic philosophy of Samkhya Yoga.

Another significant point to keep in mind is that Buddhism had started as a social reform movement. It was opposed to Brahmanic and Vedic rituals and sacrifices and to Vedic prayers of supplication to various gods. Buddhism, by 800 A.D., had spread all over India, forming monastaries, teaching centers, and a well established system of doctrines. Thus, as long as Buddhism remained free from attack, the continuity of Samkhya Yoga philosophy also remained intact, as they were closely interrelated.

But after 800 A.D., Buddhism as a religion was destroyed. Its monasteries were levelled, monks were murdered or driven into exile, books were burned, and various changes were made in ancient philosophic works to strengthen and establish the new religion, advocating the concept of God. Thus, while looking for evidence in support of the continuity of rational thought and the original Gita, we should ascertain the condition of Buddhism up to 800 A.D.

Asoka had adopted Buddhism and supported it as if it were a state religion. He promoted Buddhism not only in India but also in other countries.[70] He engraved the main doctrines of Buddhism on rocks and pillars and placed them in various parts of his empire. He appointed officers who were sent on tours of the country, preaching the doctrines of Buddhism while they performed their official duties. He assisted in convening the Third Buddhist Council, which expounded Buddhist doctrines, and sent several missionaries to various parts of the world to spread Buddhism. Thus, Buddhism, as a religion and as a doctrine, was solidly established during the reign of Asoka.

The spread of Buddhism continued up to the time of the Gupta dynasty, which ruled over a unified India until 540 A.D. and over certain parts even after 800 A.D. The Gupta period is called the 'Golden Age of Indian History', as tremendous progress was made in the fields of science, art, and literature.

Mahajan writes that during the Gupta period, "there were no sectarian gods like Siva, Vishnu, or Devi. Each god or goddess manifested himself or herself to fulfill a definite purpose and he or she was honoured by the devotees. . . A particular god was invoked for a particular purpose according to the circumstances."[71]

According to Mahajan, though the Gupta rulers patronized Hinduism, they were tolerant of other religions. Both Buddhism and Jainism were

---

[70] For details of Asoka's promotion of Buddhism, see Mahajan, *Ancient India, op. cit.*, pp. 247–255.
[71] Mahajan, *op. cit.*, p. 416.

given full religious freedom. Mahajan further writes, "we have definite evidence to show that the images of Buddha were installed here and there in the Gupta period and the old Viharas (monasteries) continued to prosper. The testimony of monuments and epigraphs shows that Buddhism continued to flourish in the time of the Guptas, as they did not interfere with the faith or its tenets. Bodhgaya, Sanchi, Mathura, and Sarnath continued to be centers of Buddhism."[72]

The Gupta rulers "possessed a scientific spirit of inquiry. They had the desire and determination to learn critically and not to follow blindly."[73] Due to their rational spirit, various literary works in the fields of science, art, architecture, and philosophy were created. Some of the prominent works of this period are: the *Panchtantra* composed by Vishnusarman; the *Hitopadesha* (the book of wise counsels); *Samkhyakarika* by Iswarakrishna; *Nyaya-bhashya* by Vatsyayana; *Vyasa-bhasya* on Yoga philosophy; *Surya Sidhanta* by Aryabhata, who explained that the earth revolves on its axis; the *Brihat Samhita* of Varahamihara, which covers astronomy, botany, natural history and physical geography; and the work of Brahmagupta declaring that all things fall to earth according to a law of nature.

Another good example of the Gupta rulers' rational outlook is the establishment of Nalanda University in Bihar during the fifth century A.D. It was a Buddhist university financed and aided by the monarchs, the rich men, and the people of the whole country. This university became an international center of learning, attracting about ten thousand students from various Buddhist countries.

Though it was a Buddhist university, "established with a view to propagate the teachings of Buddha", it was not sectarian. It welcomed ideas and knowledge from every quarter and was a center of freedom in learning. "The teachers and students were the exponents and followers of different sects or schools of thought." Subjects of study included: the Vedas, logic, Yoga, grammar, medicine, Samkhya philosophy, and Buddhist literature. [74]

Nalanda University continued to flourish until the tenth century A.D. It was destroyed when Buddhism came under violent attack in India. In the words of Mahajan, "The history of the end of the Nalanda University is in a way the history of the extinction of Buddhism from India."[75]

We have detailed accounts of the social, religious, political, economic, and literary life of India given by three Chinese travellers who visited India between the fourth and seventh centuries A.D. Fahien came to India in 399 A.D. and stayed until 411 A.D.; Hiuen Tsang came in 630 A.D. and

[72] *Ibid.*, pp. 418–419.
[73] *Ibid.*, p. 436.
[74] *Ibid.* See Nalanda University, pp. 475–478.
[75] *Ibid.*, p. 477.

visited various parts of the country until 644 A.D.; Itsing visited in 671 and remained in India until 695 A.D.[76]

From their writings, we know that Buddhism was a religion of the people and its monasteries were well maintained. According to Fahien, after the death of Buddha, the kings and householders all joined hands together in building Buddhist viharas (monasteries). He found the monastaries at Patliputra (now Patna) famous for imparting education.

From the writings of Hiuen Tasang we know that there were hundreds of *Sangharamas* (monastaries) and 200 temples in Kanauj alone. Nalanda was a great center of Buddhism. According to his account, the monastaries were great centers of education, the people had a high standard of living, the Brahmans performed the religious duties, the Kshatriyas were the governing class, the Vaisyas were the traders and merchants, and the Sudras did the agricultural and menial work. He found many persons in India who spent their whole life in study.

Itsing gives a comprehensive description of the social, political, cultural, economic, and religious life of the people. He found religious tolerance even at those places where Buddhism was a dominant religion. He "spent ten years in Nalanda, mostly copying Buddhist texts, and returned to China with 400 of them."[77]

That Buddhism flourished in India prior to 800 A.D. is also evident from the fact that King Harsha Vardhana had summoned two Buddhist assemblies in 643 A.D. to popularize Buddhism. The first assembly was held at Kanauj, which was attended by large numbers of kings, 3,000 Mahayana and Hinayana Buddhist monks, 3,000 Brahmans, and by about 1,000 Buddhist scholars from Nalanda University. The meeting lasted for 23 days.

At this assembly, King Harsha Vardhana, who had become a Buddhist, washed the image of Buddha with his own hands and carried it on his shoulders to a nearby tower. This act of the king is enough to illustrate the respect Buddhism had in India during that time. The conference at Kanauj was presided over by the famous Chinese traveler, Hiuen Tsang.

Another assembly was called at Prayaga which was attended by more than half a million people and by 18 royal families of the country. This conference lasted for 75 days. At this conference, King Harsha gave garments and gifts of pearls, gold, and silver to each participating Buddhist monk, the Brahmans, the Jains, and the representatives of other religions.[78]

From the foregoing discussion we see that freedom of expression, the pursuit of scientific inquiry and rational thought, the teaching of Yoga and

[76] *Ibid.* For the account of Fahien, see pp. 384–387; for Hiuen Tsang, see pp. 456–461; for Itsing, see pp. 478–480.

[77] A.K. Majumdar, *Concise History of Ancient India*, Vol. I (New Delhi: Munshiram Manorharlal Publishers Pvt. Ltd., 1977), pp. 35–36, 235.

[78] For details of these assemblies, see Mahajan, *Ancient India, op. cit.*, pp. 468, 470.

Samkhya philosophy, and the popularity of Buddhism all continued unhindered in India until about 800 A.D. Until then the concept of Almighty God was not part of the creed of Hinduism, even though a few Indians might have been familiar with this concept due to their contact at trade centers of the Middle East, such as Alexandria, or through their coming in contact with Christian missionaries.

It should be obvious that changes in the original Gita would not have taken place in such political, religious, social, and cultural conditions. Since the Bhagavadgita incorporated the concepts of the Almighty God, heaven, sin, and others which are of Mediterranean origin, these could have been introduced only when Buddhism had been violently attacked and destroyed.

We obtain fairly detailed information about the intellectual life of India up to the early part of eleventh century A.D. from the writings of Alberuni. He writes about Samkhya philosophy, Yoga, and Patanjali, and talks about the salient features of the Gita. What is most significant is that he does not mention the Bhagavadgita. He refers only to the Gita of Vyasa, the son of Parasara.[79]

Alberuni notes that "the Hindu text was once lost and completely forgotten. It was then rediscovered by Vyasa, the son of Parasara."[80] He refers to the 25 elements (talked about in Samkhya and also in the Gita), and seems to understand them in the secular sense of the original texts, not as such concepts were later theologically interpreted. Alberuni stated that:

> The totality of these elements is called *tattva*, and all knowledge is restricted to them. Therefore Vyasa the son of Parasara speaks: "Learn twenty-five by distinctions, definitions, and divisions, as you learn a logical syllogism, and something which is a certainty, not merely studying with the tongue. Afterwards adhere to whatever religion you like, your end will be salvation."[81]

From Alberuni's account we learn that Buddhism was eradicated from India by the end of the tenth century A.D. This is evident from the fact that during his long stay he did not meet a single Buddhist nor did he locate any of their books. In his own words, "I have never found a Buddhist book, and never knew a Buddhist from whom I might have learned their theories..."[82]

By a careful reading of Alberuni's description of the Gita it seems that the work known to him resembled the texts found in Bali, Indonesia, and in Fyzabad, India.[83] From Alberuni's account it can be conjectured that the vulgate text of Shankara Bhashya Gita was not yet in circulation. It might have been known only to a limited number of people at that time. This

---

[79] See *Alberuni's Indica, op. cit.*, pp. 62 and 73.
[80] *Ibid.*
[81] *Ibid.*, p. 73.
[82] *Ibid*, p. 121.
[83] For details on these Gitas, see Ch. V.

observation is supported by the fact that Alberuni does not even mention
Vedanta, even when he writes at great length about the Hindu religion and
its scriptures.

Alberuni knew of the early diffusion of Buddhism and mentions that, at
one time, countries all the way to the Syrian frontier were under Buddhist
influence. But he mentions that "the Buddhists were banished from those
countries, and had to emigrate to the countries east of Balkh."[84] Likewise,
Jainism seems to have been banished, as Alberuni makes only a casual
reference to it.

The attack on Buddhism coincided with several factors, the details of
which we will discuss in the next chapter. But, let it be pointed out here
that after the death of Harsha-Vardhana, India was broken into several
states which were ruled by different kings. In north and central India, the
states were ruled by the Rajput Kings, who fought amongst themselves
for supremacy. In the south, the states came under the control of several
kings who were supporters of the Brahmanic religion. The Chalukyas
(500–700 A.D.) and the Pallavas (730–800 A.D.) became great promoters
of Brahmanism.

During this time of political upheaval, Brahmanism emerged as the dominant force. According to Mahajan, the great religious reform which swept
India in the eighth century first originated in the Pallava Kingdom. The
Jains and Buddhist teachers slowly lost ground. The Pallavas were orthodox Hindus, and they laid the foundations of the great reformation which
took place in the eighth century. The Aryanization of South India was
completed during the Pallava period. Belief in a multiplicity of gods was
replaced by absolute faith in and devotion to one supreme god.

It would not have been easy to introduce the concept of Almighty God
into India where Buddhism and Jainism were well established and where
the people were used to worshipping numerous gods. The opposition to a
completely new and alien concept must have been strong. The opposition
was ruthlessly supressed in order to establish the new faith. The supporters
and promoters of the new faith destroyed all who opposed them. India
entered a Dark Age which continued for centuries.

R.C. Dutt, while describing the great changes which took place in India
on political, religious, and cultural levels writes that "the history of ancient
India ends with the eighth century and the two centuries which followed
may be justly called The Dark Ages of India. For the history of Northern
India in the ninth and tenth centuries is a perfect blank. No great dynasty
rose to power, no men of letters rose to renown, no great work of architecture was constructed. History is silent over these dark centuries."[86]

[84] *Ibid.*, p. 122.
[85] Mahajan, *Political and Cultural History of India, op. cit.*, pp. 384, 402.
[86] Romesh Chunder Dutt, *Ancient India: 12000 B.C. to 800 A.D.* (London: Longmans, Green, and Co., 1893), p. 150.

The vast destruction of men, material, and literature which took place during the religious persecution is well described by Dutt:

> For it was in the Dark Ages that religious persecution began in India. Monasteries were demolished, monks were banished, and books were burnt, and wherever the Rajputs became rulers, Buddhist edifices went down and Hindu temples arose.[87]

It was in this dark period that the original Gita was changed into the present Bhagavadgita. With the destruction of what was original, the destroyers razed the intellectual foundation of Indian civilization, reducing to rubble the heritage of centuries.

---

[87] *Ibid.*, p. 151. For a comprehensive view on Dark Ages in India and Europe, see pp. 150–151.

3
CORRUPTING THE ORIGINAL GITA

The Underlying Circumstances

The corruption of the original Gita was due to the convergence of several conditions, both internal and external. Externally, three great religions—Judaism, Christianity, and Islam—all believing in the concept of one Almighty God, were well established in the Middle East, with which India had extensive trade relationships through the port of Alexandria. By 250 A.D., Indian merchants had established colonies in Alexandria, which provided a meeting ground for Indian scholars, who could exchange philosophical ideas with the preachers, teachers, and missionaries of the new faiths. Thus, some Indians, mostly from the South, had become acquainted with the doctrines of these organized religions centuries before the actual revision of the Gita took place.

Second, it is claimed that the Syrian Christian Sect in Kerala was founded by Saint Thomas, who was martyred at Mylapore, a suburb of Madras, in 68 A.D.[1] Further, by the middle of the fourth century, the persecuted Persian Christians had set up their colonies on the Malabar Coast.[2] It is obvious that the philosophy of monotheism had made its entry into India, in some limited but concrete form, long before it was accepted and introduced through the Bhagavadgita in about 800 A.D.

Among the external factors, the most conspicuous and dominating appears to be the Islamic invasions and their subsequent conquest of Sind (then the western part of India and now in Pakistan) during the early part of the eighth century. After the death of Muhammad (570–632) the Arabs,

---

[1] Stanley Wolpert, *A New History of India*, Second ed. (New York: Oxford University Press, 1982), p. 84.

[2] Richard Garbe, *India and Christiandom*, translated by L.G. Robinson (Illinois: Open Court Publishing Company, 1959), p. 150. For a comprehensive view of Christians in India during this period and their influence on monotheistic direction of the Indian sects, see John Davies, *op. cit.*, pp. 195–201.

dedicated to the idea of one Almighty God (Allah), began a series of invasions into South Asia; they captured Sind in 712 A.D. Though the Arab
conquest of Indian territory remained limited to Sind, it provided a base for
spreading their religious creed into India. They used their political power
and resources for converting Hindus to Islam by various means, at times
by allurement, at times by force and trickery. They now began searching
for effective ways to spread Islam and expand their political power further
into India. Historians seem to agree that the Arab conquest of Sind sowed
the seed of Islam in India.

The story of how the Brahmans helped the invading Arabs in their
conquest of Sind is a treacherous history. We get a very vivid account of the
Arabs' incursions and their subsequent conquest of Sind through a book
entitled *Chachnamah*, written by Ali Kufi (of Kufah, Syria) in 1216 A.D.
The book was first translated into Persian from Arabic, and was translated
into English by Mirza Kalichbeg Fredunbeg in 1900.[3]

According to Chachnamah, Buddhism was the dominant religion in Sind
during the seventh century A.D. There were Buddhist temples and monasteries located all over Sind. The Buddhists and Brahmans lived in amity.
The various principalities and their rulers were under the king of Sind, Rai
Sahira, a Kshatriya. This kingdom fell into the hands of his chief, Chach,
who ruled for many years. After the death of Chach, his son, Dahar (Dahir)
became king. It was during his reign that the Arabs conquered Sind.

The Arabs began invading portions of Sind during the 640s. According
to the Chachnamah, during the reign of Caliph Umar (634–643) "an army
of Islam was first sent out to different parts of Hind and Sind, to carry on
religious war there."[4] But every attack of the Arabs was thwarted, their
forces destroyed, and the leader killed. Their condition changed abruptly,
however, when they began receiving support from the Brahmans. The
Brahmans had always occupied the high administrative posts before and
after Chach. They began helping the Arabs by acting as their informers;
by preaching a philosophy of surrender; by predicting victory of Islam
and defeat of the local ruler; and by working as an advance-party of the
invading Arabs. Let me give an example of how a Brahman's support
to Arabs at Debal (a small principality in Sind) provided them with their
victory in Sind.

The Arabs had invaded Debal in 711 A.D. under the command of
Muhammad Kasim (also called Muhammad Ibin Qasim). They had fought
for eight days without making any gains. Since Debal was a fortified city,

[3] Ali Kufi, *Chachnamah*, translated into English by M.K. Fredunbeg (Karachi: Gulrang Printing Corp.,
1900). The Chachnamah is the oldest history of Sind. The title of the book means the story of Chach,
who was then king of Sind. Chach was a Brahman who usurped the kingdom of Sind from a Kshatriya
king, through a palace conspiracy, when he was the chief of state.

[4] *Chachnamah, op. cit.*, p. 57.

the Arabs had encamped nearby and were waging war from their camps, without success.

In the heart of the city of Debal, there was a Buddhist temple with a high dome. On that dome, there was a high pole from which a huge flag was hoisted. This flag worked as a talisman (symbol). It meant that as long as the flag continued to be displayed, the people would be victorious. Inspired by this flag, the people and the army fought bravely, and for eight days the Arabs were held in check. On the ninth day of the battle, while the Arab army was besieging Debal, a surprising event happened:

"All of a sudden, then, a Brahmin (Brahman) came forth from the garrison, and cried for mercy. He said, "May the just governor live long! We have learnt from our science of the stars that the country of Sind will be conquered by the army of Islam, and the infidels will be put to flight. But be it known to you that the standard of the idol-house (temple), yonder, is a talisman. As long as that standard of the temple stands in its place, it is impossible for the fort to be taken by you. You must, therefore, try your best to blow off the dome of this temple, and break its flag-staff into pieces. Then only your success will be complete."[5]

After hearing the secret of the temple, the commander of the Arab army, Muhammad Kasim, called his engineer, Jaubat Salmi, and offered him a reward for devising a means of blowing off the dome of the temple. The next day, the Arabs destroyed the dome and the flag of the temple. The fall of the flag meant the fall of the Debalese people.

After the dome was demolished, the Arab army entered the temple and the fort without a fight. The people surrendered, the idol in the temple was removed, and a mosque was established. The Arabs had won their first victory, and they now knew who their collaborators would be. As a result, when Muhammad Kasim marched from one place to another, he had easy victories. And finally, he was able to conquer all of Sind.

By reading Chachnamah, one comes to see again and again that when the Arab army began marching into other areas after capturing Debal, the Brahmans worked as advance-men for them. They began telling the people, the army, and the local princes: "The sages and philosophers of Hind (India), who are the original residents of this country, have found from their books of antiquity, by use of their astrolabe and their astrology, that this empire will be conquered by an army of Islam and will come into its complete possession."[6]

Because of these predictions by the Brahmans, many chiefs and heads of various principalities surrendered to the Arabs, one after another, without a fight. The few who resisted found their military secrets turned over

---

[5] *Chachnamah, op. cit.*, p. 81–82. The name of the informing Brahman is given as Shudh-dev in Chachnamah.

[6] *Ibid.*, p. 107.

to the Arabs by Brahman informers. At one place, about one thousand Brahmans appeared before Muhammad Kasim and expressed their respect and support to him in exchange for due patronage. Kasim obliged them by appointing them to their previously held posts and also allowed them a small share in the taxes they collected from the people.[7]

The victory of the Arabs, from Debal to Sind, was greatly facilitated with the help of the Brahmans. After their conquest of Sind, the Arabs made use of Brahman administrative and priestly skills to promote the Islamic faith as well as to consolidate their power. Indeed, the conquest of India by the followers of Islam began in Sind.

It is informative to quote the view of Dayaram Gidumal, who wrote the introduction to the English edition of Chachnamah. Gidumal writes: "It is extremely doubtful if Sind could have been conquered at all, had these chiefs remained true to their king, and, curious as it may seem, it was ostensibly astrology that made traitors of them. For they said: 'Our wise men have predicted that Sind will come under the sway of Islam. Why then should we battle against Fate.' —The result of course was disastrous."[8]

Though the Islamic invaders had been trying to expand their rule to other parts of India, they were vigorously resisted by rulers outside Sind. It took them about two hundred years to finally expand into other parts of India. It took them another three hundred years to capture the whole of northern and western India and a part of South India. The invaders, no doubt impressed by the strength of the resistance, looked to Indian culture and philosophy as the likely source of this strength. This power to resist sprang from the tradition of rational philosophy, which had taught Indians to act and fight for their rights. Unless a change was brought about which would weaken their resistance, Islamic faith and power could not subdue and defeat the Indians.

Evidently, soon after getting a foothold in Sind, the Arabs invited Hindu scholars to Baghdad and asked them to translate Sanskrit books on Indian philosophy, medicine, pharmacology, astronomy, astrology, algebra, arithmetic, and other subjects into Arabic. During the days of Harun Al-Rashid (786–809), the Indian pundits (Brahmans) translated prominent Indian books into Arabic. Many Arab scholars were also sent to India for study and collection of materials. Due to these translations, the inherent philosophical sources of Indian resistance must have become apparent to Arabs. And it seems reasonable to assume that there might have been some effort on the part of Arabs to fortify their position at the intellectual level before they could hope to take command at the political level. Only further research will reveal whether Islamic power played any part directly or

[7] For details on this event, see *Ibid.*, p. 164.
[8] *Ibid.*, p. VII.

indirectly, in bringing about the revision of the original Gita, reshaping it to resemble their own book of faith—the Quran.

The suspicion that there might have been Arabic involvement in altering the original Gita springs from the fact that almost all the major concepts of the Quran have been included in the revised Gita. I will point out the similarities between the new Gita and the Quran in more detail later, but let it be mentioned here that, if we look into the motivation of external and internal agents desiring alteration in the philosophic discourse of India, the interest of the former appears no different from that of the latter. If the interest of the alien agents, whether Christians or Muslims, was to spread their faith, the interest of the Brahmans was to recapture their lost socio-religious domination. This will be evident when we examine closely the circumstances which induced the Brahmans to actively work for revision.

As pointed out in the preceding chapter, long before the advent of the Christian era the Brahmans had emerged as a priestly class and had gained some political influence due to their appointments as counselors, ministers, and *purohitas* (royal priests) to the kings. In matters of religious practice, they had become the sole authority on Vedic rituals and had controlled the socio-cultural life of the people by conducting ceremonies of marriage, birth, death, and other festivities. They had divided the people into four castes and had claimed their own superiority above all the remaining three—Kshatriyas, Vaishyas, and Sudras. Thus, in religious, social, and cultural matters, only the Brahmans could dictate what was wrong and what was right.

This dominant position of the Brahmans was challenged and gradually undermined by the teachings of Kshatriya philosophers and socio-religious reformers—Kapila, Buddha, Mahavira, and Vyasa. The spread of Buddhism and Jainism in India had much curtailed the power and influence of the Brahmans. Further curtailment of their power resulted from the popularity of Samkhya Yoga philosophy and its practice. From the period of Kapila (700 B.C.) to the time of the Gupta period (700 A.D.), the pattern of rational thought and practices had gradually become an accepted mode of life of the people. This trend continued until the end of the seventh century A.D.

For the Brahmans, the villain most responsible for their diminished status was this whole group of rational thinkers, philosophers, and yoga practitioners. The teachings and practices of Kapila, Buddha, Mahavira, Patanjali and Vyasa had not only overshadowed and invalidated what Brahmanism preached, but also made them look small-minded, insignificant, and self-serving.

How the Brahmans reacted to this changed condition is well explained by Monier-Williams. The Brahmans planned to deify the most eminent Kshatriya heroes and incorporate them into their system. This was done out of necessity rather than from any wish to honour the warrior caste. Any circumstance which appeared opposed to the Brahmanical system was speciously explained away, glossed over, or mystified. The ambitious Brahmans who aimed at religious and intellectual supremacy gradually saw the policy of converting the great national epics, which they could not suppress, into instruments for moulding the popular mind in accordance with their own pattern. They proceeded to brahmanize what was before the property of the Kshatriya or warrior caste.[9]

The motivation of the Brahmans to destroy the influence of the rational thinkers coincided with that of the alien powers, especially the Moslems, who had already been engaged in steady expansion since they captured the Sind. Ironically, the revival of Brahmanism became aggressive during this same period under the leadership of Shankaracharya, who accepted the concept of monotheism and certain tenets of both Christianity and Islam and waged a 'holy war' of religious conquest all over India.

The Revival of Brahmanism

Though the organized movement for the revival of Brahmanism began in the eighth century A.D., the Brahmanical religion began to regain its lost position in the seventh century A.D. due to the patronage of South Indian kings—the Chalukyas and the Pallavas. During this period, the unified nature of Indian rule had broken down and India had come under the rulership of numerous kings. Two prominent kingdoms of South India, the Chalukyas and Pallavas, accepted the Brahmanical religion and promoted it through Vedic rituals, temple building, and by granting favours and royal patronage. Further research would reveal to what extent the Chalukyas and Pallavas were motivated by the presence of Christian and Islamic missionaries, who were quite active in South India by the seventh century. It appears plausible that the Chalukyas and the Pallavas might have decided to support Brahmanism as a way to check the spread of alien religions.

The Brahmanic religion in this period continued to follow the Vedic tradition of polytheism. Up to this time religious tolerance was shown towards the opposing indigenous religions, Buddhism and Jainism, even by those kings who accepted Brahmanism. Religious persecution had yet to take place. Monier-Williams in his book *Indian Wisdom* observes,"Hinduism and Buddhism coexisted and were tolerant of each other in India till about the end of the eighth century of our era."[10]

---

[9] Monier-Williams, *Indian Wisdom*, pp. 317–321.
[10] *Ibid.*, p. XXXVI.

However, this condition changed when the Brahmans accepted monotheism and began interpreting the whole religious history of India, from Vedas to Upanishads, in a completely new way. The most interesting points in this interpretation were that the status of Brahmans as a caste and class was strengthened, all the gods and goddesses of Vedas were superseded by a single Almighty God, and religious persecution began with a sense of crushing the enemies. It happened with the coming of Shankaracharya.

This is emphatically pointed out by Monier-Williams when he says: "Undoubtedly Sankara was the very incarnation of strict Brahmanism; and if it be possible to name any one real historical concrete personality as a typical representative of Brahmanical doctrines, it is undeniable that we must point to Sankara."[11]

Shankaracharya

Shankaracharya, popularly known as Shankara, was born in a Nambudri Brahman family of Kerala (Malabar coast) in 788 A.D. and died aged 32 in 820 A.D. His father Sivaguru died when Shankara was seven. His mother Aryamba sent him to study the Vedas and Vedangas with a Brahman guru Govinda, who lived on the banks of the Narmada river.

He was well educated in Vedic philosophy by his guru. After completing his formal education, he took a vow of sanyasa (renouncing the worldly life), remained a bachelor, and dedicated his life to spreading and teaching his newly found philosophy of *Advaita* (non-dualism, absolutism), *Vedanta* (the end of Vedas), *Mayavada* (the illusory character of the dualistic world and the reality of the Brahman alone); and *Moksha* (the union of beings with Brahman).

He travelled all around India, debating and challenging his adversaries and discussing his philosophy with those who held different views. He established four *Mathas* (religious centers) in different parts of India for the propagation and perpetuation of his philosophy. These Mathas are still maintained by his Brahman successors, who are all called Shankaracharyas and are considered to be the guardians and spokesmen of Hinduism. The Mathas founded by Shankaracharya are: Sarda Pitha at Dwarka in Maharashtra, Jyotir Matha at Badrikasrama in the Himalayas, Govardhana Matha at Jagannath (Orrisa), and Sarda Pitha at Sringeri (Mysore).

Shankaracharya did not write any book of philosophy of his own but expounded his views by writing bhasya (commentary) on the writings of others. He introduced his philosophy of monotheism through various

[11] Monier-Williams, *Brahmanism and Hinduism* (London: John Murray, 1891), p. 55.

commentaries. Though there are several commentaries now ascribed to Shankara, only the following three are accepted as authentic: (i) Brahma Sutra Bhasya, (ii) Bhagavadgita Bhasya, and (iii) Upanishads Bhasya (about ten Upanishads).

Shankara expounded his philosophy of Advaita (non-dualism) by declaring Isvara (God) as omnipresent, omnipotent, infinite, and absolute. God is the creator, preserver, and destroyer of the world. He can be approached by devotional worship and desireless action.

To Shankara, God is the material and efficient cause of the world. Godhead or Brahman is that from which beings arise, in which they reside after arising and into which they disappear at the end. He resides within the souls and rules them. Prosperity whether in this world or the next is temporal. The supreme good is to achieve release from the bondage of the temporal process by craving the grace of God.

The devotees worship God in various forms under different names. It is the same God that takes on a variety of forms and names through his power of *maya*. Whenever dharma (religion) is threatened, God incarnates Himself in order to preserve it for the world. The highest way of worship is to see God everywhere, as all in all.[12]

Shankara interpreted the word Brahman, at times making it synonymous with Brahma but at others with God, by using his concept of maya (illusion). According to Shankara, "God, thus, is conditioned Brahman; the conditioning principle is called maya. As maya is not a reality alongside or apart from Brahman, it does not make for the introduction of any real quality. All that Godhead requires for its status is assumed duality, and not real duality."[13]

Maya is that which does not exist. It is in fact non-existent. As dream and illusion are observed to be unreal, even so all this universe of duality in its entirety is seen to be non-real.

Man achieves happiness by devotion to God. Without being nearer to God, man cannot achieve happiness. God is the fountain of man's knowledge. When the soul unites with God, one obtains moksha (salvation, release, or liberation). According to Shankara, moksha is for the man of wisdom who has renounced desire and who strives for wisdom. It is not for the one who has not renounced and continues to have desires.

Renouncing action, Shankara says that "one desirous of moksha (release) should always renounce action along with its means. It is only by one that so renounces that the inner self which is the supreme goal is realized."[14] By an action which is contrary to scriptural injunctions, one goes along the

---

[12] T.M.P. Mahadevan, *Sankaracharya* (New Delhi: National Book Trust, India, 1968), pp. 58–67. For details on Advaita philosophy of Shankara, see Ch. V. For Shankara's monotheistic view see his *Bhagavadgita-Bhashya*, IV 6; XV 8, 17; XVI 14, and XVIII 61.

[13] *Ibid.*, p. 60.

[14] *Ibid.*, p. 103–104.

downward path of animals. But to those who are without desires, who are not attached to the relation of means and ends, there arises the eagerness to inquire into the nature of inner-self.

Shankara advocated renunciation of all desires and argued that the knowledge of Brahman which is the inner self is opposed to being associated with action. Karma Yoga, according to Shankara, is not possible even in dreams, as it is based on erroneous knowledge.

He rejected Kapila's Samkhya philosophy arguing that, since Kapila had accepted the unconscious Pradhana (mool prakriti, nature) as the cause of the world, it goes against the teachings of smritis (teachings of the sages), which declare God to be the cause of the world. Since Yoga also accepts prakriti as the independent cause of the world, it was also rejected. Yoga practices, he said, are good for spiritual advancement, but he rejected all its theoretical and philosophical doctrines.

Likewise, he refuted the doctrines of both Buddhism and Jainism, arguing that, in the absence of an abiding self or controlling God, the groupings and complexes of elements of existence are unintelligible. The Buddhist doctrine of cause and effect, antecedent and consequent, organization and destruction was termed meaningless. The talk of Buddhists, which ignores the truth of identity or of at least relative permanence, is characterized by Shankara as vain and pointless.[15] The talk of Jainas of seven categories and non-persuasiveness of the soul was rejected on the ground that they did not make a categorical statement and used a peculiar kind of logic.[16]

In the words of Bazaz, "In advancing his doctrines, Shankara was motivated by a desire for the reestablishment of Brahminism which object could be achieved by refutation of Buddhism and Jainism, particularly the former. He was an ideologist of Brahmanical reaction and patriarchal sacerdotal society. . . . Shankara examined different philosophies in his own way and came to the conclusion that every one except his own had shortcomings."[17]

An Appraisal of Shankaracharya

Shankaracharya was the first Indian to openly accept, propagate, and expound the concept of monotheism as a part of Hindu religion. From pre-Vedic time up to the end of the eighth century A.D., polytheism continued to be practiced as a religious creed by Brahmans and non-Brahmans alike, even though all forms of worship were rejected by Buddhism and Jainism. Against such a background, the vigorous campaign to popularize monotheism as a religious philosophy of Hinduism appears abrupt and intriguing.

---

[15] J.L. Mehta, editor, *Vedanta and Buddhism* (Varanasi: Banaras Hindu University, 1968), pp. 13–15.
[16] Sri Sankaracarya, *Brahma-Sutra*, translated by Swami Gambhiranand (Calcutta: Advaita Ashrama, 1965), pp. 402–432.
[17] Prem Nath Bazaz, *op. cit.*, pp. 278–279.

When we look into the geographical and environmental background of Shankara's upbringing, it becomes obvious that he borrowed the concept of monotheism from the foreign sources at work in his area. As mentioned earlier, Shankara was born on the Malabar coast, where the Christian missionaries and the Jewish community had been active for centuries. Further, the agents of Islam had penetrated the Malabar coastal area decades before the religious training of Shankara had begun. Thus, by the time Shankara was mastering the religious philosophy, concepts, and practices of Hinduism from his guru Govinda, three versions of monotheism—Judaism, Christianity, and Islam—were quite familiar to the intellectuals and religious men of his area. Evidently, Shankara, his guru Govinda, and other students of the school were acquainted with monotheism and other theistic doctrines of these organized religions. It was easy for Shankara to foresee the formation of a fourth version—Hinduism—by using the same basic tenets of monotheism to serve the purposes of Brahmanic revival. According to R.C. Majumdar, the respected historian of India, "Sankara's monism was based upon the Islamic creed which he had learnt from the forefathers of the Moplahs, Navayats and Labbes of South India."[18]

Shankara seems to have borrowed from both Christianity and Islam. His lifestyle of sanyasa, wearing a ceremonial garment, carrying a long staff, founding of mathas (religious centers), setting up a system of succession of Shankaracharyas on the pattern of the papacy, and a form of devotional worship may all have been copied from Christianity. From Islam he borrowed a style of philosophic interpretation and presentation, the notion of gaining victory by crushing opponents; uplifting the position of Brahmans from the level of mere caste to the level of divine messenger like the 'prophets' of the faith.

Though Shankaracharya wrote several commentaries, he presented his basic tenets similarly in all of them. Whether we read his Brahma Sutra Bhasya or his Bhagavadgita Bhasya, we find that he was concerned with the same basic themes: expounding the concept of Almighty God, advaita (non-dualism), maya (illusion), Brahmanism, and refuting the doctrines of Samkhya, Buddhism, Jainism, and Yoga.

The significance of Shankara's commentary on the Bhagavadgita is well explained by E.G. Parrinder in his book *The Significance of the Bhagavadgita for Christian Theology*. He writes: "The place of the Bhagavadgita in the debate between non-dualism or monism and personal theism is central . . . Sankara, the prince of monists, tried to force it all into his own philosophy, considering that the Gita was based upon the same assumptions. This made him delight in some of its apparently monistic passages, but slur over or twist around other verses that demand personal or transcendental theism. And when the Gita clearly recommends devotion

---

18 R.C. Majumdar, *Readings in Political History of India* (New Delhi: B.R. Publishing Corp., 1976), p. 228. For details on Christian, Jewish, and Islamic operation in South India, see pp. 227–228.

to God above wisdom or even duty, Sankara tries to force it into his own mould of identification with the Absolute."[19]

The basic difference, however, between his Brahma Sutra Bhasya and the Bhagavadgita Bhasya is that, whereas the former contains only his doctrine of monotheism, maya, and Brahmanism, the latter also contains all that was in the original Gita, even when it had been altered. And this is the reason that, of all the books written for propagating the doctrines of Brahmanic revival, none could become as popular as the Bhagavadgita.

If we carefully examine the contents of the Bhagavadgita, especially Chapters IV–XVIII, it would appear as if it were written by a contemporary of Shankaracharya. The contention that the Bhagavadgita had already long existed is rejected on the grounds: (i) that there is no historical evidence of the Bhagavadgita's existence prior to Shankara's time; and (ii) that there is no evidence of monotheism in Indian culture prior to his time.

There are scholars, both Indian and Western, who hold the view that the doctrine of monotheism developed from monism as expressed through the concept of Atman and Brahman in several of the Upanishads, such as Brihadaranyaka, Svetasvatara, and Chhandogya. It is true that we find references to Atman or Brahman identified with the universe, with the only reality, and as the essence of man. It was taught that when the Brahman is known everything is known. But the fact is that these ideas were nowhere worked out as a theological system and the latter-day theistic interpretation of 'Brahman as the Lord controlling the world' is not in itself sufficient to justify a claim that monotheism arose indigenously in India.

Further, these scholars might bear in mind that as yet there is no reliable chronology of Indian philosophical history. This fact is underscored in the work of S.N. Dasgupta, A History of Indian Philosophy, which is regarded as the single most trustworthy work in the field. Therein Dasgupta acknowledges: "I had to leave out many discussions of difficult problems and diverse important bearings of each of the systems to many interesting aspects of philosophy. This, I hope, may be excused in a history of philosophy which does not aim at completeness."[20]

As Macdonell points out in his History of Sanskrit Literature: "History is the one weak spot in Indian literature. It is, in fact, non-existent. The total lack of the historical sense is so characteristic, that the whole course of Sanskrit literature is darkened by the shadow of this defect, suffering as it does from an entire absence of exact chronology . . . Such being the case, definite dates do not begin to appear in Indian literary history till about 500 A.D."[21]

---

[19] Edward Geoffrey Parrinder, The Significance of the Bhagavadgita for Christian Theology (London: Dr. Williams' Trust, 1968), p. 8.

[20] Dasgupta, A History of Indian Philosophy, op. cit., Vol. I, p. 4.

[21] A.A. Macdonell, A History of Sanskrit Literature (New York: Haskell House Publishers Ltd., 1968), pp. 10–11.

In the absence of any chronology it is risky to claim that monotheism as advocated by Shankara is an indigenous concept and not one brought in from outside India. Let me quote the view of Dasgupta, who is competent to clarify this question of monotheism in the context of India.

According to Dasgupta there is no historical evidence of monistic doctrine in Indian culture prior to Shankaracharya or Gaudapada. He makes a categorical statement on this point: "I do not know of any evidence that would come in conflict with this supposition. The fact that we do not know of any Hindu writer who held such monistic views as Gaudapada or Shankara, and who interpreted the Brahma-Sutras in accordance with those monistic ideas, when combined with the fact that the dualists had been writing commentaries on the Brahma-Sutras, goes to show that the Brahma-Sutras were originally regarded as an authoritative work of the dualists."[22]

Dasgupta goes on to explain: "I do not know of any Hindu writer previous to Gaudapada who attempted to give an exposition of the monistic doctrine, either by writing a commentary as did Shankara, or by writing an independent work as did Gaudapada."[23]

Dasgupta cites instances of dualistic interpretations of the Upanishads and the Brahma-Sutras and argues that "Shankara carried on the work of his teacher Gaudapada and by writing commentaries on the ten Upanishads and the Brahma-Sutras tried to prove that the absolutist creed was the one which was intended to be preached in the Upanishads and the Brahma-Sutras."[24]

Several scholars, both Indian and Western, have pointed out that Shankara has misrepresented the original view of the Brahma-Sutras. A.B. Keith in his *History of Sanskrit Literature* categorically states that Shankara "doubtless misrepresents Badarayana".[25] Swami Vireswarananda in his work *Brahma-Sutras* expresses a similar view, saying that there is a strong opinion current amongst scholars today that whatever be the merit of Shankara's metaphysical doctrines, he is not faithful to Badarayana in his interpretation of the Sutras.[26]

Further, if we critically examine the authorship of some prominent doctrinal texts of this period, one suspects that they were composed or reworked by the same group of Brahman scholars. For example, the Brahma-Sutras (also called Vedanta-Sutras) is said to be written by Badarayana, but there is no historical record of his life.[27]

What is most intriguing is that the texts of both the Brahma-Sutras

---

[22] *Ibid.*, p. 422. For more on Gaudapada and Shankara, see pp. 422–439.

[23] *Ibid.* Gaudapada was the teacher of Govinda (the teacher of Shankaracharya). According to Dasgupta, Gaudapada was living during the time Shankara was a student.

[24] *Ibid.*, p. 432.

[25] A.B. Keith, *A History of Sanskrit Literature* (Oxford: The Clarendon Press, 1928), p. 477.

[26] Swami Vireswarananda, *Brahma-Sutras* (Calcutta: Advaita Ashrama, 1962), p. XIII.

[27] *Ibid.*, p. V.

and the Bhagavadgita, on which Shankaracharya wrote his commentaries, cross-reference each other. Sutras 2.3.45 and 4.2. 21 of the Brahma-Sutras talk about the Bhagavadgita, and sutra XIII, 4 of the Bhagavadgita talks about the Brahma-Sutras. This exposes the fact that these two works are the product of the same period expounding similar doctrines. Since the author of the Brahma-Sutras was a Brahman (Badarayana), and Brahmanization of the original epic Mahabharata is proven by such scholars as Monier-Williams, Holtzmann, Belvalkar, John Davies, and Richard Garbe, it seems evident that the author of the Bhagavadgita (The Song of the Supreme) was also a Brahman.[28]

Monier-Williams argues "The work, as we now possess it, cannot possibly be regarded as representing the original form of the poem. Its compilation appears to have proceeded gradually for centuries. At any rate, as we have already indicated, it seems to have passed through several stages of construction and reconstruction, until finally arranged and reduced to orderly written shape by a Brahman or Brahmans, whose names have not been preserved."[29]

Since the Bhagavadgita is now a part of the epic Mahabharata, it is evident that the authorship of the former was also the same Brahman or Brahmans. Richard V. De Smet holds the view that the chief author was a Bhargava Brahman of Mathura region.[30] As already mentioned, Garbe, Otto, and Davies have all expressed their view that the present Bhagavadgita is the product of a Brahman.[31]

Why did Brahmans select the original Gita for alteration when other writings then in existence advanced the same monotheistic teachings? If we look into the various commentaries of Shankara wherein he expounded his theories, none of them could become popular amongst the masses. Neither his Brahma Sutras nor any of his Upanishad Sutras has ever been accepted by the masses as popular books of philosophy and guidance. None of his works could touch the heart and mind of Indians as did the original Gita and the Yoga Sutra. It was to win greater acceptance and mass appeal that they selected the original Gita for revision, as it contained the gist of all the rational philosophy advocated by the sages from Kapila to Vyasa, and its teachings and practices had been adopted as a way of life by the people.

Furthermore, if we look into the records of the literary history of India it will be found that Samkhya and Yoga have been referred to as the same. This is evident from the fact that "in the epic Mahabharata the two systems are actually spoken of as one and the same."[32] Since the composition of the original Gita was primarily based on the doctrines of Samkhya Yoga, by

[28] For a comprehensive view on Brahmanization of Epics Ramayana and Mahabharata, see Monier-Williams, *Indian Wisdom*, *op. cit.*, pp. 309–374.
[29] *Ibid.*, pp. 371–372.
[30] B.R. Kulkarni (Ed.),*The Bhagavadgita and the Bible*, (Delhi: Unity Books, 1972), p. 2.
[31] For their views, see Chapter 2.
[32] Macdonell, *History of Sanskrit Literature*, p. 396.

tracing the popularity of the latter in Indian antiquity, we can gain a clear view of the mass appeal and acceptance of the former. And this should also provide a clue as to why the original Gita was selected for alteration.

An early account of Samkhya's popularity is well recorded by Macdonell in his *History of Sanskrit Literature*. In Macdonell's words, "At the time of the great Vedantist, Shankara (800 A.D.), the Samkhya system was held in high honour. The law book of Manu followed this doctrine, though with an admixture of the theistic notions of the *Mimamsa* and *Vedanta* systems as well as of popular mythology. The *Mahabharata*, especially Book XII, is full of Samkhya doctrines; indeed almost every detail of the teachings of this system is to be found somewhere in the great epic. . . Nearly half the *Puranas* follow the cosmogony of the Samkhya, and even those which are Vedantic are largely influenced by its doctrines."[33]

I mentioned in chapter one that changes were made not only in the Gita but also in various other writings of that time to establish the historical legitimacy of the monotheistic concept inserted into the Bhagavadgita. It was for this purpose that the redactors added Chapters I and X to the Rig Veda; reconstructed the epics Ramayana and Mahabharata by identifying Rama and Krishna with The Supreme Being; added several verses to Samkhya Karika to change the original concept of bhavas (basic strivings of man), and the concept of purusha and prakriti; and added more than 100 verses to the Yoga Sutra of Patanjali to introduce the concept of Iswara (God) and to interpret Yoga as union with God.

It is obvious that the interpolations of such varied and vast nature would not have been possible without the collaboration of some capable persons. The needed mobilization of like-minded Brahmans would not have been difficult when we take into account the probable arousal of their sentiment under the banner of 'Revival of Brahmanism.'

The fact that Shankara was widely opposed by members of his own caste and other prominent Brahmans of his time, indicates that the altering of the original Gita may have been done by a small circle of ambitious Brahmans. For example, when Shankara's mother died, none of the Brahmans of his village or anyone else came to participate in the funeral. He was boycotted by his caste and others alike. Shankara had to perform the cremation of his mother all by himself.

Further, Shankara was challenged by several prominent Brahman intellectuals of his time. It is said that Shankara defeated them in debate. But if we consider his debate with Mandana Mishra, Shankara could not defeat the latter on philosophic grounds but only on some trivial question. Even this was due to the mediation of Mishra's wife, Bharati, who was acting as an umpire in the discussion, which lasted for 18 days.

[33] *Ibid.*, p. 394.

The greatest opposition to what Shankara preached was from the Buddhists, Jains, and the followers and teachers of Samkhya Yoga. These opponents were crushed by the burning of their books, by the demolishing of their teaching centers and monasteries, and by the murdering of the preachers of Buddhism and Jainism. Brahmanical revivalism continued for centuries after Shankaracharya. India entered into a dark age with the coming of Shankaracharya.

While discussing religious development in India, Macnicol rightly observes "The whole period has aspects of similarity in the history of Hinduism to the 'dark ages' of Mediaevalism in the history of the Christian Church, and what Thomas Aquinas and the great school men were in one development, Sankara and Ramanuja were in the other."[34]

Before concluding this section, it would be appropriate to point out the similarity between the Bhagavadgita and the Quran and also the Bible to show the sources from which Shankara's monotheistic doctrine were borrowed. We will first discuss the similarity between the Bhagavadgita and the Quran.

The Bhagavadgita and the Quran

There have been numerous studies by Western, Eastern and Indian scholars who have pointed out the fundamental sameness of Hinduism with other major religions. The study of Pandit Sunderlal comparing the identical doctrines and views of the Bhagavadgita and Quran seems to be quite comprehensive and objective.

Talking about the Gita and the Quran, Sunderlal says, "The Gita is, as recognized on all hands, the quintessence of the Hindu faith. If the two sacred books are approached with an open mind, and without entertaining any predilections, it will be found that the basic truth which they impart is precisely one and the same."[35]

Pointing out the identical doctrine expounded in the Gita and the Quran, Sunderlal writes, "We shall first present the concept of Iswara or Allah. The Gita and the Quran hold exactly the same view of Him. Iswara is styled by Gita as the Light of Lights (G. 13:17) and the Light of the Sun and the moon (G. 7:8). The Quran calls Allah the Light upon Light (Q. 30:5) and the Light of the heavens and the earth (Q. 30:5). According to the Gita, Iswara carries people from darkness toward light (G. 10:11). Likewise, the

[34] Nicol Macnicol, *Indian Theism*, p. 98.
[35] Pandit Sunderlal, *The Gita and the Quran*, translated by Syed Asadullah (Hyderabad, India: Institute of Indo-Middle East Cultural Studies, 1957), p. 7.

Quran speaks of Allah as He who carries people from darkness toward light (2:257)."[36]

The Gita says: "The entire world is encompassed by Iswara" (9:4, 11:33). The Quran says: "verily Allah encompasseth all things" (Q. 41:54). The Gita calls Iswara the Lord of the Worlds (G. 5:29). The Quran also calls Allah the Lord of the Worlds (Q. 1:1). The Gita talks of Iswara as the beginning of all living objects, their middle and their end (G. 10:20). The Quran speaks of Allah: "He is the first; He the last; He the manifest and the Hidden; and He is the Knower of all things" (Q. 57:3). The Gita speaks of God as the supreme source of everything, and the soul as the manifestation of Iswara (G. 15:5, 6, 7). The same view is expressed in the Quran in various ways, such as: "We all are Allah's and to Him shall we return."(Q. 2:156); " He is the maker of the Heavens and the Earth! He hath created everything. Lord! for unto Thee must we return" (Q. 2:285). A close study of the contents of the Bhagavadgita and the Quran would reveal that on basic ideas related to man, the universe, the prophets (avataras), and devotion to God, both express highly similar views. Even where there are linguistic and stylistic differences, the underlying sameness of ideas on the fundamentals can be easily discerned.

As mentioned earlier, the leaders of the Brahmanic revival seem to have adopted their monotheistic model from the Quranic source and elaborated and expanded the basic structure by adding things which suited their aims. This seems to be the reason that at places we find an almost word-for-word copying of Quranic passages into the Bhagavadgita. But we also notice the presentation of differing views in it, especially on matters related to refutation of Samkhya Yoga doctrines, such as satkaryavada, samyaka jnana, gunas, desires, the concepts of purusha-prakriti; and condemnation of Buddhism and Jainism.

The Bhagavadgita and the Bible

There are numerous scholarly studies now available which point out the similarities between the Bhagavadgita and the Bible and also mention the Christian influence on the monotheistic concept of Hinduism. I have selected the work of Garbe, *India and Christendom*, for citation and reference, primarily because of his deep-rooted interest in tracing the original Gita and his noteworthy contribution.

While discussing the Christian influence on the Bhagavadgita, Garbe points out that there is some difference of opinion between European

[36] *Ibid.*, p. 11.

scholars and traditional Hindus. The latter claim that the monotheistic concept of the Bhagavadgita is older than its presentation in the New Testament. The European scholars hold completely the opposite view. According to Garbe, "European scholars have thought that no other Indian work bears such abundant evidence of Christian influence as the Bhagavad Gita."[37]

Pointing out the Christian views expressed in the Bhagavadgita, Garbe mentions two identical presentations: "(i) faith in God's love to man and in His mercy and forgiveness of sins arising therefrom; and (ii) the requirement laid upon man of devout love of God. From these agreements have arisen all sorts of reminiscences of New Testament modes of expression, which naturally suggested the thought of a loan."[38]

Garbe quotes the view of Lorinser who, in his introduction to his metrical translation of the Bhagavadgita into German, has observed: "the author of the Bhagavad Gita not only was acquainted with the writings of the New Testament and made frequent use of them, but wove Christian ideas and views into his system." Lorinser goes on to say: "this much admired monument of the spirit of ancient India, this most beautiful and exalted didactic poem, which can well be regarded as one of the noblest flowers of pagan wisdom, owes precisely its purest and highest praised teachings for the most part to Christian sources."[39]

Garbe quotes the following similarities of the Bhagavadgita to the New Testament which were pointed out by Paul Deussen in his translation of the Bhagavadgita:[40]

In the Bhagavadgita, Ch. IV, 4 and 5: On the question of birth, Krishna tells Arjuna: "Many have been my past births. I know them all, whilst thou knowest not." This view is expressed in the New Testament, John VIII: 57, 58: "Jesus said unto them, Verily, verily I say unto you, Before Abraham was, I am."

In the Bhagavadgita, Ch. IX, 29: "I am the same to all beings; no one is hateful to Me and no one dear. But those who worship Me with devotion, are in Me, and I too am in them". John XIV: 20: "At that day ye shall know that I am in my Father, and ye in Me, and I in you."

In the Bhagavadgita, Ch. IX, 32: "For, taking refuge in Me, they also, O Son of Pritha, who are of inferior birth—women, Vaishyas, as well as Shudras—even they attain to the Supreme Goal." In Galations III: 28: "There is neither Jew nor Greek, there is neither bond nor free, there is neither male nor female: for ye are all one in Christ Jesus."

[37] Richard Garbe, *India and Christendom*, translated by Lydia G. Robinson (Illinois: Open Court Publishing Company, 1959), p. 222.
[38] *Ibid.*, p. 237.
[39] *Ibid.*
[40] *Ibid.*, p. 240.

A comparative study of the Bhagavadgita and the New Testament would reveal that on major doctrines of theism, they present identical views: the concept of Almighty God, the creation of the Universe, soul, sin, heaven, hell, devotion, and worship of God, the concept of the savior, the emphasis on surrender to the will of God, and the notion of salvation.

We have pointed out instances where the original Gita was altered by incorporating alien doctrines. This does not mean that Christianity or Islam have not borrowed from Indian sources. There are several areas of Christianity and Islam where one can see Indian influence. The setting up of the system of missionaries for propagating Christian doctrines is patterned after the Buddhistic system of missionaries, who were organized and sent abroad during the time of Asoka (273–236 B.C.). The dress of the Christian clergy, their practice of depending upon charity, and the dedication of their entire lives to promoting their religion all seem to be influenced by Buddhism. The sufferings of Christ remind one of the sufferings of Mahavira and Buddha, and the glorification of suffering in Christianity seems likewise to be influenced by Buddhism and Jainism.

Furthermore, Indian influence can be detected in the Suffi sect of Islam, especially in the manner of devotion, meditation, and dress. As pointed out earlier, much of Indian literature was translated into Arabic and Arab scholars were sent to India to study. Indian influence on Islamic religion and culture is noticeable in the mode of prayer, the wearing of beads, and certain celebrations.

4
CONSEQUENCES OF CHANGING THE GITA

Reworking the original Gita to form the Bhagavadgita was not merely the modification of a book. It was a surreptitious plot to dismantle the whole intellectual edifice of Indian culture which had been built up over a thousand years. The changers not only stopped the tide of rationalism in Indian life but also seduced people into believing and accepting the false as genuine, alien as indigenous, religious as political, and mystical as rational. The consequences were deep, all-encompassing, and bewildering. India, indeed, was pushed into a 'dark age'.

It has already been mentioned that when the original Gita was altered, the interpolators also made changes in many other works of that time to establish textual support in their favor. It was for this reason that the interpolations were made in the Rig Veda, the Epics, Samkhya Karika, and Yoga Sutra. It is obvious that there could have been numerous alterations in many other texts, still to be detected.

It has also been pointed out that bands of proselytizers for the new Brahmanic faith were organized at four different centers (mathas) during the time of Shankaracharya. These teachers received increasing political protection and patronage. At the same time, the national opponents of the new faith were forced into silence. In such an atmosphere, the people had to accept the doctrines of the new faith even when they did not agree with them. This enforced obedience of the Indian people towards the newly coined doctrines and codes of behavior which, though beneficial to the Brahmans as a caste, were disastrous to India as a nation, as a political entity, and as a culture.

The repercussions of these changes were so far-reaching that they cannot be adequately discussed under any single category. I have, therefore, preferred to cover them under four different subheadings: (i) political submissiveness; (ii) philosophical distortions; (iii) mystification of Yoga; and (iv) religious and cultural effects.

Political Submissiveness

The revisors of the Gita and other ancient Indian texts seem to have become so obsessed with their notion of religious domination that they failed to foresee the political consequences of their actions and thoughts. To Indians, the concept of a nation was well-known since the time of Asoka (273–236 B.C.), who ruled the whole of India as one nation. The concepts of sovereignty and the sovereign state, polity, and separation of religious institutions from political ones were known to the elite. The duty of the king to his people and theirs towards the kingship were discussed by Kautilya in his *Arthasastra* (The Science of Polity), whose time is generally accepted to be about 300 B.C.[1]

Given such a political background, the promoters of the new Brahmanic religion should have dedicated themselves to protecting the interests of the sovereign state. This was expected from the Brahmans more than other social groups because for centuries they had occupied most of the high political and religious posts. Because of these appointments and their priestly duties, the Brahmans had acquired the most privileged positions on both social and political levels. Being privileged as they were, their writings and teachings had a profound and lasting effect on the thought and actions of the people.

The teachings of the new Brahmanic religion replaced political and secular values with religious ones. They interpreted the world, the kingdom, and the state as maya (illusionary). The highest good in life was to surrender to the will of God, render devotion to God, strive to go to heaven, and be free from the bondage of birth and death. God is the protector, preserver, and destroyer of the world. Man can do only what he is predestined to do. The knowledge of God was the highest knowledge, and to render service to him was the highest action. The Brahman represented the godhead on earth. To know the Brahman was to know God. Fate dictated the destiny of man, and it could not be changed.

These teachings destroyed the political will of the Indian polity. To Indians it now made little difference who controlled the political power or who ruled the state. The most important goal in life was to obtain moksha (liberation from birth and death) by rendering devotion to God. The pain, sorrow, and miseries in this life were because of the Karma (deeds) of the previous life. Only by obtaining moksha could one achieve everlasting freedom.

Further, the caste system was made more rigid and discriminatory through the Bhagavadgita. For example, Krishna (who is the creator of

---

[1] Those scholars who consider the date of Kautilya as 400 A.D. have been opposed by a number of Indian historians. The Indian historians give ample evidence to prove that the Arthasastra was written around 300–400 B.C.

the Universe) says: "The fourfold caste system has been created by Me in accordance with their differentiation of Guna and Karma" (G IV, 13). Their duties are distributed in accordance with the qualities they are born with (G XVIII, 41–48). Women, sudras, and vaishyas are inferior by birth (G IX, 32).

The sudras (the manual workers) were now untouchables. Social intermingling with them was not permitted. Educational opportunities were not available to them. The Vaishyas (the farmers and the traders) were put in the third category. Though they were not untouchables, they were not accorded the prestige enjoyed by the upper caste. The Kshatriyas (the warrior and ruling caste) were put in the second position and had to follow the counsel and guidance of the Brahmans. The Brahmans now raised their position from mere caste level to the level of godhood. Though still labelled as a caste, they came to occupy the status of Brahma, which was invariably interpreted as 'god' (G IV:24, 31, 34).

This caste division of the Indian polity broke the spine of social cohesiveness. In a country where the great majority was comprised of sudras and vaishyas, the rigid caste system made them apathetic towards questions of national destiny. Reduced in social position and taught a philosophy of surrender, the vast majority of the Indian population became submissive and remained paralyzed and uncaring spectators of foreign conquest.

It is not surprising that prior to 800 A.D. no foreign power could subjugate the Indian people. The foreign invaders did do some harm here and there on several occasions, but they could not establish themselves for long. Nor could they expand to other parts of India, even when its central rule was broken and it began to be ruled by numerous kings. This condition, however, changed after the eighth century A.D. when the Brahmans began playing an active role in social-political-religious fields.

Had it not been for the active support and collaboration of the Brahmans, the Arabs would not have been able to conquer Sind and expand gradually into the other parts of India. After capturing Sind in 712 A.D., the Arabs actively planned and prepared for the conquest of India. From their experiences in Sind, the Arabs saw that their goal of expansion throughout India would be achieved only when they could receive the support of the Brahmans. They began cultivating the Brahmans. Centers were established, not only in Sind but also in Baghdad and Syria, where Brahman and Islamic scholars collaborated in the translation of Indian literature. These centers also secretly produced new literature which was claimed to be very old. Now Hinduism was made to resemble Islam on a philosophical level. A sense of passivity, submissiveness, and inertia was created among the masses under the guise of a new religious doctrine. Having achieved this, the internal stage of India was set for Islamic conquest and rule.

It has been observed by Max Weber that "Brahmanical theory served in an unequalled manner to religiously tame the subjects. Finally, the invasion and domination of foreign conquerors benefited the power monopoly of the Brahmans. After a period of fanatical iconoclasm and Islamic propaganda, the conqueror resigned himself to accept the continued existence of Hindu culture."[2]

It is an irony of history that the Indians, who prided themselves on being warriors and war heroes and who preferred to die rather than surrender, now began acting so submissively to foreign invasions. Let me quote the view of a historian who depicts this changed mental condition of the Indians after the teachings of Shankaracharya came into prominence. He tells us how ultimately India came under Islamic rule:

> The degraded level to which the majority were pushed down made them indifferent to country-wide dangers and kindred problems. This alone made possible the woeful situation that while the invaders swept across the country, the masses mostly remained inert. The people of the land, with a few exceptions, were indifferent to what was happening around them. Their voice had been hushed in silence by a religio-social tyranny. No public upheaval greets the foreigners, nor are any organized efforts made to stop their progress. Like a paralyzed body, the Indian people helplessly look on, while the conqueror marches on their corpses. They look staggered, only to sink back into a pitiable acquiescence to the inevitable to which they have been taught to submit.[3]

Islamic domination of India, which began in Debal, a small area of Sind, in 712 A.D., was completed by the sixteenth century. Muslim rule over India remained intact for more than three hundred years. Then came the British occupation of India in the eighteenth century, which lasted until 1947. Thus, colonization of India, which began in the eighth century, continued under one or the other alien power until the twentieth century. This prolonged colonization would never have lasted so long if the people had not been taught doctrines of submissiveness, political and worldly indifference, and maya, through the medium of the Bhagavadgita.

In his book, *The Crux of the Indian Problem*, written prior to Indian independence, Dr. Paranjpye expressed his "profound conviction that the current ideas of religion form the great stumbling-block in the way of Indian progress", and argued that "If one looks below the surface of actual events in India, one is inevitably led to the conclusion that the excessive deference to authority in all spheres, and the slight regard paid to the reasoning faculty, are the main characteristics of the Indian people and the cause of most of the troubles from which their country is suffering."[4]

---

[2] Max Weber, *The Hindu Social System*, translated by H. Gerth and D. Martindale (Minnesota: University of Minnesota Sociology Club, 1950), Vol. I, p. 125. See also pp. 121–127.

[3] A.K. Majumdar, *Concise History of Ancient India*, Vol. I (New Delhi: Munshiram Manoharlal Publishers Pvt. Ltd., 1977), p. 389. See also pp. 385–389. The above quotation taken from 'History and Culture of the Indian People', Ed. by R.C. Majumdar (V5, p. 127).

[4] Dr. R.P. Paranjpye, *The Crux of the Indian Problem* (London: Watts & Company, 1931), p. IX. For more on Dr. Paranjpye's views see pp. VII–XVI.

Another scholar who tried to investigate "the root cause of the socio-economic problems of India" during the pre-independence days expresses a similar view. Prabhaker S. Shilotri in his *Indo-Aryan Thought and Culture (And Their Bearing on Present Day Problems in India)* observes: "Something is radically wrong in a country where hundreds of millions of people in a perpetual low standard of life succumb to a condition of chronic poverty, restless political discontent, and misery. Superficial analyses have simply resulted in remedial measures—while the fundamental conditions remain practically unchanged."[5] According to Shilotri, Indians have developed a "fixed attitude" and "the philosophy that has the greatest hold on the Indian mind today is represented by the more eclectic teachings of Krishna in Bhagavadgita."[6]

Shilotri finds faults with the educational system of the country which does not encourage inquiry and investigation of various problems facing India: "Unfortunately, it is a defective system of education in which we are drilled at home. It trains our memory and teaches us to perform some intellectual feats, but creates in us no inquiry and unbiased attitude towards social, political and economic problems. This neglect of the teaching of social sciences is largely responsible for the unsatisfactory intellectual leadership that we find in India today."[7]

In Shilotri's own words, "My main thesis is that the abnormal mental evolution of the Indo-Aryan stock has been largely responsible for the chaotic political, social and economic conditions that we find in India as the curtain rises on her authentic political history."[8]

Philosophical Distortions

The distortion of the major philosophical concepts of ancient India through the corruption of the Bhagavadgita had a crippling effect on the creative and rational thinking of the Indian people. The damage was not the result of the introduction of monotheism as such, but was due to the deliberate alteration of long established philosophical ideas which had inspired and guided the people of India. If philosophical-rational concepts can be considered as the social or mental wealth of a culture, the protagonists of the new Brahmanic religion introduced a conterfeit currency.

It has already been mentioned (Ch. I) that the Age of Indian Philosophy began with the work of Kapila (700 B.C.). He is the earliest systematic

---

[5] P.S. Shilotri, *Indo-Aryan Thought and Culture* (New York: The Evening Post Job Printing Office, 1913), p. 12.
[6] *Ibid.*, p. 54.
[7] *Ibid.*, pp. 14–15.
[8] *Ibid.*, p. 9.

and rational thinker of India whose thoughts permeated all segments of the society and influenced subsequent thinkers for centuries. In order to comprehend the distortions of Kapila's thought brought about through the corruption of the Bhagavadgita, we need to remember the basic tenets of his philosophy and also the major thoughts of later thinkers. Only by knowing what the original thoughts were can we see how they were systematically distorted.

Since a discussion of early Indian thinkers has already been presented, we will point out only their salient features here to avoid repetition. Kapila's main concerns had been: what causes sorrow (dukha) in human beings, how it can be eliminated, and how happiness (sukha) can be achieved in life. He considers various facets of this problem as a systematic thinker and points out the remedy for sorrow and the way to achieve happiness.

According to Samkhya philosophy, when man (purusha) acquires proper knowledge of himself, nature (prakriti), the gunas (everlasting operating forces and constituents of nature), the emergence and functions of the twenty-five elements (tattvas), and the cause-effect relationships, and acts correctly, then he, by his own power, eliminates sorrow and achieves happiness. He explains these ideas in detail under two theories: the theory of right action (satkarya-vada) and the theory of proper knowledge (samyaka-jana).

Both of these theories of Kapila are interwoven to emphasize the importance of taking correct actions in order to obtain the desired results. According to Kapila, though people act variably due to different motivations (bhavas), they all work for the fulfillment of their desires. The fruit of action depends on the knowledge and mode of action of the doer. Every person possesses the same basic qualities, faculties, and properties on both the physical and the mental level. All his faculties, the gunas, and nature (prakriti) work to fulfill one purpose—the enjoyment and happiness of the purusha. Man, so knowledgeable when he acts rightly, eliminates sorrow and achieves happiness on his own.

The basic philosophical tenets of Kapila have been shared by all subsequent rational thinkers of India. This is evident when we examine the teachings of Buddha, founder of Buddhism, and Mahavira, the great teacher of Jainism (both 500–600 B.C.), both of whom emphasized right action and proper knowledge. Both were equally concerned with the basic problem of human beings: how to eliminate sorrow and how to achieve happiness in life.

A comprehensive presentation of the basic ideas and philosophy of Kapila is found in the work of Patanjali (400 B.C.). In his Yoga Sutra, Patanjali talks about right action by introducing the concept of pratyahara (visualizing the opposite of what is undesirable so that ensuing action will bring the proper result), and he covers the theory of proper knowledge by introducing the concepts of yama, niyama, and samyama.

According to Patanjali, to obtain the desired result of any action, one should visualize the opposite of what is presently undesirable. This act of visualizing the opposite would cause the sense organs, action organs, and all the internal faculties (intellect, self-consciousness, and the mind) of the man (purusha) to work co-operatively in the direction of materializing the desired result.

In the Yoga Sutra, Patanjali combined the theoretical and philosophical teachings of Kapila with the eight steps of Yoga. It is assumed that any person who follows these principles and practices the steps of Yoga becomes capable of eliminating sorrow and of achieving a healthy, happy, and prosperous life.

A culmination of these ideas and practices came in the writings of Vyasa, who composed the orignal Gita in about 400 B.C. Vyasa presents the basic philosophy of Kapila, Buddha, Mahavira, and Patanjali in a unique way. The Gita presented the essence of all the masters of Indian culture in the form of a song (gita), which made it very popular with the masses.

By changing the original Gita into the Bhagavadgita, all these philosophical and practical teachings were completely distorted. The Bhagavadgita presented quite the opposite of what was taught by all the rational thinkers and Yoga practitioners of ancient India. In reading the Bhagavadgita, one gets the impression that its main target of attack is the ideas of all the rational thinkers—from Kapila to Vyasa. There is repeated denunciation of action, fruits of action and desire. Expressing his view on the changes made in the Bhagavadgita, Max Weber observes, "Samkhya doctrine formed the basis for the original version. Only later were correct Vedantic features added through a classicist Brahmanical revision."[9] Let me quote a few verses from the Bhagavadgita to illustrate philosophic distortions:

Krishna tells Arjuna: "Action can never affect me. I have no desire for the fruits of actions. He who knows me thus is not bound by actions" (IV, 14). "Thy right is to work only, but not with its fruits. Let not the fruits of action be thy motive" (II, 47). "Action is inferior to discipline of mental attitude. Wretched are those whose motive is the fruit (of action)" (II, 49). "I am the father of this world, the mother, the dispenser of the fruits of actions" (IX, 17).

Krishna says that the person who sees inaction in action and action in inaction is wise among his fellows, is enlightened, and a performer of all actions. He whose every enterprise is without desire or motive and whose

[9] Max Weber, *The Religion of India*, translated by H.H. Gerth and D. Martindale (Illinois: The Free Press, 1958), p. 183.

actions are burnt up by the fire of knowledge, he is called a sage by the wise (IV, 18–19).

Krishna goes on to say that he whose actions are offered to Brahman and who acts without attachment is not soiled by sin (V, 10). By abandoning the fruits of actions, the disciplined man attains abiding peace. By acting due to desire and by being attached to the fruits of action, the undisciplined man is bound (V, 12). The man who, abandoning all desires, moves about without longing, without self-interest, and without self-awareness attains peace (II, 71). The man who has controlled the senses, renouncing all actions mentally, happily rests in the nine-gated city.[10] He neither works nor causes others to work (V, 13). While talking about the cause-effect relationship, the Bhagavadgita says that nature is the cause, but in experiencing pleasure and pain, the purusha is the cause (XIII, 20). Besides the prakriti (nature), there is another superior prakriti, which maintains this world. The supreme soul in this body is the great Lord who is the highest self (XIII, 22). All actions are performed by nature alone, and the self is actionless (XIII, 29).

In various ways, the Bhagavadgita decried all actions other than for bodily care, self-purification, sacrifice, and prayer. The actions involved in fulfilling worldly goals were denounced and the life of *sanyasa* (renunciation) and devotion to God were acclaimed.

A society which advocates the philosophy of inaction and fruitless action cannot be expected to innovate when faced with the challenges of life. This is exactly what happened in the case of India. The creativity and will to make a better society were stifled.

The preoccupation of society became how to escape the cycle of rebirth and how to be assured of a better life after the present one. The life of the present meant little. As a result, the society became paralyzed. Deterioration followed. Impoverishment was the natural outcome.

If we observe the behavior and thought of the Indian populace in our own day, we will find that from farmers to industrialists, students to teachers, politicians to social workers, and from housewives to men on the street, with few exceptions, the teachings of the Bhagavadgita are followed. It seems as if India as a nation fails to recognize any heritage prior to the period of Brahmanic revivalism. The teachings of Kapila, Mahavira, Buddha, Patanjali, and Vyasa do not seem to have any link with the India of today. Keith has observed, "The scientific attitude of mind which seeks to find natural causes for events of nature is not normal in India".[11]

---

[10] The nine-gated city refers to the body. The two eyes, the two ears, two nostrils, the mouth, the organ of generation and the anus have been referred to as the nine doors of the body.

[11] A.B. Keith, *A History of Sanskrit Literature* (Oxford: The Clarendon Press, 1928), p. 146.

Mystification of Yoga

By changing the original Yoga Sutra of Patanjali and Samkhya Karika of Kapila and by presenting Yoga quite differently in the Bhagavadgita, the pragmatic qualities of Yoga were completely replaced by religious, spiritual, and mystical preoccupations. Further, by naming all 18 chapters of the Bhagavadgita after some form of Yoga, by defining its aim as achieving unity with God, and by making renunciation (sanyasa) a part of its practices, Yoga was incorporated into Hindu religion. Thus, a system which had been in practice since the Harappa-Mohenjodaro civilization of 3000 B.C. or even earlier and which had developed into a comprehensive discipline of rational philosophy and practice was made a sectarian vehicle of religious propaganda. As a rational system, Yoga was lost.

To comprehend this change, one must look into the historical development of Yoga from the earliest times to 800 A.D., when substantial changes were made in the literature of ancient India. It has already been observed that when Patanjali wrote his Yoga Sutra he incorporated all the basic tenets of Samkhya philosophy and presented Yoga as a rational system of study and practice. His system comprised eight definite steps. The method of practicing each step and the results of practicing each were distinctly explained. By following these steps any person could expect to achieve identical results.

Just before outlining the eight steps of Yoga, Patanjali writes that by practicing them impurities are destroyed, knowledge shines forth, and wisdom radiates (Ch. II, 28). By practicing samyama (a combined form of concentration, meditation, and deep meditation), one derives various kinds of mental power and develops knowledge which helps achieve the goals of one's life. Thus, the Yoga practitioner of Patanjali maintains not only excellent physical and mental health, but is capable also of fulfilling his desires and thereby leading a happy life.

This Yoga system reached its culmination when it was presented in song form in the original Gita. By summarizing the gist of Indian philosophy, by emphasizing prominent facets of Yoga, and by highlighting the value of action, duty, and responsibility, Vyasa made the original Gita a 'handbook of life' for the masses. It became not only a source of inspiration but also a guide for the totality of life. Again, there was no inclusion of any religious vocabulary or concepts in it. And it remained unchanged up to 800 A.D.

In order to change Yoga into a religious cult, the revisionists had to alter not only the original Gita but also the original Yoga Sutra of Patanjali and the original Samkhya Karika of Kapila in order to create the impression that Yoga was in fact a religious system from the time of its origin.[12] Let me quote a few verses from the Bhagavadgita to show the contrast between the secular and religious nature of Yoga.

In answer to a question raised by Arjuna as to who are better versed in yoga, Krishna says: "Those who fix their mind on me, worship me, with highest faith are the best in yoga, in my opinion" (XII, 2). "If you are unable to fix your mind on me, then seek to reach me by constant practice of yoga, O Arjuna" (XII, 9). "But, if you are unable to do even this, then, seek union with me and renounce the fruits of all actions while controlling your mind" (XII, 11). "When a man is not attached to objects of sense nor to actions and has renounced all thoughts, then he is established in Yoga" (VI, 4).

Krishna goes on to say: "Knowledge is better than practice; better than knowledge is meditation, but better than meditation is the reununciation of the fruits of actions. Renunciation leads immediately to peace" (XII, 12). "I am the origin of everything, and all things spring from me. Knowing this, the wise men meditatively worship me" (X, 8).

Talking about renunciation, Krishna declares: "When a man whose intellect is unattached everywhere has controlled his mind and has given up all desires by renunciation, he attains the highest perfection by non-action" (XVIII, 49). "Dedicate all actions to me mentally, make me your goal, keep your mind always fixed on me by practicing yoga of reason" (XVIII, 57). "Abandoning all duties, surrender yourself to me alone; I will liberate you from all your sins, do not be afraid" (XVIII, 66). "This knowledge is the mystery of all mysteries" (XVIII, 63).

The above quotations indicate that Yoga was made to resemble a system of worship, devotion (bhakti), and renunciation (sanyasa). Yoga lost its distinct identity. Almost any activity, idea or practice could now be called Yoga. As a result, we find people calling diverse forms of physical exercise Yoga asanas and interpreting their cultic practices as belonging to numerous types of Yoga, such as Japa Yoga, Kriya Yoga, Laya Yoga, Bhakti Yoga, and so forth.

There is little wonder then that Yoga could no longer remain a secular system. It could neither become popular with the masses nor be taught in the academic institutions of India—until recently. Yoga became a system of practice mixed with religious, spiritual, and cultic values, and it remained confined to *ashrams* (centers dedicated to religious values and practices). The cult of guruism developed. Those learning and practicing Yoga in the ashrams became disciples of the guru (master of the center) and worked as devout followers of the cult. Being cultic, it thrived on secrecy, mysticism, rituals, superstitions, and devotion. Yoga became sectarian.

---

[12] For details on interpolations in the Yoga Sutra of Patanjali and in Samkhya Karika of Kapila, see Chapter 1, the sections on Kapila and Patanjali.

Religious and Cultural Effects

The Bhagavadgita's effect on Hinduism remained mostly on a doctrinal level without causing any substantial change in the mode of religious practices. Though philosophy changed, image worship continued. Thus, Hinduism could not be transformed into a religion in the sense that organized religions of our time are known to us.

When monotheistic doctrine made its entry into Hinduism, it could not be a substitute for the entrenched idol-worship. The pattern of idol-worship, rituals, religious offerings, and observances could not be replaced. Pantheism continued. Popular deities (like Rama, Krishna, and Shiva), mother goddesses (like Durga, Kali, and Devi) and *grama devata* (village divinities) continued to be worshipped. Hinduism could not be made into a coherent religion like Christianity or Islam. It remained more like a cultural group rather than an organized religion. This is the reason that most Indian scholars define Hinduism as 'a way of life' or a culture rather than a religion. As Max Weber has pointed out, "Only in recent literature have the Indians themselves begun to designate their religious affiliation as Hinduism. It is the official designation of the English census for the complex of religion also described in Germany as Brahmanism.[13] And he goes on to explain: "In truth, it may well be concluded that Hinduism is simply not a 'religion' in our sense of the word."[14]

One wonders why the places of worship of Hindus have idols, unlike the synagogue, church, or mosque. Why did the Hindus not build their temples in accordance with their faith preached in the Bhagavadgita? What has caused this difference in mode of worship, which would generally follow the mode of belief?

To answer this question, we have to look into the history of Hinduism. The religious history of India can be divided into three phases: pre-Vedic, Vedic, and post-Vedic. In the pre-Vedic period, as discussed in chapter one, the most organized forms of religious practices were found among the Dravidians. They worshipped the pipal tree, stones, snakes, and village divinities. Their mode of worship and belief system differed from the Aryans. The Vedic period is generally viewed as commencing with the coming of the Aryans, who worshipped 33 gods. From these, Hindu pantheism developed.

In the post-Vedic period, certain deities became popular, perhaps due to the composition of such epics as the Ramayana and the Mahabharata. Now Rama, Krishna, and Shiva became the most popularly worshipped gods of Hinduism. Along with this pantheism, the worship of mother-goddesses, such as Durga, Kali, and Devi also emerged. Worship of the

[13] Max Weber, *The Hindu Social System*, op. cit., p. 32.
[14] *Ibid.*, p. 44.

pipal tree, village divinities (grama devata), and household family deities continued. The Buddhist monasteries enshrined the idols of Buddha, and Jain temples had images of Mahavira and other Tirthankaras (gurus). This diverse system of worship remained a part of Indian culture.

During the post-Vedic period, large temples were built for particular deities such as Rama or Krishna or for aggregates of deities. Pantheism had taken root.

It was against this background of pantheism that monotheism was brought into Hinduism. Since monotheistic doctrine was imposed on a system where pantheism was deeply rooted, it could not go much beyond the philosophical level. As a result, the advaita philosophy of Shankara, though fully depicted in the Bhagavadgita, could not be incorporated into religious practices of the masses.

There are other differences between Hinduism and the major world religions. For example, there is no single word in Hinduism which refers to the concept of Almighty, such as 'Yahweh' in Judaism or 'Allah' in Islam. There are numerous designations for God in Hinduism, such as Isvara, Bhagavana, Prabhu, Hari, Narayana, and so on. Surprisingly, all these terms are commonly used as personal names. No one would dare have the name of Allah or Yahweh as a personal name, but it is not offensive to have Hindu divine appellations as personal names. Had the concept of God emerged in Hinduism as it evolved in Christianity and Islam, there would have been a unique name. But we find that every word used to refer to God has numerous other meanings.

Furthermore, there is no equivalent word for religion in Hinduism. The generally used word, dharma, means duty or obligation and not religion. For example, one might say 'family dharma','husband dharma', 'caste dharma' and so on to connote their respective duties or obligations. According to Max Weber, the concept of religion is closer to the Hindu concept of *Sampradaya*, which refers to sacred paths or groups.[15] This is enough to indicate that Hinduism could not be transmuted into a religion.

Monier-Williams in his book *Brahmanism and Hinduism*, written in 1891, makes a distinction between Brahmanism and Hinduism. And he gives a detailed account of the intertwining of religion with social and domestic life in every part of India, commenting:

> It is often asserted that the Hindus are the most religious people in the world. Those who make this assertion ought, of course, to define what they mean by the word 'religious'. What is really meant, I think, is that among all the races of mankind the Hindus are the greatest slaves to the bondage of immemorial tradition not so much in its bearing on religious beliefs, or even on moral conduct, as on social usages, caste practices, and domestic ceremonial observances.[16]

---

[15] *Ibid.*, pp. 44–45.

[16] Monier-Williams, *Brahmanism and Hinduism* (London: John Murray, 1891), p. VII.

Explaining the religious outlook of a Hindu, he notes: "While accepting Hinduism he may be at the same time a believer in Buddhism, in Muhammadanism, in Judaism, in Christianity; or may call himself a Theist, a Deist, a Polytheist, a Theosophist, or even an Agnostic . . . all the diversities of sceptical belief are, so to speak, 'roped together' by one rigid and unyielding line of Brahmanical pantheistic doctrine."[17]

Before summing up this section, a word about the overall effect of the Bhagavadgita on Indian culture and society is in order. The most outstanding cultural effect seems to be that the people, especially the younger people, have lost faith in the genuineness of the ancient Indian texts. They find contradictory thoughts and confusion in most of what is claimed to be ancient. It appears as if there was never any Indian prior to the modern period who could think rationally or clearly without being obscure or religious.

Unless a student is religiously motivated, he finds no ancient Indian text which seems relevant to modern times. As a result, the Indian past remains unlinked with the present. Lack of trust, interest, and credibility in what belongs to the past does not allow for national growth rooted in its own sources. "The mind of the Indian youth now craves a consistent theory that will explain to him his situation and offer him a clue towards its solution."[18]

[17] *Ibid.*, p. 9. For more on Brahmanism-Hinduism, see his Preface and pp. 54–72.
[18] Shilotri, *op. cit.*, p. 13.

5
THE REDISCOVERY
OF THE ORIGINAL GITA

In this section I wish to discuss: (i) how I rediscovered the original Gita; and (ii), why similar efforts by other scholars, both Western and Indian, produced little but frustration and failure. Before describing the research of other scholars, it may be helpful to relate the story of my own search.

As mentioned in the preface, my research began during the early part of the 1970s when I founded the Indian Institute of Yoga at Patna, India, and resumed teaching Yoga. During this initial phase of research, I was quite unaware of the works of German scholars such as Richard Garbe, Rudolf Otto, J.W. Hauer, and others, nor had I seen the versions of the Gita found in Bali (Indonesia) and Farrukhabad, Uttar Pradesh. My research up to this point was mainly to satisfy a personal curiosity and was limited to investigating Yoga as a rational system by reviewing the original texts of Kapila, Patanjali, and other classical Indian philosophers.

My effort was to find out: What was the philosophic base from which Yoga derived its philosophy and what was the historical evidence that Yoga was practiced in Indian antiquity? When and how did it mature as a discipline of thought and practice? What caused the decline of Yoga as a rational system? With these questions in mind, I went through the pertinent literature then available to me in Patna and, in this process, finally reached the point of critically reading the Bhagavadgita.

While reading the Bhagavadgita, I became disheartened and confused. I was disturbed because my image of Yoga as a rational system, which had emerged by reading Kapila and Patanjali, was distorted by its religious and mystical coloring in the Bhagavadgita. I felt confused because of the countless contradictory assertions in the Bhagavadgita. At times, I wondered whether Indians had ever had the ability to think coherently! Thinking that I might be wrong in my understanding of the meaning or the content, I read it quite carefully again and again. It was during this phase of the critical reading of the Bhagavadgita that I came to the following conclusions:

(i) That there was a separate Gita prior to this Bhagavadgita, which I called the 'original Gita'.

(ii) That the original Gita began with verse 28 (Ch. I) of the present Bhagavadgita.

(iii) That the text of the original Gita (the ur-text) is intact within the first three chapters of the extant Bhagavadgita.

(iv) That fifteen new chapters were added to the original Gita when it was altered. Twenty-seven verses were appended before verse 28 and numerous verses were inserted among the verses of the first three chapters to create a supportive link for the vast interpolations.

(v) That the original Gita was altered during the time of Brahmanic revivalism around 800 A.D. to propagate the doctrine of non-dualism (advaita) and Vedanta (the end of the Vedas).

My aforesaid conclusions, at this point, were quite tentative. They were based upon my personal hunches formed during my reading of the primary and secondary source materials then available to me. Since I was not very certain of my findings, I continued my research to ascertain the truth.

Soon afterwards, I became aware of an article entitled, "The Bhagavadgita From the Island of Bali," written by N.G. Sardesai and published in the *Modern Review* of July 1914.[1] Sardesai had been in Indonesia for some time and, after searching through local archives of Indian literature, he found a copy of the Gita, written on palm leaves in the Kavi (Balinese) language.

It was most fascinating for me to find that the Gita discovered in Bali also began with verse 28 of the extant Bhagavadgita, as I had independently concluded. This finding emboldened me in my convictions. Though this Gita of Bali did not quite appear to me to be the ur-text, it did reveal several facts of great importance which strengthened my notion about the Bhagavadgita as an altered form of the original.

In the Gita of Bali there are no chapters as we see in the extant Bhagavadgita. The total number of verses in this Gita is only 86 instead of the 700 verses of the extant Bhagavadgita.

Later, I was equally fascinated to see that the Gita found in Farrukhabad also begins with verse 28, does not have any chapters, and the total number of verses is only 84.[2] But this Gita also did not appear to me quite to be the original.

Both the Gita of Bali and that of Farrukhabad suggested that the initial alteration in the original might have been done with the idea of keeping the

---

[1] N.G. Sardesai, 'The Bhagavadgita From the Island of Bali' (*Modern Review*, Calcutta, July 1914), pp. 32–38.

[2] See Shanti Prakash, *The Adi Bhagavad Gita* (Fyzabad, U.P., India: The Sadharana Dharma Sangha, 1936). It is in Hindi. The title of the book means the Original Bhagavad Gita.

total number of verses the same as that with which people were familiar. At this stage of alteration it seems likely that only about half of the verses of the original were replaced with the verses representing monotheistic doctrines. Its elaborate expansion with all 18 chapters and seven hundred verses might have been done some time afterwards, during the early part of the Indian Dark Age.

Before describing the particulars of the original Gita, let me mention two most important findings in the process of my research without which perhaps I would not have been able to complete the present work. These findings are: (i) the original Samkhya Karika, and (ii) the original Yoga Sutra. The reader will at once comprehend the significance of these books when I explain what the originals contained and how they were changed to support the major alteration in the Gita.

The Original Samkhya Karika

Since the Bhagavadgita is predominantly an exposition of philosophical assertions found in the Samkhya, I tried to determine the exact content of this source text. In going through the Samkhya Karika, I found that this too had been corrupted by later amendment (for details on these interpolations, see chapter one). These interpolations are so evident that they should have been noticed by the many scholars who have written on Samkhya philosophy. Most interestingly, these interpolations betray themselves when the Samkhya Karika is referred to as the *shasti-tantra* (the science of sixty verses).[3] Our suspicions are immediately aroused, seeing that there are 73 verses, 13 too many.

By interpolating these 13 extra verses, numerous theistic concepts were inserted into the original text of the Samkhya to dilute its rational, non-theistic nature. Thus, we find such Hindu religious concepts as Brahma (one of the gods), the three divisions of the universe *(tridha sargah)*, charity *(dana)*, spirituality *(adhyatmika)*, fate *(bhagya)*, divinity *(daiva)*, and the word 'manusha' for the 'purusha' of Kapila. All these terms appear only in the interpolated 13 verses and nowhere else.

It can easily be understood that if the original Samkhya is not first identified, it is impossible to determine the authentic teachings of Kapila as presented in the Bhagavadgita. And this has been, to my mind, the basic failure of previous attempts to recover the original Gita. They all, without exception, failed to find the key to unravelling the mystery shrouding the original Gita.

[3] Samkhya Karika, verse 72.

Even those scholars who have detected interpolations in the Samkhya Karika have pointed to only ten verses, not all 13. Larson in his book *Classical Samkhya* and Keith in his *A History of the Samkhya Philosophy* mention the interpolations but do not cite all the amendments.[4] They have mentioned only verses 46–51 related to bhavas (motivations) and three or four verses at the end as interpolated. They do not identify the interpolation of verses 52, 53, and 54.

The Original Yoga Sutra

In retrospect, I must admit that it was not easy for me to identify the original Yoga Sutra of Patanjali. It took years of pondering the extant text before reaching my conclusions. The key difficulty I faced was seeing the dual personality of Patanjali—that of a rationalist and that of a religious man, both at the same time.

During the initial stage of my research, with the little knowledge I had of Patanjali, he appeared to me mostly a man of rational and non-theistic outlook. This was because he tried to explain every aspect of Yoga in a systematic and rational way: its steps, methodology, and obtainable results. But while going through his Yoga Sutra time and again, I began doubting his commitment to rationality when he also talked about god (isvara) and the deity *(devata)* and at places made unrelated and even contradictory statements concerning Yoga.

This confusion about Patanjali was resolved only when I began going through all the pertinent literature related to the original Gita, especially during the latter part of my research. The picture of the original Yoga Sutra emerged quite clearly after I had determined the original Samkhya Karika and after I had read and evaluated all three books together: Samkhya Karika, Yoga Sutra, and the Bhagavadgita. It became apparent to me how interpolations were made in all the three books by using almost the same concepts, style, and even vocabulary.

Here I must acknowledge that the work of J.W. Hauer and S.N. Dasgupta has been of immense help in my identification of the original Yoga Sutra. Though Dasgupta did not point out all the interpolations in the Yoga Sutra, he did provide solid evidence for identifying the interpolation of Chapter IV in its entirety. It is the work of J.W. Hauer which explains when later sections of the Yoga Sutra were added to the main body of the text.[5]

---

[4] See Larson, *op. cit.*, pp. 193–194 and Keith, *op.cit.*, pp. 96–97.
[5] For details on the view of Hauer and Dasgupta, see chapter one, the section on Patanjali.

The original Yoga Sutra has only 82 verses. The original begins with verse 28 of Ch. II and ends with verse 55 of Ch. III of the present text. The original did not have any chapters as it has now. The verses in the original appeared one after another in an uninterrupted sequence.

In the original—except Ch. II, 44 and 45, in which words devata (deity) and isvara (God) have been inserted—there is nowhere any mention of religious concepts. Even when we delete these insertions from the original, it in no way disturbs the actual meaning of those two verses. Most of the religious terminology which has been interpolated occurs in Ch. I, Ch. II, 1–27, and Ch. IV. In these interpolated sections, theistic concepts such as faith *(shradha)*, guru *(teacher)*, piety *(punya)*, spirituality *(adhyatma)*, spiritual master *(swami)*, incantation *(mantra* and *japa)*, god *(prabhu)* and kriya Yoga (devotional Yoga) have been inserted.

The Yoga Sutra as it stands today is indeed in line with the extant text of Samkhya and also the extant Bhagavadgita. In order to recognize the original Gita, it is imperative that one first identify the original Samkhya and the original Yoga Sutra. Having done this, anyone can tell where the original Gita lies buried in the expanded and camouflaged structure of the present Bhagavadgita.

The main reason why scholars who have tried to uncover the original Gita have not been successful is that they have investigated the Bhagavadgita in isolation without judging it in its historical context of thought and practice. Had they scrutinized the Bhagavadgita on the basis of its own internal evidence, such as Ch. II, 39 and Ch. III, 3, where it categorically states that the discussion is based on the Samkhya and Yoga, they would not, perhaps, have neglected to look first for the originals of the Samkhya and Yoga Sutra.

Scholarly Works on the Original Gita

Of the scholars who have tried to identify the original Gita, one of the earliest and most noteworthy is Richard Garbe. He tried to point out which sections and verses were interpolated and which were the original. In his book *Introduction to the Bhagavadgita*, he excluded a total number of 170 verses as not belonging to the original Gita. He excluded the first 24 verses (in Ch. I, 1–24) and 146 verses at other places which represent Vedantic and Mimansic thoughts.

Garbe was unable to identify all the interpolated verses in the original: "I do not cherish the illusion that I have succeeded, in the way which I have chosen, in eliminating all the ungenuine portions of the Bhagavadgita. In the recension many verses besides have been inserted of which not a word existed in the original poem; the means of recognizing these as ungenuine are wanting, and I am not inclined to commit myself to mere conjecture."[6]

The main difficulty of Garbe, as it appears, was that though he had written extensively on Samkhya, Yoga, and Indian philosophy, he had not determined all the interpolations in the Samkhya Karika or in the Yoga Sutra. For example, he pointed out only seven verses of the Yoga Sutra (which talk about God) as interpolated and of a contradictory nature. He could not identify all the interpolations in it, as has been done by J.W. Hauer.

Had Garbe known the original Samkhya and the original Yoga Sutra, he might have identified all the interpolations in the original Gita. This is based upon the assumption that Garbe understood the basic character and structure of the original Gita and the nature of its interpolations, as is evident from statements such as this: "In the old poem Krsnaism philosophy based on the Samkhya-Yoga is proclaimed; in the additions made in the recension, the Vedanta philosophy is taught." He goes on to declare that in comparison to Samkhya Yoga philosophical discussion, the discussion of ". . . Vedanta takes a considerably inferior place."[7]

Another work of significance is *The Original Gita* by Rudolf Otto. Like Garbe, Otto wrote extensively about Indian philosophy and thoughts, but his research on the original Gita is centered around the text of the Bhagavadgita without any investigation of the original Samkhya and Yoga Sutra. He seems to be concerned with identifying the original Gita by analyzing only the contradictory thoughts and philosophic distortions of the Bhagavadgita.

According to Otto, "The present day guise of The Bhagavadgita, however, is not its original version; and I trust that I have succeeded in proving, in Chapter IV [of his book], that it is actually based upon a primitive text—The Original Gita—which itself was in no sense whatever specifically doctrinal writ, and therefore no 'Upanishad', but simply a fragment of a most magnificent epic narrative."[8] He goes on to say that "It was, then, into this old and primitive fragment of the Epic itself, as the matrix, that doctrinal writ subsequently became inserted, with the view of securing for it the authority of Krishna's divine form. . ."[9]

The reasons Otto could not succeed in identifying the original Gita, even though he felt strongly about it, were: (i) he did not consider it in the context of Samkhya and Yoga; and (ii) he himself, being a theologian,

---

[6] Richard Garbe, *Introduction to the Bhagavadgita* (Bombay: The University of Bombay, 1918), p. 11. For the views of other German and American scholars who have talked about the original Gita, see pp. 2–12.

[7] *Ibid.*, p. 8.

[8] Rudolf Otto, *The Original Gita*, translated by J.E. Turner (London: George Allen and Unwin Ltd., 1939), p. 10.

[9] *Ibid.*, p. 12.

did not differentiate between the rationalistic and theistic assertions of the Bhagavadgita.

But in spite of these shortcomings, Otto did try to identify the original Gita. According to him, the original Gita contained only 128 verses which are spread out in five chapters of the Bhagavadgita, mostly in Ch. I and II, the remainder in Chs. X, XI, and XVIII. He did not accept any verses of the remaining 13 chapters.

Amongst the Indian scholars who have tried to identify the original Gita, the work of G.S. Khair is noteworthy, though disappointing. In his book, *Quest for the Original Gita*, he has pointed out the verses belonging to the original Gita and the verses which were interpolated in two phases by two different authors.

Like Otto, Khair limited his study to the main text of the Bhagavadgita, without making any effort to investigate the interpolations in the context of historical fact. As he himself admits: "After an intensive study of the poem I have come to the conclusion that the Gita was written by three philosopher-poets, during three different periods, for different types of audiences. This inference is reached after a number of textual analyses and other methods of classification which are described in detail. The conclusions are based on the contents of the text itself."[10]

According to Khair, the original Gita had only certain portions of the first six chapters of the present Bhagavadgita. The second author added six more chapters (VIII, XIII, XIV, XV, XVII, and XVIII). The third author recast the whole poem, added six entirely new chapters, inserted them in the body of the poem, and shifted the chapters.[11]

The original Gita, as Khair points out, begins with verse number 20 of Ch. I, and the total number of verses belonging to it is 121, which are spread throughout the first six chapters. The verses of the original Gita according to Khair, are noted below along with their respective chapters and numbers:

Chart Showing Where the Verses of the Original Gita Occur in The Bhagavadgita (According to Khair):

Chapter	Verse Number	Total
I.	20-37	21
	45-47	
II.	10-13	
	18-30	
	39	
	47-52	24

[10] Gajanan Shripat Khair, *Quest for the Original Gita* (Bombay: Somaiya Publications Pvt. Ltd., 1969), pp. XII–XIII.

[11] *Ibid.*

III.	1-16	
	19	
	26-29	24
	33-34	
	42	
IV.	16-19	
	23-33	21
	37-42	
V.	1-2	
	4-6	10
	8-17	
VI.	1-6	
	10-12	
	18-28	21
	46	
	Total	121

The recent work of another Indian scholar, Bazaz, even though not primarily concerned with finding the original Gita, is informative. In his book *The Role of Bhagavad Gita in Indian History*, he makes penetrating historical inquires about the composition of the Bhagavadgita and points out how and when it was brought about in support of Brahmanic revivalism. He is very outspoken about the repercussions of the Bhagavadgita on the thought and practice of Indian civilization and holds the view that "On the whole its teachings can help (and have helped) only to subvert human progress and nourish social evils."[12]

Had Bazaz been fully acquainted with the original Samkhya and the original Yoga Sutra, he would have been more specific in pointing out the true characteristics of the original Gita, even though he was not directly concerned with it. What is significant about his work is that it raises important questions and provides clues to the suppressed, distorted, and altered state of Indian philosophy and literary culture.

Another relevant work in this respect is by S.D. Pendse.[13] Though his book *Pouranika Bhagawata Dharma* is in the Marathi language and not directly concerned with the original Gita as such, he is quite categorical in his findings. Pendse observes that only the first three chapters of the Bhagavadgita are original and all the other 15 chapters have been added later. His work is in Marathi, with which I am not familiar, but he seems to have grasped the main body of the original, in a general way. The truth

12 Prem Nath Bazaz, *The Role of Bhagavad Gita in Indian History* (New Delhi: Sterling Publishers Pvt. Ltd. 1975), p. X.
13 S.D. Pendse, *Pouranika Bhagwata Dharma* (Poona: Venus Prakashana, 1967).

is, in my view, that not all of the first three chapters are original, though the original is within these three.

Since the whole of the Bhagavadgita appears in the epic Mahabharata (Bhishma Parva, Ch. 42), there have been several scholarly studies of the epic to determine its actual date, historicity, textual integrity, and so forth. All the recent studies show that there have been several recensions of the Mahabharata. Obviously, the original Gita which might have been a part of the original epic, has also gone through several recensions.

These studies reveal that the original epic had only 8,800 verses and its name was Jaya. It was expanded to 24,000 verses and its name was changed to Jaya Bharata and then to Bharatetihas. At a much later time, the epic was expanded to 100,000 verses and got its present name, Mahabharata.[14]

According to Vaidya, "The philosophic portion named Gita was a part of the original Jaya". After its first alteration, the expanded Gita was called Harigita or Anugita. And finally it was altered into the present Bhagavadgita. Vaidya holds the view that the original has been twice altered and cites much evidence in support of his view.[15]

Talking about the original Gita of Vyasa, Vaidya writes: "Ever since I became a student of Indian Philosophy, particularly a reader of Bhagavadgita, it had been my feeling that the work of Sage Vyasa has not been handed down to us in its original form and that later writers have made some additions and alterations."[16] One interesting finding of Vaidya is that in the original Gita, Krishna used to be addressed as Keshava, Madhava, and Achyuta, and not as Bhagawan (God) described in the present-day Bhagavadgita. The epithet Bhagawan (God) when applied to Lord Krishna clearly indicates a composition made some thousand years after the sage Vyasa.[17]

In spite of his herculean work in search of the original Gita, Vaidya could not identify it. The main reason for his failure is that he centered his studies on the internal evidence of the epic without giving consideration to the Samkhya Yoga philosophy on which the original Gita is based.

Among numerous recent studies of the Mahabharata, the work of S.P. Gupta is noteworthy. We get valuable information about its date, place, nature, composition, contents, and so on from his book: *Mahabharat: Myth and Reality*. According to this study, there is no reference to the Mahabharata in the Vedic literature; until the fourth century B.C. no Indian literature mentions it; and there is no consensus among scholars

[14] For detail see R.V. Vaidya. *A Study of Mahabharat: (A Research)* (Poona: A.V.G. Prakashan, 1967) p. 11; and S.P. Gupta (ed.), *Mahabharat: Myth and Reality* (Delhi: Agam Prakashan, 1976), pp. 3–4.

[15] Vaidya, *Ibid.*, pp. 33–46.

[16] *Ibid.*, p. 33.

[17] *Ibid.*, p. 23. For details on three recensions of the Mahabharata and the Gita, see pp. 3–12 and also pp. 33–46.

about its date, some putting it at 600 B.C. or earlier while others claim the date to be 400 B.C.[18]

While summarizing the views and opinions of various scholars who have contributed to his book, S.P. Gupta writes, "These facts of history, archaeology, art, epigraphy and astronomy collectively support the internal evidence of the text, that the Mahabharat as we have it today had grown in stages; from 8,800 verses of the Jaya, through 24,000 verses of the Bharata, to the present-day 100,000 verses of the Mahabharat, over a considerable period of time."[19]

Even though the work of Gupta is not concerned with the original Gita, the information provided therein is very helpful in determining the redactions of the epic as well as the Gita.

There are numerous scholars, both Western and Indian, who have commented on the original Gita without being specific about its identity. The works and comments of these scholars are listed by Garbe, Khair, and also by Bazaz.[20] Therefore, without going into any further discussion about the views of these scholars, let me now reveal the key to finding the original Gita.

The Key to the Original Gita

It is imperative that the key to identifying the Gita be clearly stated so that others may independently reach the same conclusion. My guidelines for textual analysis are briefly stated below:

(i) Identification of the Original Samkhya Karika. Since most of the available books on Samkhya have been written by scholars who have accepted all the 73 verses in the extant text, they have not been able to discuss all aspects of this philosophy correctly. Their misinterpretation, distortion and lack of proper understanding was due to the contents of the 13 interpolated verses in the present text.

Therefore, it has been necessary to: (i) eliminate the interpolated verses (see chapter one); and (ii) make my own independent study of each verse without accepting the interpretations of others.

(ii) Identification of the Original Yoga Sutra. All the interpolated verses (see chapter one) in the Yoga Sutra needed to be eliminated. Each verse of the original text had to be correlated with the following verse or verses. Here again, I could not accept the interpretations of any writer on the Yoga

---

[18] S.P. Gupta (ed.), op. cit., pp. 3–51.
[19] Ibid., p. 255.
[20] For details on these, see Garbe, op. cit., pp. 2–12; Khair, op. cit., pp. 8–12; and Bazaz, op.cit., pp. 164–172.

Sutra because, to my knowledge, there is no book in the English language which is based on the original.

Since the interpolated verses both in the Samkhya Karika and the Yoga Sutra speak of religious views and concepts, books based on the existing texts are highly misleading and untrustworthy. Therefore, I had to make my own study of Samkhya and Yoga and to delete those verses which contained religious, devotional, and spiritual concepts of Hinduism.

This was imperative because neither Samkhya nor the Yoga Sutra advocated religion. Since the original Gita is an expansion of Samkhya and Yoga, religious, spiritual, or devotional ideas have no place in the original Gita.

(iii) Internal Evidence. The original Gita has been identified also on the basis of its own internal evidence as clearly stated in II, 39, III 1, 2, and 3. Let me describe these crucially important sources of identification:

As stated earlier, the contents of the original Gita are in the form of a dialogue between the warrior prince Arjuna and his counsellor charioteer Krishna. Arjuna had expressed his unwillingness to fight, as he foresaw tragic consequences of the war. Arjuna described his physical-mental condition in 11 verses (see Part Two of this book). Krishna tried to convince Arjuna that he should fight. After explaining various aspects of Samkhya philosophy in 25 verses (see the text of the original Gita, in Part Two of this book), Krishna says:

> This wisdom explained to you is according to Samkhya (philosophy). Now listen to wisdom according to Yoga, knowing which, O Partha (Arjuna), you will get rid of the restraints on action (II, 39).

After this statement, Krishna talks to Arjuna about the teachings of Yoga in 16 verses. Then Arjuna says:

> O Krishna, if you consider that knowledge is superior to action, then why do you urge me to engage in this terrible action (war). By your equivocal instructions, you seem to be confusing my understanding. Therefore, tell me definitely only one thing by which I can attain the highest good (III, 1–2).

Replying to the question of Arjuna, Krishna says:

> O Arjuna! as I have said before, there is a twofold path in this world: the path of knowledge (Jnana Yoga) is that of Samkhya, and the path of action (Karma Yoga) is that of yogins (practitioners of yoga) (III, 3).

Krishna then explains the importance of taking action in 28 follow-up verses and ends the talk. The original Gita has a total of 84 verses. These verses are spread throughout Chs. II and III, and only eleven are in the later section of Ch. I of the Bhagavadgita.

On the basis of this internal evidence, it can be seen that, unless one knows what the original Samkhya and original Yoga were, one would not be able to correctly identify the original verses of the Gita, as the talk is exclusively based on these two texts. Further, this internal evidence helps us in judging which verses of the Bhagavadgita are authentic and which are later additions.

To complicate our task, there are some verses in certain chapters of the Bhagavadgita which appear, on the face of it, genuine, such as III, 8, XIII, 19, and XVII, 8–10. It should be remembered that these verses are used now and then as camouflage to justify interpolations. Even where a particular verse appears quite genuine, it either repeats what has been said in the original Gita about Samkhya philosophy or it tells about an aspect of Yoga which was unknown to Patanjali.

Now let me explain the criteria by which 84 verses of the extant Bhagavadgita have been identified as genuine and 616 verses have been revealed to be interpolation. My effort will be to provide some detailed explanation about the verses of the first three chapters and offer only a more general discussion of the verses in the remaining 15 chapters. But before going into this explanation, some pertinent facts about the original Gita are stated.

Pertinent Facts About the Original Gita

The total number of verses in the original Gita is 84. The original begins with verse number 28 of the Bhagavadgita and ends with verse 43 in Chapter III. Thus, the content of the original Gita is found within the first three chapters of the extant Bhagavadgita. The remaining fifteen chapters (from Ch. IV to XVIII), containing 538 verses, have been interpolated.

There are 162 verses in the first three chapters of the Bhagavadgita, of which 78 verses are additions and only 84 are original. The sequence of presentation in the original Gita is in the following order.[21]

The problem of Arjuna, his unwillingness to fight the war, is stated first, in 11 verses in Chapter I, 28–34, 37, 40, 46, and 47.

Then Krishna replies in 42 verses in Chapter II, 3, 11–31, 34–36, 39–41, 48, 50, 53, 56–58, 60, and 64–70. His reply based on Samkhya philosophy takes up 25 verses, up to verse 36. His reply based on Yoga, comprises 16 verses, up to verse 70. Verse 39 explains the distinction between Samkhya and Yoga.

Upon hearing the inspiring reply of Krishna, Arjuna raises the question in two verses (Ch. III, 1–2) about the superiority of knowledge or action.

In answering Arjuna's question, Krishna explains the paramount importance of action in life as the means of performing one's duty, achieving social justice, and setting an honorable precedent. The teaching of Krishna is based on Samkhya and Yoga and takes up 31 verses of Ch. III, 3–9,

---

[21] The text of the original Gita with its English transliteration, translation, and my comments are presented in Part Two of this book.

16–21, 23–29, 32–35, 38–40, and 42–43. The content of these verses is based mainly on Karma Yoga (Yoga of action).

Interpolated Verses in the First Three Chapters

The sequence of interpolation and my exposition for each interpolated verse in the first three chapters of the Bhagavadgita now follows:

Chapter I.

In the first chapter, entitled 'Yoga of Dejection of Arjuna', a total of 36 verses are interpolated: verses 1–27, 35–36, 38–39 and 41–45. The first 27 verses recount the condition of readiness for war, describe the armies on both sides, and state the question of Dhritarashtra and the reply of Sanjaya. These verses do not contain any philosophic dialogue. And above all, they are not related to the main problem of Arjuna and the theme of the original.

In verses 35–36, the concepts of the threefold division of the universe *(trailokya rajya)* and sin *(papa)* are discussed. It is obvious that any such argument is quite contrary to the views of Samkhya and Yoga in its original form. Therefore these two verses cannot belong to the original. Likewise, verses 38 and 39 both talk about sin and hence are easily recognized as not belonging to the original. Verses 41–45 talk about caste intermingling *(varna shankara)*, hell *(naraka)*, caste-duty *(jati-dharma)* and sin *(mahat-papa)*. These concepts are obviously religious and Brahmanic.

In all these 36 interpolated verses there is no philosophic content. Nor is there any thought based on rational considerations. Seen in this context, to any student of the original Samkhya Karika and original Yoga Sutra, these verses in Chapter I appear to be alien intrusions.

Chapter II.

The second chapter, entitled 'Yoga of Samkhya System', has a total of 72 verses. Among these, 42 belong to the original and 30 verses are interpolated.

The first verse is the narrative statement of Sanjaya, and the second verse (II, 2) talks about heaven *(swarga)*. Because the first is quite unrelated and because the second argues a religious doctrine, one can easily recognize the verses as interpolated. Verses 4–10 deal with worship *(puja)*, the teacher (guru), alms *(bhaikshyam)*, discipleship *(shishya)*, the sovereignty of the gods *(suranam rajyam)*, and repeat the statement of Arjuna. Again, there is no philosophic content in any of these verses. They in no way relate to Samkhya and the Yoga Sutra.

Verses 32–33 and 37–38 mention such concepts as heaven (swarga-dwara) and sin.

Verses 42–47 talk about Veda, heaven, and Brahman, and one verse (47) advises one not to care about the fruit of action, saying: "thy right is to work and never at all to its fruits."

Since these statements have been made while Krishna is explaining Yoga discipline, it is evident that these views and concepts are contrary to the original Yoga Sutra.

Verses 49 and 51 condemn those whose motive is to realize the fruit of action and speak about being free from the bonds of birth and reaching a sorrowless state after renouncing action. Verse 52 merely refers to the preceding verse.

As stated earlier, action (work) and the fruits of action have been strongly emphasized in Samkhya philosophy and in the Yoga Sutra of Patanjali. The verses cited above are quite contradictory, even antagonistic, to Samkhya Yoga.

Likewise, verse 54 states an irrelevant question of Arjuna, and verse 55 talks about giving up all desire (a philosophy of sanyasa which is contradictory to the Samkhya Yoga view).

Verses 59 and 61 refer to the concept of the Supreme (Almighty God), and 62–63 again talk about desire, saying that it arises because of the attachment of the senses to objects and that anger arises from desire. None of these interpretations of desire and its consequences are authentic teachings. According to Samkhya, desire may arise without attachment of the senses, and anger does not arise only from desire.

Verse 71 again condemns desire, and verse 72 talks about the divine state *(Brahmi Sthiti)* and oneness with Brahman *(brahmanirvana)*, which is interpreted by various scholars as the attainment of the bliss of God.[22]

Chapter III.

This chapter is entitled 'Yoga of Right Action' (Karma Yoga) and has 43 verses. Among these, 31 verses belong to the original and 12 verses are interpolated.

Verses 10–15 talk about Prajapati (one of the post-Vedic gods), *deva* (deity), *yajna* (vedic sacrificial ceremony), *santa* (sainthood), *papa* (sin), and Brahma (one of the post-Vedic gods). None of these concepts belong to Samkhya or the original Yoga.

Verse 22 refers to the three worlds *(trishu lokeshu)*, and verses 30–31 speak about sanyasa (renunciation), adhyatma (spirituality), and shradha (faith). Verses 36, 37, and 41 deal with sin.

The following table shows which verses of the extant Bhagavadgita are original and which were interpolated. There is a total of 616 interpolated verses, of which 78 are inserted in the first three chapters among the original verses, and the remaining 538 verses, contained within 15 different chapters, are added to the main body of the original text.

---

[22] See S. Radhakrishnan, *The Bhagavadgita, op. cit.,* p. 129.

The Original and Interpolated Verses in the Extant Bhagavadgita

Chapter	Original Verses	Total Original	Interpolated Verses	Total Inter-polation	Total Verses
Ch. I	28–34, 37, 40 46–47	11	1–27, 35–36 38–39, 41–45	36	47
Ch. II	3, 11–31, 34–36, 39–41, 48, 50, 53, 56–58, 60, 64–70	42	1–2, 4–10, 32–33, 37–38, 42–47, 49, 51–52, 54–55, 59, 61, 62–63, 71–72	30	72
Ch. III	1–9, 16–21, 23–39, 32–35, 38–40, 42–43	31	10–15, 22, 30–31, 36–37, 41	12	53
Chs. IV–XVIII	—	—	all the verses	538	538
TOTAL		84		616	700

Verses of the Fifteen Interpolated Chapters[23]

Chapter IV is entitled 'Jnana-Karma-Sanyasa Yoga' (Yoga of Knowledge, Action, and Renunciation). The title suggests that one can expect to find some philosophical deliberations, but there is not a single verse which can be judged to contain any rational or philosophic thought. The whole chapter is primarily concerned with the idea of incarnation, maya (illusion), Brahman, worship of deities, the fourfold caste system, yajna (sacrifices), sin, faith, and 'action in inaction'.

Action is described as sacrifice to the gods (IV, 12). Further, one should offer the self as sacrifice to Brahman. According to verse 37, "as fire reduces fuel to ashes, so fire of knowledge reduces all actions to ashes". Evidently, unless religiously motivated, one can scarcely find any wisdom in the entire chapter.

Chapter V is entitled 'Karma-Sanyasa Yoga' (Yoga of Action and Renunciation). It talks about renunciation and Yoga of action, but declares both to be identical in principle. And it argues that renunciation is hard to obtain without Yoga and that a person achieving harmony through Yoga goes to Brahman. Yoga is interpreted as the performance of action as an offering or as an act of self-purification.

The chapter offers a confused combination of pranayama (breathing) and dharana (concentration). It recommends practicing concentration by

[23] For the original Sanskrit title of each chapter, its translation, and the number of verses in each, see Chapter 2 (the Contents of the Bhagavadgita).

gazing between the eyebrows and by equalizing the ratio of exhalation and inhalation through the nostrils (V, 27), claiming that when the mind is controlled through this practice, one is liberated.

Obviously, though the names of Samkhya and Yoga are invoked, not a single verse discusses these without distortion. Rather, we are taught that a life of renunciation is in accordance with some sort of superior action.

Chapter VI is called Dhyana Yoga (Yoga of Meditation). It defines what Yoga is, gives instruction on the practice of meditation, prescribes diet, and gives direction on the practice of Yoga. But in all these, the precepts of the original Yoga Sutra are violated.

Yoga practitioners are advised to seek solitude, to abstain from hope (to be nirashi), and not to be greedy. They are instructed that the location of Yoga practice should be neither too elevated nor too low, that the practitioner should sit on a piece of cloth placed over a straw mat (kusha-grass) and practice Yoga for purification of the self (VI, 12). They should keep the head, neck, and body straight and should gaze at the tip of the nose, without looking around (VI, 13). Further, Yoga is not possible for those who eat too much or too little, nor for those who sleep excessively or stay too often awake. The practitioner of Yoga, following this advice, enjoys infinite bliss upon contact with Brahman (the Eternal). Such a yogi becomes fit to worship (VI, 30–31) and achieves unity with God.

None of these prescriptions for the renunciatory life are in accordance with Patanjali and the Yoga Sutra.

Chapter VII is entitled 'Jnana-Vijnana Yoga' (Yoga of Knowledge and Science), but it is mainly concerned with monotheism. It talks about God, faith, maya (illusion), Brahman, and spirituality. It also talks about prakriti (nature) but says this is inferior to a higher prakriti (God). Krishna says: "I am the source of creation and dissolution of the whole universe" (VII, 5–6). Likewise, it talks about Guna, but interprets it as maya.

It tells us that there are four types of devotees and they are fruitful to the extent of their faith in God. While discussing *avyakta* (unmanifest) and *vyakta* (manifest), Krishna says, "I am manifest but veiled by yoga-maya (yogic illusion) (24–25).

Although some basic concepts of Samkhya philosophy are retained, they are all misinterpreted and distorted. Further, as the title of this chapter suggests, one would expect some philosophical and rational discussion here. But there is no verse in this whole chapter which can be considered consonant with the Samkhya and Yoga Sutra. Therefore, I concluded that none of these verses were part of the original corpus.[24]

Chapter VIII is entitled 'Yoga of the Word Brahma' and contains 28 verses. The entire chapter is concerned with Brahman, God, spirituality

---

[24] For Samkhya views on prakriti, avyakta, vyakta, guna, and purusha, see Chapter 1, the section on Kapila.

(adhyatma), rebirth, worship, Veda, and Brahma, and repeats the process of yoga practice. None of this chapter can be regarded as accurately reflecting the views of Samkhya or Yoga Sutra.

Chapter IX is entitled 'Yoga of Kingship and Its Insights' and has 34 verses. These verses speak about devotion and worship. Krishna says: "Under my supervision, nature produces, the world revolves" (IX, 10). "Worship me with a single mind (13). "I am the father, the mother, the grandfather of this world, and the dispenser of the fruits of action" (17). "I am in them who worship me" (29). The chapter is primarily concerned with monotheistic ideas, all of which are later interpolations.

Chapter X, 'Yoga of Manifestations' discusses monotheism in phrases which are almost biblical. In this chapter, Krishna declares: "I am the source of all" (X, 8). "I am the self, the beginning, the middle, and the end of all beings" (20). Among the sages I am Kapila" (26). Krishna further explains how he is everywhere and says that "nothing exists without Me" (19–40).

Obviously, none of these verses belongs to the original.

Chapter XI, entitled 'Yoga of Seeing the Universal Form', is again concerned with monotheism. In this chapter, Krishna shows his divine form to Arjuna (XI, 5–8). The chapter says that Krishna as God (the Supreme) has been addressed by various names. "Thou are the Father of this world, moving and unmoving" (43), "primal God" (38). Devotion is the only means by which one can realize God (54–55).

The title of Chapter XII is 'Yoga of Devotion' (Bhakti Yoga). As the name suggests, it is primarily concerned with the devotional aspects of theism. It talks about forms of worship (XII, 1–11) and emphasizes abandonment of the fruits of action (13–19).

'Yoga of the Division of the Field and the Knower of the Field' is the title of Chapter XIII. Though the verses of this chapter speak about purusha, prakriti (nature), Jnana (knowledge), cause-effect, sukha (happiness), and dukha (sorrow) and give the impression that Samkhya philosophy is being presented, it in fact interprets all these concepts from a theistic point of view by talking about worship, union with God, devotion, realization of Brahman, and renunciation.

A close study of these verses would reveal that the basic concepts of Samkhya are merely cited and are not explained in their original form. These concepts, it appears, are used only as a camouflage for legitimizing the insertion of monotheistic views by giving the impression that they are in accordance with Samkhya and Yoga.

For example, verse 19 says that prakriti and purusha are beginningless (anadee). According to Samkhya, prakriti is beginningless but the purusha are born of fathers and mothers, possessing both indestructible and perishable qualities. Likewise, verse 20 explains that nature is the cause of effect and purusha is the cause of experiencing pleasure and pain. But verse 22 declares that the supreme spectator in this body is God (Maheshwara and Parmatma).[25] No verse is genuinely expressive of the original Samkhya. Theism intrudes into each verse.

Chapter XIV is entitled 'Yoga of Three Guna Constituents'. It talks about sattva, rajas, and tamas gunas but attaches a theistic interpretation to each guna in the course of describing their qualities and functions. Just before describing gunas, Krishna says, "my womb is the great Brahma, in that I put the germ, then is the birth of all beings (XIV, 3). Whatever forms are produced, I am the seed-giving father" (4).

According to Samkhya philosophy, various manifestations of nature take place because of the gunas, which are the ever-present, ever-changing, indestructible constituents of nature.[26] But here all forms of manifestation are declared to be the work of God. Thus verses 5–18, which talk about gunas, their qualities and functions, do not belong to the original, even though they may appear to be authentic. They are used here only as a cover-up for theistic assertions, as evidenced by verse 19 which says, "Knowing that which is higher than these gunas, attains to My Being".

Chapter XV is called 'Yoga of the Highest Purusha' and has 20 verses. This chapter is mainly concerned with Vedanta, Supreme Purusha, God, and the knower of Vedas. It follows the Samkhya in describing the emergence and working of the senses, but then says that when God (isvara) takes leave of bodily form, He takes the senses and mind with him "as the wind carries away perfumes from their places (flowers)" (XV, 7–8).

It talks about two types of purusha: perishable and imperishable, giving the impression that the Samkhya philosophy is discussed. But it says the Supreme Purusha is isvara (God), who pervades and sustains the threefold world (lokatrayam) (16–17). In verse 18, Krishna says: "As I transcend the perishable, and am even higher than the imperishable, I am declared to be the Supreme Purusha in the world and in the Veda." Verse 20 says that by knowing what has just been taught, a man becomes wise and all his duties are accomplished.

Chapter XVI is entitled 'Yoga of the Distinction Between Devil and Godly' and has 24 verses, all concerned with theistic beliefs. It discusses acts of alms giving and austerity, sacrifice, the study of scriptures, and deity and condemns those who do not believe in theistic concepts (XVI, 7–21) saying that they go to hell and are thrown into the womb of demons (19).

Chapter XVII, 'Yoga of Distinction Between Three Kinds of Faith', says there are three kinds of faith of the embodied, born of their nature: sattvic (good), rajasic (passionate), and tamasic (dull). The faith of every individ-

---

[25] For proper view of Samkhya philosophy concerning the concepts referred to in this chapter, see Chapter 1 of this book.

[26] See Samkhya Karika, verses 16–18.

ual is in accordance with his nature. Good men worship gods, the passionate worship the demigods, and the dull worship the spirits and ghosts (XVII 2–4).

Then it talks about food, saying that these three kinds of people prefer three different kinds of food, according to their nature. It categorizes food as sattvic, rajasic, and tamasic and explains the effect of each on the consumers. The talk about food, although superficially unrelated to theism, does not belong to the original for two reasons: first, Patanjali never categorized food on the pattern of gunas, and second, he did not designate any type of food as essential for the performance of asanas and pranayamas; nor did he recommend any special category of food for the practice of samyama (a combined form of dharana, dhyana, and samadhi). Had food been considered an important factor, Patanjali would surely have included it in his description of the principles of yama, niyama, or pratyahara! But his general advice on things not specifically dealt with in the Yoga Sutra is to maintain a condition of sattva (a harmonious state).[27]

The main motive for discussing food on the pattern of the three guna principles of Samkhya is to link it with the idea of renunciation, devotion (bhakti), and sacrificial rituals (yajna). This becomes evident when one looks at the verses which follow the description of food. For example, verse 11 says that sacrifice offered without desire and with firm faith is sattvic, sacrifice offered in order to seek reward is rajasic, and sacrifices in which no food is distributed and which are devoid of mantras and faith are tamasic (12–13). Further, it declares 'Om Tat Sat' as the triple designation of Brahman (the Brahman, the Vedas, and the sacrifices) and explains its value in six verses (23–28).

Chapter XVIII is entitled 'Yoga of Liberation and Renunciation' and contains 78 verses. In the first part of this chapter (verses 7–12), the talks concern renunciation, desireless action, and abandonment of all fruits of action (sarva karma phala tyaga).

Preceding these talks, verse 2 defines renunciation as 'action without desire'. Verse 3 refers to the view of philosophers (manisinah), saying that according to some of them, "action should be given up as an evil". And then verse 5 makes action conditional, saying that acts of sacrifice (yajna), almsgiving (dana), and austerity (tapa) should not be relinquished but should be performed.

The chapter is concerned with the three divisions of the universe and the three constituents of nature. It considers all actions on the basis of three gunas (a Samkhya concept) on which food and devotional worship have been earlier discussed. Then it talks about caste division, arguing that the duties of different castes are distributed according to the qualities caste members are born with and according to their nature (41–45).

---

[27] See Yoga Sutra II 30–44 and 50.

Though this chapter talks about Dhyana Yoga (Yoga of meditation) in verse 52 and Buddhi Yoga (Yoga of intellect) in verse 57, both types of Yoga are described as suited to devotion and worship. For example, Krishna says: "Renouncing mentally all actions in Me, regarding Me as the Supreme and resorting to the Yoga of intellect (Buddhi Yoga), do thou ever fix thy mind on Me"(57).

Throughout we find a Yoga being put forth in the Bhagavadgita which is not the Yoga of the Yoga Sutra. Wherever Yoga or Samkhya concepts are invoked, they are invariably distorted and misinterpreted. For example, verse 13 quotes Samkhya, saying that there are five causes for taking any action, and in verse 14 it declares that the fifth is the presiding deity. If we examine this interpretation closely, we will notice that Samkhya never mentioned five causes of action. According to Samkhya, people work for the fulfillment of their desires, motivated by one of the eight bhavas (motivations). Samkhya mentions five fundamental principles of cause and effect (satkarya).[28] This is only one of countless examples of the distortion of Samkhya.

In this chapter, we also encounter the concept of a covenant between worshippers and God which has a pronounced biblical resonance. This idea of covenant is depicted by verse 65, wherein Krishna says: "Fix your mind on Me; be devoted to Me; sacrifice to Me; prostrate thyself before Me; so shall you without doubt reach Me. This I truly promise to you, for you are dear to Me." The following verse emphasizes this view saying, "Abandoning all duties, come to Me alone for shelter. I will liberate you from all sins, grieve not." To this promise of Krishna, Arjuna responds saying, "Destroyed is my ignorance; and through your grace I have gained a proper way of thinking. I am free from doubts. I will act according to Thy word"(73).

From the foregoing, it is obvious that there is no verse in this last chapter which belongs to the original Gita. The dialogues on Samkhya and Yoga, although at times appearing authentic, are found distorted upon close scrutiny. In all these chapters (IV–XVIII), Samkhya and Yoga are used only as disguises and are never prescribed in their original forms. Every statement is tied up with theistic, devotional, and renunciatory ideas. For these reasons, all these verses are identified as interpolated.

I do not claim that all possible sources of investigation have been exhausted. My effort has been to take into consideration the views and opinions of all those scholars, both Indian and Western, who have questioned the genuineness of the Bhagavadgita and have tried to reveal the contents of the original Gita. But I have ignored the views and opinions of those commentators and scholars (from the eighth century onward) who

---

[28] See Samkhya Karika, Sutra 9, Sutras 43–44, and also the table of 25 elements in Chapter 1 of this book, under Samkhya.

have written or commented on Samkhya, Yoga, or the Gita with a notion to support theism and Brahmanic revivalism. This research, therefore, has taken into consideration all those primary and secondary source materials which have appeared pertinent, objective, and revealing.

It is probable that somewhere certain works remain undiscovered which might have a great bearing on the contents of the original Gita. With this notion in mind, I had once planned to visit Bali, Java, Sumatra, Cambodia, Tibet, Sri Lanka, and certain places in India hoping that in these areas of ancient Indian influence an intact copy of the original Gita might be unearthed. But I gave up this idea when I became thoroughly convinced of the correctness and genuineness of my finding. I no longer considered it necessary to search far and wide for the ur-text of the Gita when all the essential clues were to be found in the Gita itself.

Though my search has occupied 15 years and has imposed its share of personal hardship, there is a feeling of great accomplishment in presenting the Gita in its true original form. I hope this work will inspire and aid in unearthing other lost treasures of ancient India, the knowledge of which will help to enrich our understanding of the foundations of Indian civilization.

6
CONCLUDING OBSERVATIONS

The rediscovery of the original Gita draws our attention to a crucial missing element of Indian civilization: its philosophic history is incomplete and mostly unwritten. Though India has produced renowned historians and scholars, their work is mostly concerned with narrating and assessing major events in the socio-political and cultural realms. The few who have written on the history of Indian philosophy, such as S.N. Dasgupta, Belvalkar, Radhakrishnan, and C.D. Sharma have not dealt with the widespread revision of ancient rational philosophy which signalled the onset of the dark age of Indian culture. Although these historians do point out certain distortions and redactions, their work has not been conducted in the investigative spirit. We do not find in their accounts any identification of those responsible for these changes, their motives, and the ensuing impact on Indian thought and practice.

Scholars, both Indian and Western, need to be reminded here of the observation that an internationally-known scholar, R.C. Dutt, made decades ago: "The history of ancient India ends with the eighth century." And further: "History is silent over these dark centuries."[1] It follows that in the absence of historical research into distortions and redactions of philosophical and literary texts perpetrated during the dark centuries, a clear picture of their thought processes can hardly be comprehended and there can be no meaningful appreciation by present-day India of its own past.

The value of such historical research should not be underestimated. The renowned British historian, H. Butterfield, has observed, "We should study problems rather than periods." Concerning the importance of historical education and explanation, Butterfield advised his colleagues: "We may hold the view that the aim of an historical education is the training and exercise of certain faculties of the mind. We may consider that it is important to learn how our civilization developed or to see modern political problems against the background of history."[2]

Butterfield emphasizes the internal examination of problems saying that historians should 'resurrect' what has happened in the past. He goes on

[1] R.C. Dutt, op. cit., p. 150.
[2] H. Butterfield, The Study of Modern History (London: G. Bell and Sons, Ltd. 1944), p. 27.

to specify, "we must have more of the kind of history which is not mere narrative but exposition—the history which takes account of the differences between the centuries, between stages of intellectual development, even between types of social structure."[3]

A civilization grows and flourishes on the nourishment it receives from accumulated wisdom, teachings, and the practices of its heritage. The feeling of belonging to a particular cultural heritage, makes the past inspiring and educational. But when this natural source of nourishment is blocked by distorting and concealing the historical record, the individual becomes alienated and is unable to trace his cultural lineage. He cannot take advantage of what was left behind by his forefathers.

Indian history as portrayed by scholars is for the most part misleading and untrustworthy. Present-day India cannot thrive without a corrected knowledge of its past.

It is not uncommon to find scholars discussing ancient Indian philosophy by quoting thinkers who wrote during and after the ninth century A.D. More often than not, these scholars, both Indian and Western, try to link the Vedic period with the thinkers and commentators of the ninth to twentieth centuries to validate the expansion and growth of Indian thought, as if nothing worth mentioning existed between the Vedic period and the ninth century A.D. One finds that the thoughts and practices of thinkers between 700 B.C. and 800 A.D. are being played down, distorted, or completely ignored.[4]

As a result, the picture of ancient India we obtain through the accounts of these scholars is: 1. that India is the birth place of religious, spiritual, and mystic thought; 2. that the development and expansion of all religious doctrines can be traced to sources in Indian antiquity; 3. that from the days of the Vedas, India is a land of theologians, mystics, and spiritualists; and 4. that it continues to produce gurus, swamis, sanyasins, tantrics, and mystics as torch-bearers of divinity in the world. To many Indians, this depiction of India does indeed provide a sense of cultural superiority, even when they find themselves surrounded by unspeakable human degradation and impoverishment. It seems as if there is a tendency to cover up or ignore what in fact is a national and social shame with a make-believe feeling of being superior in the world of spirituality and divinity.

It is this all-engulfing, one-sided account of Indian history which needs to be corrected. A new philosophic history of India must reveal: What actually was India?[5] Why and how did it fall into dark ages and why

---

[3] Ibid., p. 12–13.

[4] For example, see Radhakrishnan, op. cit., 'Periods of Indian Thought', pp. 56–60; C. Sharma, op. cit., pp. 1–40; S.N. Dasgupta, A History of Indian Philosophy, Vol. I, pp. 67–77; Belvalkar, op. cit., 'Evaluation of Upanishadic Philosophy', pp. 327–42.

[5] An objective and investigative presentation of Indian philosophic history is attempted by Erich Frauwallner, History of Indian Philosophy, translated from German into English by V.M. Bedekar (New York: Humanities Press, 1974). This work can be regarded as a model, even though it does not answer all the pertinent issues of the period.

did it remain colonized for more that a thousand years? What is wrong with India that it fails to achieve overall prosperity and remains instead a paralyzed socio-economic-political power?

If we look closely into the causes of India's being as it is, especially in the light of what has already been revealed through this limited research, it will be seen that as a cultural entity, it does not stand on its true parental and hereditary foundations. By blocking, ignoring, and distorting the major rational thoughts and practices of its heritage, it has prevented the precious flow of those hereditary foundations which would have enriched its mental faculties, nourished its growth, and aided in its prosperity. Consequently, for an average aspiring Indian, there is very little available outside the religious-spiritual domain to which he can look for guidance, inspiration, self-confidence, and pride. Thus, an investigative and objective presentation of Indian philosophic history becomes a vitally important task for the scholars of Indology.

Furthermore, a correct account of the Indian past will be valued properly when we take into consideration what it has to offer as a solution to such issues of universal concern as sorrow (dukha), happiness (sukha), and universal welfare. Since what India is experiencing is much the same as what many societies of Asia, Africa, America, and Europe are faced with, the observations and recommendations of ancient Indian thinkers and Yoga practitioners might be of equal interest to people in every society. The validity of this view can be readily seen when we proceed to examine an issue of universal concern: Advancement vs. Impoverishment.

The Cause of Social Advancement or Impoverishment

Employing the concepts of Samkhya philosophy, let us consider a pivotal question: What causes the advancement or impoverishment of a society? Answers can be provided on the basis of the cause-effect concept of Samkhya philosophy: The effect exists in the cause. In the case of a society, its people are the cause and its quality of life is the effect. As is the cause, Samkhya teaches, so is the effect. The effect can never contain what is not already present in its cause. The people (agent) can produce only what they are capable of producing. Significantly, humans possess the ability to acquire what is not readily available, alter what is not suitable, and create alternative ways to achieve desired ends. The making of a society, therefore, primarily depends upon the quality of the human cause.[6] Material cause, though important, is not the decisive factor. This is evident when

---

[6] For a detailed discussion on cause-effect relationship and on human cause, see Chapter 1, the section on Theory of Right Action.

we look at the achievements of societies which, though poor in natural resources, nevertheless found ways to circumvent this handicap.

Moreover, human cause is not immutable, and a people can enrich itself through the acquisition of skill and knowledge. Samkhya teaches us that in order to produce beneficial effects the human cause must first acquire proper knowledge (samyak jnana), must be inspired by proper motivation (bhavas), must be able to take right action (satkarya), and must strive for the fulfillment of desires *(autsukya nivrittyartham)*. Action of the people, when influenced by these qualities, brings excellence to their work and thereby advances the society. The absence of such action, on the other hand, causes impoverishment and sorrow (dukha). The original Gita dramatizes this view well by saying that achieving excellence in action is Yoga. It implies that mere work is not enough. Rather, one should aim at excellence in whatever one is engaged.

In the light of the foregoing discussion, it can be argued that the cause of impoverishment in Indian society is due to its own human cause. It is not the outcome of any material cause. If a plenitude of resources be considered as the cause of prosperity, India should be among the happiest lands on earth. It possesses a wealth of resources—land, water, minerals, favorable climate, strategic geographical location and above all, vast manpower. What has so conditioned and transformed the human cause of India that it fails to achieve prosperity?

As explained earlier, after the revival of Hinduism in about 800 A.D., the philosophic outlook and the thought pattern of the people were transformed through the Bhagavadgita. This was done in two ways: (i) by distorting the basic concepts of the rational thinkers of ancient India, such as Kapila, Buddha, Mahavira, Patanjali, and Vyasa; and (ii) by suppressing free thought.

It has been pointed out (Chapter 1) that all rational thinkers of ancient India had emphasized: (i) taking right action and (ii) acquiring proper knowledge. Both these major concepts were distorted, even denied, in countless ways. For example, though action was talked about, it was considered worthwhile only for bodily purification, devotion, and worship. Action for personal, family, and social betterment was dismissed as insignificant. The life of renunciation (sanyasa) and desireless action was glorified. Action and inaction were reinterpreted to mean the same. Material wealth and prosperity were called maya (illusionary). Knowledge meant knowing theistic doctrine, the Vedanta, the Brahman, and the Supreme God.

Further, Hindu revivalism promoted the philosophy that men are not born equal. The division of the populace into four caste groups was legitimized by the Bhagavadgita. Women were subjugated, and people of lower caste were declared untouchable for life. The Brahman caste, on the other hand, was declared synonymous with godhood. A vast majority of the polity was thus degraded in terms of human values and power. A sense of inferiority, due to birth and fate, was instilled in the masses.

However, it should be clearly stated that it was not and is not the teaching of theism and religious doctrines which has adversely affected the Indian masses. Had the Bhagavadgita been concerned with promoting only religious doctrine and not with distorting rational philosophy, it would not have had the ruinous effects we now observe. Historically, it is as amazing as it is perplexing to see that no other religion in the world denigrates and devalues the role of action in life as do the teachings of the Bhagavadgita. By negating action and rejecting knowledge, by interpreting material wealth as illusion (maya), and by glorifying renunciation (sanyasa), the distorted teachings of the Bhagavadgita have produced inertia and indifference to human problems among its adherents. In the case of India, the entry of monotheism is inseparably allied with the distortion and denigration of existing rational thoughts. What this distortion of rational thought has done to the Indian polity can be fathomed better when we examine the relationship of actions and thought.

Action Versus Thought

In order to better understand how thought conditions and motivates action, we must review what has been taught by Patanjali in his Yoga Sutra and by Kapila in his Samkhya philosophy.

According to Samkhya Yoga, men are equal. Each person possesses the same faculties. The mind, intellect, self-consciousness, the sense organs and the action organs (the thirteen instruments) of each person possess the same basic capabilities. The mind works as an action organ as well as a sense organ. The purusha (man) can improve the quality, power, and function of his mind and any other organ by means of the eight steps of Yoga.

Yoga maintains that a man forms himself through mental visualization. His action is conditioned by his thought. The level of performance is equal to his level of thought. His becoming unfolds, in due time, gradually but surely, in conformity with what he perceives and visualizes in his mind. Mental visualization causes likewise materialization.

Further, Yoga holds that visualization of the mind begins at a very early age. The learning process of a child begins with conception and continues through all the stages of pregnancy. By the time a child is two years old, (s)he draws a rudimentary sketch, through the process of mental visualization, of what (s)he would like to be. This outline is modified with age and becomes clearer. This mental imagery, good or bad, conditions and shapes personality, behavior, and action. How this shaping of the mind of an average Indian takes place, from his childhood to adulthood, is not difficult to comprehend when we consider it in the light of the prevalence of the Bhagavadgita's teachings among the Indian masses.

By applying the principles of Samkhya Yoga to the problem of man and his society, it can be argued that an individual is a part of the whole. The quality of the whole is reflected in the part. By looking at the part, one gets an idea of the whole. The whole can be bettered only be bettering the parts. The impact of Yoga teaching on the whole (the society) can very well be comprehended when we see what it teaches and recommends for the betterment of the individuals (parts). In this context Patanjali's recommendation of pratyahara and samyama is worth considering.

Pratyahara is mentally visualizing the opposite of what is presently undesirable. Since visualization causes materialization, pratyahara practice will eliminate the unwanted and effectuate the desired. According to the Yogic view, mental visualization mobilizes all physical and mental faculties in an automatic way towards the realization of what is so visualized. This mental visualization may be called a mental picture, a thought or the voice of the brain. If mental visualization can be considered a thought, it follows that it (thought) influences and actuates action.

Samyama is a combined form of dharana (concentration) dhyana (meditation), and samadhi (deep meditation). By the process of samyama, the mind is better prepared for pratyahara. By samyama, the one-pointedness of the mind is perfected, its fluctuation and dissipative nature is controlled, and the holding of an image is prolonged. With this acquired ability, an individual is better able to mentally withdraw from the unpleasant and become attached to what is desirable. Thus, by knowing and applying pratyahara and samyama, an individual becomes capable of achieving excellence in all his actions.

The original Gita emphasizes the value and importance of excellence in action, of setting good precedents, of working with a sense of responsibility, justice, and duty; and it teaches how the common welfare can be improved, how sorrow (dukha) can be eliminated, and how happiness (sukha) can be obtained. Thus, judging on the basis of what it teaches, the original Gita becomes a most valuable guide and a 'handbook' for individuals in every society.

The problem of human and social well-being has always been, in all ages, a matter of deep concern to the great philosophers. We find ancient thinkers such as Kapila, Buddha, Mahavira, Patanjali, and Vyasa in India; Confucius and Lao-tse in China; and Plato and Aristotle in Greece sharing the same basic concern—how to improve and maintain individual and social well-being.

As noted earlier, the growth of a civilization is rooted in what it has learned from its past. The past becomes educational and inspirational only when it commands the trust and respect of the generations that follow. Without trust, even the most treasured ideas and teachings get rejected. On the other hand, with trust, even the follies, mistakes, and shortcomings of the past or present get talked about, examined, improved, or refined with pride. The rediscovery of the original Gita will restore that missing trust of the Indians in their own treasures of intellectual wealth left behind by their forefathers. The present India will be linked properly with its past and will stand on its hereditary foundations.

The value of this work outside India can be better gauged if one considers the universality of the Gita's teachings. This world of our's, though miraculously advancing in science and technology and causing unprecedented escalation of change in numerous areas of human concern, has failed or is miserably failing in one area of universal concern: sorrow (dukha). For millions around the world, obtaining proper food, clothing, shelter, health care, and education still remain a dream. Even in the most affluent societies, the question of dukha (sorrow) remains unchanged. For example, concern about health, longevity, stress, and fear cause sorrow to millions even when they are privileged to possess all the amenities of the good life. To this vast mass of people, from the most affluent to the most lowly, an answer to human basic problems needs to be provided. The teachings of the original Gita provide an answer.

The author holds the view that our world can be made much happier than what we see. Any human society possessing two things—land and water—need not starve, face sorrow, or permit human degradation to continue. The suffering in all societies—advancing and advanced—is perpetuated for two basic reasons: (i) lack of proper knowledge and (ii) lack of excellence in action. Human suffering everywhere is due to human cause. By improving human cause, dukha (sorrow) can be eliminated and sukha (happiness) can be achieved universally. This is what was taught by Kapila, Buddha, Mahavira, Patanjali, and Vyasa. This is the question that was raised by Arjuna and the answer to it is what comprises the original Gita. Since the question is universal, the teachings of the Gita will remain universally valid.

PART TWO

THE MAHABHARATA:
BACKGROUND OF THE ORIGINAL GITA

The original Gita was composed in the form of a dialogue between Arjuna (the warrior king and hero of the war) and Krishna (the counsellor charioteer of Arjuna) which took place just before the actual fighting commenced during the Mahabharata (the great war). It is called the great war because all the kings and tribes of northern India participated in it, either on the side of the Pandavas or the Kauravas—the two Aryan royal families. In order to fully comprehend the text of the Gita, it is necessary to understand the background of this great war.

In northern India, there was a kingdom of the Kurus, also known as the Bharatas. The king of the Kurus had two sons, Dhritarashtra, the elder, and Pandu, the younger. Dhritarashtra was blind and had one hundred sons, who were called the Kauravas. Pandu had five sons, who were called the Pandavas. Due to the blindness of Dhritarashtra, his younger brother Pandu became king.

Pandu, who died at an early age, was succeeded by Dhritarashtra. Dhritarashtra brought up the young Pandava brothers together with his own hundred sons, thoroughly educating them in warfare and the military arts. After some time, jealousy developed between the sons of Dhritarashtra and the Pandavas, which ultimately led them to war.

Among the Pandavas the eldest was Yudhishthira, a righteous man, but with a weakness for gambling. The second oldest was Bhima, a man of great strength and size. The third brother was Arjuna, the real hero of the epic Mahabharata. He possessed great skill in warfare and arms. Nakula, the fourth, knew how to care for horses. And the fifth, Sahadeva was well versed in astronomy. Due to these accomplishments of the Pandavas, the sons of Dhritarashtra—the Kauravas—became envious. Duryodhana, eldest son of Dhritarashtra, became the leader of his brothers and they were able to banish the Pandavas.

The Pandavas, now in exile, reached the kingdom of Panchala. It happened that the daughter of the Panchala king, Draupadi had to choose her husband in accordance with the ancient Indian ritual, called *Swayam-vara* a ceremonial competition in which all the warriors had to show their prowess in warfare and archery. The winner received a garland from the hands of his wife to be. Arjuna, a warrior of extraordinary skill in archery, won over the other suitors and thus married Princess Draupadi.

The Pandava brothers, with the help of the Panchala king, recovered a portion of their old kingdom and built their new capital at Indraprastha (near modern Delhi). By this time, Krishna, son of Vasudeva, became a strong supporter of the Pandavas. The resurgence of the Pandavas caused even greater jealousy among the Kauravas and they began plotting to completely ruin the Pandavas.

Their scheme called for Duryodhana (the eldest son of Dhritarashtra) to challenge Yudhishthira to a gambling tournament. The game was rigged, the Pandavas were cheated, and as a consequence, had to forfeit their newly restored kingdom. Duryodhana insulted Draupadi before the assembly of princes and kings and forced the Pandavas into an exile of twelve years. They were promised that if, at the end of the period of their exile, they spent an additional year hidden away in complete seclusion, their kingdom would be returned to them.

After their exile was ended, the Pandavas returned and claimed their kingdom from Duryodhana. But their rightful claim was refused. As a result, both parties began preparing for war.

Krishna tried to mediate and went, with a peace proposal, to see Dhritarashtra. According to this proposal, five villages were to be given to the Pandavas, and the war would be averted. This humble request of Krishna was also not heeded. The war, thus, became inevitable. Krishna sided with the Pandavas, and acted as the charioteer and counsellor to Arjuna in this war.

The Mahabharata lasted for 18 days and it was fought on the plains of Kurukshetra (north of Delhi). It is against this background of the great war that a dialogue took place between Arjuna and Krishna. It occurred just before the battle commenced, on the battlefield, while both the armies were awaiting the signal to attack. Arjuna had come to the battlefield in his chariot driven by Krishna. It is this dialogue which makes up the original Gita.

A verse in the original Sanskrit is given first. It is followed by its English transliteration. Then comes the English translation of the verse. My comments are provided only where necessary to clarify the meaning, especially as it relates to Samkhya and Yoga.

TEXT OF THE ORIGINAL GITA

1

दृष्ट्वेमं स्वजनं कृष्ण युयुत्सुं समुपस्थितम् ॥

arjuna uvāca:

> *dṛṣṭve 'maṁ svajanaṁ kṛṣṇa*
> *yuyutsuṁ samupasthitam*

Arjuna said:
O Krishna, when I see my kinsmen assembled here and eager to fight,

2

सीदन्ति मम गात्राणि मुखं च परिशुष्यति ।
वेपथुश्च शरीरे मे रोमहर्षश्च जायते ॥

sīdanti mama gātrāṇi
mukham ca pariśus yati
vepathuś ca śarīre me
romaharsaś ca jāyate

My limbs falter, my mouth becomes dry, my body shivers, and my hairs stand on end.

3

गाण्डीवं स्रंसते हस्तात्त्वक्चैव परिदह्यते ।
न च शक्नोम्यवस्थातुं भ्रमतीव च मे मनः ॥

gāṇḍīvaṁ sraṁsate hastāt
tvak cai 'va paridahyate
na ca śaknomy avasthātuṁ
bhramatī 'va ca me manaḥ

Gandiva (the bow) slips from my hand, and my skin is burning all over. I cannot stand still. My mind seems to whirl.

4

निमित्तानि च पश्यामि विपरीतानि केशव ।
न   च श्रेयोऽनुपश्यामि हत्वा स्वजनमाहवे ॥

nimittāni ca paśyāmi
viparītāni keśava
na ca śreyo 'nupaśyāmi
hatvā svajanam āhave

And I see adverse portents O Keshava (Krishna). I do not foresee
any good will come from killing my family in this battle.

5

न काङ्क्षे विजयं कृष्ण न च राज्यं सुखानि च ।
किं नो राज्येन गोविन्द किं भोगैर्जीवितेन वा ॥

na kāṅkṣe vijayaṁ krsna
na ca rājyaṁ sukhāni ca
kiṁ no rājyena govinda
kiṁ bhogair jīvitena vā

I wish no victory, nor kingdom nor things of pleasure, O Krishna!
What should I do with a kingdom? O Govinda, of what use is
having sovereignty, or enjoyment, or life itself to us?

6

येषामर्थे काङ्क्षितं नो राज्यं भोगाः सुखानि च ।
त इमेऽवस्थिता युद्धे प्राणांस्त्यक्त्वा धनानि च ॥

yesām arthe kānksitam no
rājyam bhogāh sukhāni ca
ta ime 'vasthitā yuddhe
prānāms tyaktvā dhanāni ca

Those for whom we desire sovereignty, enjoyment, and things of
pleasure, stand here in readiness to fight, having given up (the hope
of) life and wealth;

7

आचार्याः पितरः पुत्रास्तथैव च पितामहाः ।
मातुलाः श्वशुराः पौत्राः श्यालाः संबन्धिनस्तथा ॥

*ācāryāḥ pitaraḥ putrās
tathai 'va ca pitāmahāḥ
mātulāḥ śvaśurāḥ pautrāḥ
śvālāḥ sambandhinas tathā*

Teachers, fathers, sons and also grandfathers, uncles, fathers-in-law, grandsons, brothers-in-law, and other relatives.

8

तस्मान्नाहीं वयं हन्तुं धार्तराष्ट्रान्स्वबान्धवान् ।
स्वजनं हि कथं हत्वा सुखिनः स्याम माधव ॥

tasmān nā 'rhā vayaṁ hantuṁ
dhārtarāṣṭrān svabāndhavān
svajanaṁ hi kathaṁ hatvā
sukhinaḥ syāma mādhava

Therefore, it is not right that we slay our kinsmen, the sons of
Dhritarashtra. How can we be happy by killing our own people,
O Madhava (Krishna)?

9

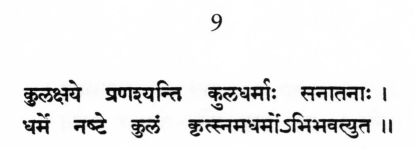

kulakṣaye pranaśyanti
kuladharmāḥ sanātanāḥ
dharme naṣṭe kulaṁ kṛtsnam
adharmo 'bhibhavaty uta

With the destruction of the family, the eternal family laws are destroyed; and when Law is destroyed, lawlessness prevails over the whole family.

10

यदि   मामप्रतीकारमशस्त्रं   शस्त्रपाणयः ।
धार्तराष्ट्रा रणे हन्युस्तन्मे क्षेमतरं भवेत् ॥

yadi mām apratīkāram
aśastraṁ śastrapāṇayaḥ
dhārtarāṣṭrā raṇe hanyus
tan me kṣemataraṁ bhavet

It would be better for me if the sons of Dhritarashtra (the Kauravas), with weapons in their hands, should slay me in the battle, while I remain unresisting and unarmed.

11

एवमुक्त्वार्जुनः संख्ये रथोपस्थ उपाविशत् ।
विसृज्य सशरं चापं शोकसंविग्नमानसः ॥

evam uktvā 'rjunaḥ saṁkhye
rathopastha upāviśat
visṛjya saśaraṁ cāpaṁ
śokasaṁvignamānasaḥ

Having spoken thus on the battlefield, Arjuna sat down on the seat
of his chariot, throwing away his bow and arrow, overwhelmed with
grief.

12

कृष्ण उवाच

क्लैब्यं मा स्म गमः पार्थ नैतत्त्वय्युपपद्यते ।
क्षुद्रं हृदयदौर्बल्यं त्यक्त्वोत्तिष्ठ परंतप ॥

krishna uvāca:

> *klaibyaṁ mā sma gamaḥ pārtha*
> *nai 'tat tvayy upapadyate*
> *kṣudraṁ hṛdayadaurbalyaṁ*
> *tyaktvo 'ttiṣṭha paraṁtapa*

Krishna said:
O Partha (Arjuna), do not yield to unmanliness. It does not befit thee. Cast off this petty weakness of the heart! And stand up, O scorcher of the foes!

13

अशोच्यानन्वशोचस्त्वं प्रज्ञावादांश्च भाषसे ।
गतासूनगतासूंश्च नानुशोचन्ति पण्डिताः ॥

aśocyān anvaśocas tvaṁ
prajñāvādāṁś ca bhāṣase
gatāsūn agatāsūṁś ca
nā 'nuśocanti paṇḍitāḥ

You are lamenting for those whom you should not lament for. And yet you speak words of wisdom. Wise men do not grieve for the dead or for the living.

14

न त्वेवाहं जातु नासं न त्वं नेमे जनाधिपाः ।
न चैव न भविष्यामः सर्वे वयमतः परम् ॥

na tv evā 'haṁ jātu nā 'sam
na tvaṁ ne 'me janādhipāḥ
na cai 'va na bhaviṣyāmaḥ
sarve vayam ataḥ param

There was never a time when I did not exist, or you, or these kings, nor shall any of us cease to exist hereafter.

Comment: Krishna here proclaims the everlasting presence both of purusha (man) and prakriti (nature), as taught in Samkhya philosophy.

15

देहिनोऽस्मिन्यथा देहे कौमारं यौवनं जरा ।
तथा देहान्तरप्राप्तिर्धीरस्तत्र न मुह्यति ॥

dehino 'smin yathā dehe
kaumāraṁ yauvanaṁ jarā
tathā dehāntaraprāptir
dhīras tatra na muhyati

Just as this body passes through childhood, youth, and old age, so also does it pass into another body. The wise man is not perplexed about it.

Comment: Krishna refers to the Samkhya teaching (Karika 39) concerning the difference between the enduring subtle bodies (comprised of tanmatra or subtle elements) and the perishable bodies (comprised of mahabhuta or gross elements). This teaching is also found in Karika 65.

16

मात्रास्पर्शास्तु कौन्तेय शीतोष्णसुखदुःखदाः ।
आगमापायिनोऽनित्यास्तांस्तितिक्षस्व भारत ॥

mātrāsparśās tu kaunteya
śītoṣṇasukhaduḥkhadāḥ
āgamāpāyino 'nityās
tāṁs titikṣasva bhārata

The contacts of the senses with the objects, O son of Kunti (Arjuna),
cause heat and cold, happiness (sukha) and sorrow (dukha), have a
beginning and an end. They are impermanent. O Bharata, endure
them.

Comment: This refers to perception and its effect, as explained in Karika
35 and 36. It is stated that the senses register the presence of objects and
relay them to the mind, which synthesizes them and takes them to self-
consciousness (ahamkara). This faculty in turn refers percepts to the self,
which finally brings them before the intellect (buddhi), which ascertains
their nature.

Since these organs (ahamkara, manas, and the senses) differ from one
another and are distinct specifications of the gunas (sattva, rajas, and
tamas), they differ in their effects on the body, although all effects are
transient.

The attachment of senses to the object, as referred here, does not mean
any particular object. Rather, it refers to any event, imaginary visualization,
experience of witnessing some incidents, the ideas related to love, romance,
anger, evil design and so on. In all these conditions, when the senses get
attached to any such object (Vishaya), thing, or subject, there is likewise
a conditioning effect, in accordance with the nature of that object on the
body. For example, when attached to soothing music, relaxation; when to
anger, heat; when to love and romance, pleasure; when to death of a loved
one, sorrow; and so on. But none of these effects are permanent. They
come and go.

17

यं हि न व्ययन्त्येते पुरुषं पुरुषर्षभ ।
समदुःखसुखं धीरं सोऽमृततत्वाय कल्पते ॥

yaṁ hi na vyathayanty ete
purusaṁ purusarsabha
samaduḥkhasukhaṁ dhīraṁ
so 'mṛtatvāya kalpate

O prince of men, the wise man who is not disturbed by these and to whom happiness and sorrow are alike, is fit for immortality.

Comment: In Samkhya philosophy it has been explained that the purusha experiences suffering due to decay and death until his deliverance from the subtle body. And therefore, pain is in the nature of things (Karika 55). Further, the purusha feels pleasure and pain because of everlasting presence of the three gunas whose nature is pleasure, pain, and insensitivity (Karika 13). Thus, the knowledgeable man is not preoccupied by these.

18

नासतो विद्यते भावो नाभावो विद्यते सतः ।
उभयोरपि   दृष्टोऽन्तस्त्वनयोस्तत्त्वदर्शिभिः ॥

nā 'sato vidyate bhāvo
nā 'bhāvo vidyate satah
ubhayor api drsto 'ntas tv
anayos tattvadarśibhih

There is no coming into being of what is non-existent; nor does the existent cease to be. The truth about these two has been perceived by the knowers of the tattvas (elements).

Comment: The cause and effect relationship of the satkaryavada theory of Kapila is explained in this verse (see Samkhya Karika, sutra IX). According to Samkhya, the non-existent cannot be brought into existence; and an effect exists in its cause.

19

अविनाशि तु तद्विद्धि येन सर्वमिदं ततम् ।
विनाशमव्ययस्यास्य   न   कश्चित्कर्तुमर्हति ॥

avināśi tu tad viddhi
  yena sarvam idaṁ tatam
vināśam avyayasyā 'sya
  na kaścit kartum arhati

Know that by which all that is pervaded is indestructible. None can cause the destruction of that—the imperishable (gunas).

Comment: This verse refers to Karika 11 wherein it is explained how the three gunas pervade the manifest, unmanifest, and the knower. The gunas are everlasting and indestructible. Though they change form, they are never destroyed.

20

अन्तवन्त इमे देहा नित्यस्योक्ताः शरीरिणः ।
अनाशिनोऽप्रमेयस्य तस्माद्युध्यस्व भारत ॥

antavanta ime dehā
nityasyo 'ktāḥ śarīriṇaḥ
anāśino 'prameyasya
tasmād yudhyasva bhārata

These bodies which embody the indestructible, immeasurable, and everlasting are said to have an end. Therefore fight, O Bharata.

Comment: Here Krishna refers to Samkhya Karika 39 wherein it has been explained that the bodies born of father and mother are perishable, whereas the subtle bodies (comprised of subtle elements) are constant. Though our bodies possess the characteristics of the three gunas (which are everlasting) they come to an end because of the perishable nature of the gross elements (which come into existence with birth).

21

य एनं वेत्ति हन्तारं यश्चैनं मन्यते हतम् ।
उभौ तौ न विजानीतो नायं हन्ति न हन्यते ॥

ya enaṁ vetti hantāraṁ
yaś cai 'naṁ manyate hatam
ubhau tau na vijānīto
nā 'yaṁ hanti na hanyate

He who thinks that this being is a slayer, and he who thinks that it is slain, both of them do not possess true knowledge. He neither slays nor is he slain.

Comment: Here, the reference is to the working of prakriti (nature) and its relationship with the purusha (man) as stated in Karika 62 and in several other verses. It has been explained that no one is bound, no one is released. Only prakriti in its various forms transmigrates, is bound, and is released. The purusha, like a spectator, sees prakriti, whose activity has ceased due to the completion of her purpose (Karika 65). Further clarification of this view is provided by the following verse of the original Gita.

22

न जायते म्रियते वा कदाचिन्नायं भूत्वाऽभविता वा न भूयः ।
अजो नित्यः शाश्वतोऽयं पुराणो न हन्यते हन्यमाने शरीरे ॥

na jāyate mriyate vā kadācin
nā 'yaṁ bhūtvā bhavitā vā na bhūyaḥ
ajo nityaḥ śāśvato 'yaṁ purāṇo
na hanyate hanyamāne śarīre

It is not born, nor does it ever die. After having been, it again ceases
not to be. It is unborn, everlasting, permanent, and primeval. It is
not killed when the body is slain.

*Comment: Here the distinction between the purusha and prakriti, as
depicted in Samkhya philosophy, is described. Prakriti (nature) is uncreated, unborn, and everlasting, whereas purusha (person) is born, impermanent and possesses both perishable and imperishable tattvas (elements). See
Karika X and XI. Due to these characteristics of purusha, the emergents
of nature (produced by nature) in him are never destroyed, even when the
body is destroyed.*

23

वेदाविनाशिनं नित्यं य एनमजमव्ययम् ।
कथं स पुरुषः पार्थं कं घातयति हन्ति कम् ॥

vedā 'vināśinaṁ nityaṁ
ya enam ajam avyayam
kathaṁ sa puruṣaḥ pārtha
kaṁ ghātayati hanti kam

He who knows that it is indestructible, eternal, unborn, and inexhaustible—how and whom can he cause to be killed, and how and whom can he kill?

Comment: This verse also refers to Samkhya Karika X and XI.

24

वासांसि जीर्णानि यथा विहाय नवानि गृह्णाति नरोऽपराणि ।
तथा शरीराणि विहाय जीर्णान्यन्यानि संयाति नवानि देही ॥

*vāsāṁsi jīrṇāni yathā vihāya
navāni gṛhṇāti naro 'parāṇi
tathā śarīrāṇi vihāya jīrṇāny
anyāni saṁyāti navāni dehī*

Just as a person casts off worn-out garments and puts on different
ones that are new, so also the individual casts off a worn-out body
and joins with other ones that are new.

*Comment: Krishna invokes the Samkhya philosophy about life and death.
Several sutras of Karika explain this aspect of our life. Sutra 63 says that
prakriti binds herself by herself by means of seven forms (rupa) and releases
herself by means of one form. Sutra 65 explains that due to its purpose
having been accomplished, the activity of prakriti ceases and the subtle
body takes another form (see also Karika 66 and 67).*

25

नैनं छिन्दन्ति शस्त्राणि नैनं दहति पावकः ।
न चैनं क्लेदयन्त्यापो न शोषयति मारुतः ॥

nai 'naṁ chindanti śastrāni
nai 'naṁ dahati pāvakaḥ
na cai 'naṁ kledayanty āpo
na śoṣayati mārutaḥ

Weapons cannot cut it (the subtle body), fire does not burn it; water does not make it wet, nor does the wind make it dry.

26

अच्छेद्योऽयमदाह्योऽयमक्लेद्योऽशोष्य   एव   च ।
नित्यः   सर्वगतः   स्थाणुरचलोऽयं   सनातनः ।।

acchedyo 'yam adāhyo 'yam
akledyo 'śoṣya eva ca
nityaḥ sarvagataḥ sthānur
acalo 'yam sanātanaḥ

This cannot be cut, cannot be burnt. It can neither be wetted nor dried. It is eternal, all-pervading, stable, immovable, and forever.

Comment: In Samkhya Karika the difference between the subtle bodies and the bodies born of father and mother is explained. The subtle bodies are indestructible and non-specific, whereas the bodies born of parents are comprised of specific and hence perishable elements. See Karika 38–39 for understanding the difference between tanmatras (subtle elements) and bhutani (gross elements).

27

अव्यक्तोऽयमचिन्त्योऽयमविकार्योंऽयमुच्यते ।
तस्मादेवं विदित्वैनं नानुशोचितुमर्हसि ॥

avyakto 'yam acintyo 'yam
avikāryo 'yam ucyate
tasmād evaṁ viditvai 'naṁ
nā 'nuśocitum arhasi

This (mool-prakriti) is said to be unmanifest, unthinkable and unchangeable. Therefore, knowing it to be such, thou shouldst not grieve.

Comment: The avyakta (unmanifest state of nature) is unthinkable and unchangeable. For understanding avyakta, see Karika 3 and chapter one, the section on Kapila, in this book.

28

अथ चैनं नित्यजातं नित्यं वा मन्यसे मृतम् ।
तथापि त्वं महाबाहो नैवं शोचितुमर्हसि ॥

atha cai 'nam nityajātam
    nityam vā manyase mṛtam
tathā 'pi tvam mahābāho
nai 'nam śocitum arhasi

Even if you think that this body is constantly born and constantly
dying, even then, O mighty-armed, you should not grieve.

29

जातस्य हि ध्रुवो मृत्युर्ध्रुवं जन्म मृतस्य च ।
तस्मादपरिहार्येऽर्थे   न   त्वं   शोचितुमर्हसि ॥

jātasya hi dhruvo mṛtyur
dhruvaṁ janma mṛtasya ca
tasmād aparihārye 'rthe
na tvaṁ śocitum arhasi

For the one who is born, death is certain; and certain is the birth for the one that has died. Therefore, you should not grieve over what is inevitable.

Comment: Samkhya Karika, sutras 18–19, explains birth, death, and the plurality of purasha.

30

अव्यक्तादीनि भूतानि व्यक्तमध्यानि भारत ।
अव्यक्तनिधनान्येव तत्र का परिदेवना ॥

avyaktādīni bhūtāni
vyaktamadhyāni bhārata·
avyaktanidhanāny eva
tatra kā paridevanā

Beings are unmanifested in their beginning, manifested in their
middle state, and unmanifested again in their ends. O Bharata, what
is there in this to grieve?

*Comment: In Samkhya philosophy it is explained that only prakriti mani-
fests. The purusha born of parents is in the unmanifest state in the beginning (embryonic) stage; passes through the state of the manifest when intellect, consciousness, senses, and subtle elements develop or emerge as the
purusha comes into proximity with nature; and when these organs cease
to function, the purusha returns to the unmanifest state. See Karika 40 and
the chart of 25 tattvas (in chapter one of this book).*

31

आश्चर्यवत्पश्यति कश्चिदेनमाश्चर्यवद्वदति तथैव चान्यः ।
आश्चर्यवच्चैनमन्यः शृणोति श्रुत्वाप्येनं वेद न चैव कश्चित् ॥

āścaryavat paśyati kaścid enam
āścaryavad vadati tathai 'va cā 'nyaḥ
āścaryavac cai 'nam anyaḥ śṛṇoti
śrutvā 'py enaṁ veda na cai 'va kaścit

One looks upon it as a marvel, another speaks of it as astonishing,
others hear of it as a wonder. Yet having heard of it, no one
whatsoever knows it.

*Comment: Krishna refers to the difficulty in understanding prakriti (na-
ture), its constituents, its qualities and functions; and also the concept of
25 tattvas. For details on the 25 tattvas, see chapter one (the chart).*

32

देही नित्यमवध्योऽयं देहे सर्वस्य भारत ।
तस्मात्सर्वाणि भूतानि न त्वं शोचितुमर्हसि ॥

dehī nityam avadhyo 'yaṁ
dehe sarvasya bhārata
tasmāt sarvāṇi bhūtāni
na tvaṁ śocitum arhasi

The dweller in the body of everyone is eternal and indestructible.
Therefore, O Bharata, you have no cause to sorrow over any
creatures.

Comment: This refers to the emergence (in our bodies) of intellect, self-
consciousness and the tanmatras (subtle elements) due to the working of
nature (prakriti). Thus, nature dwells in our body due to these emergent
properties (vikriti-prakriti). Since nature is eternal, that which belongs to
nature, in our bodies, does not die out even when the gross body perishes
upon death. See Karika 21–23.

33

स्वधर्ममपि चावेक्ष्य न विकम्पितुमर्हसि ।
धर्म्याद्धि युद्धाच्छ्रेयोऽन्यरक्षत्रियस्य न विद्यते ॥

svadharmam api cā 'veksya
na vikampitum arhasi
dharmyād dhi yuddhāc chreyo 'nyat
kṣatriyasya na vidyate

Further, even if you consider your own duty, you should not falter because there is nothing higher for a Kshatriya than to fight a righteous war.

Comment: Here, the reference is to the concept of bhavas (motivations) which impel man to work or act, as discussed in detail in Samkhya Karika, sutras 43–45 and also in 58. Here, Vyasa is emphasizing the duty and responsibility of a man of princely class.

34

अकीर्तिं चापि भूतानि कथयिष्यन्ति तेऽव्ययाम् ।
संभावितस्य   चाकीर्तिर्मरणादतिरिच्यते ।।

akīrtiṁ cā 'pi bhūtāni
  kathayiṣyanti te 'vyayām
saṁbhāvitasya cā 'kīrtir
  maraṇād atiricyate

And also, people will speak of your everlasting dishonor. And for one who has been honored, dishonor is worse than death.

Comment: Here and in the following two verses, Vyasa explains the value of living an honorable life, setting good precedents, and fulfilling one's responsibility.

35

भयाद्रणादुपरतं मंस्यन्ते त्वां महारथाः ।
येषां च त्वं बहुमतो भूत्वा यास्यसि लाघवम् ।।

bhayād raṇād uparataṁ
  maṁsyante tvaṁ mahārathāḥ
yeṣāṁ ca tvaṁ bahumato
  bhūtvā yāsyasi lāghavam

The great warriors will think that you withdrew from the battle on account of fear; and you will be held in less esteem by those who hold you high.

36

अवाच्यवादांश्च बहून्वदिष्यन्ति तवाहिताः ।
निन्दन्तस्तव सामर्थ्यं ततो दुःखतरं नु किम् ॥

avācyavādāṁś ca bahūn
vadiṣyanti tavā 'hitāḥ
nindantas tava sāmarthyaṁ
tato duḥkhataraṁ nu kim

Also, your enemies will spread many unspeakable tales about you, condemning your skill. What is more painful than that?

37

एषा तेऽभिहिता सांख्ये बुद्धियोंगे त्विमां श्रृणु ।
बुद्ध्या युक्तो यया पार्थ कर्मबन्धं प्रहास्यसि ॥

eṣā te 'bhihitā sāṁkhye
buddhir yoge tv imāṁ śṛṇu
buddhyā yukto yayā pārtha
karmabandhaṁ prahāsyasi

This wisdom explained to you is according to Samkhya. Now listen to wisdom according to Yoga, knowing which, O Partha, you will get rid of the restraints on action.

Comment: In this verse, Vyasa has made it clear that what has been explained up to this point is in accordance with the Samkhya philosophy. And what follows is in accordance with Yoga.

This verse provides an internal clue for determining the verses of the original Gita. It should be obvious that the verses not belonging to Samkhya or Yoga are interpolated and hence are not a part of the original Gita.

38

नेहाभिक्रमनाशोऽस्ति प्रत्यवायो न विद्यते ।
स्वल्पमप्यस्य धर्मस्य त्रायते महतो भयात् ॥

ne 'hā 'bhikramanāśo 'sti
pratyavāyo na vidyate
svalpam apy asya dharmasya
trāyate mahato bhayāt

Herein (that is, in this path of Yoga) action commenced is not lost,
(and afterwards) obstacles do not arise. Even a little practice of this
discipline (Yoga) will protect you from great fear.

Comment: This verse explains the Yogic principle that no action is with-
out a result. An action unfailingly brings a result, whether good or bad.
When people act with aishvarya bhava (power motive), the obstacles are
destroyed. But when one acts with anaishvarya bhava (feebleness), obstruc-
tions arise.
Further, an action originates in the mind. In order for an action to be
correctly taken and its result desirable, Patanjali advocated the practice of
Pratyahara (visualizing the opposite of what is presently undesirable). By
visualizing the opposite of the undesirable, the ensuing action would be
taken correctly. According to Yogic principles, all the internal and external
organs of our bodily system work cooperatively for the materialization
of what is visualized by the mind. Thus, by practicing Yogic steps one
becomes confident of deriving the desirable result and, hence, need not be
afraid of the consequences of action. For details on Pratyahara, see chapter
one, the section on Patanjali.

39

 व्यवसायात्मिका बुद्धिरेकेह कुरुनन्दन ।
बहुशाखा ह्यनन्ताश्च बुद्धयोऽव्यवसायिनाम् ॥

vyavasāyātmikā buddhir
eke 'ha kurunandana
bahuśākhā hy anantāś ca
buddhayo 'vyavasāyinām

O Kuru Nandana (descendant of Kuru, Arjuna), in this path (Yoga discipline) there is one-pointed determination; but the thoughts of the irresolute are many-branched and endless.

Comment: Yoga Sutra III, 11, is referred to here where Patanjali has discussed Samadhi parinama. This is the state in which many-pointedness of the mind subsides and one-pointedness arises, due to the practice of samyama. Those whose minds are not disciplined in samyama, will wander endlessly in their thoughts.

40

योगस्थः कुरु कर्माणि सङ्गं त्यक्त्वा धनंजय ।
सिद्ध्यसिद्ध्योः समो भूत्वा समत्वं योग उच्यते ॥

*yogasthaḥ kuru karmāṇi
saṅgam tyaktvā dhanaṁjaya
siddhyasiddhyoḥ samo bhūtvā
samatvaṁ yoga ucyate*

O Dhananjaya (Arjuna), perform action being firm in Yogastha (Yoga). Abandon attachment and be balanced in success and failure. The state of equilibrium is known as Yoga.

Comment: Krishna advises Arjuna to act and alludes to the value of the component practice of Yoga, as stated in Yoga Sutra II, 28. Therein Patanjali has stated that, by practicing the eight steps of Yoga, impurities are destroyed while knowledge and wisdom are acquired. One gains a harmonious state of mind through the practice of yama, niyama, and samyama.

41

बुद्धियुक्तो जहातीह उभे सुकृतदुष्कृते ।
तस्माद्योगाय युज्यस्व योगः कर्मसु कौशलम् ॥

buddhiyukto jahātī 'ha
ubhe sukrtaduskrte
tasmād yogāya yujyasva
yogah karmasu kauśalam

Those with proper knowledge *(buddhi-yuktah)* leave behind both
good and evil deeds in this life. Therefore, discipline yourself in
Yoga, for achieving excellence in action is called Yoga.

Comment: Yoga Sutra II, 36 and III, 23, emphasize the theme of achiev-
ing excellence in action. The observance and practice of those steps (as
explained in Yoga Sutra) enable the individual to achieve excellence in
whatever is undertaken.

42.

श्रुतिविप्रतिपन्ना ते यदा स्थास्यति निश्चला ।
समाधावचला बुद्धिस्तदा योगमवाप्स्यसि ॥

śrutivipratipannā te
yadā sthāsyati niścalā
samādhāv acalā buddhis
tadā yogam avāpsyasi

When your intellect, which is puzzled by the *(Shruti)* Veda text you have heard, will become fixed and immovable in samadhi, you shall attain this Yoga.

Comment: Several verses of the Yoga Sutra (see II, 33–34) explain the value of pondering the opposite (pratyahara). Also see III: 9,10, and 12, wherein the practice and results of nirodha, samadhi, and ekagrata forms of samyama are explained.

43.

दुःखेष्वनुद्विग्नमनाः   सुखेषु   विगतस्पृहः ।
वीतरागभयक्रोधः   स्थितधीर्मुनिरुच्यते ॥

*duhkhesv anudvignamanāh
sukhesu vigatasprhah
vītarāgabhayakrodhah
sthitadhīr munir ucyate*

He whose mind is not distressed in adversities, who does not hanker after pleasures, and is free from passion, fear, and anger, is called a *muni* (sage) of steady wisdom.

Comment: In Yoga Sutra III, 48–50, it is stated that by performing samyama upon the process of apprehension, one gains mastery over the sense organs. At that stage, there is complete mastery over the Pradhana (nature), and there arises supremacy over all states and forms of existence, and one gains all-encompassing knowledge.

44.

यः सर्वत्रानभिस्नेहस्तत्तत्प्राप्य शुभाशुभम् ।
नाभिनन्दति न द्वेष्टि तस्य प्रज्ञा प्रतिष्ठिता ॥

yaḥ sarvatrā 'nabhisnehas
    tat-tat prāpya śubhāśubham
nā 'bhinandati na dveṣṭi
    tasya prajñā pratiṣṭhitā

He who is without attachment on any side, and who feels no
exultation or aversion about the agreeable or disagreeable, his
wisdom is firmly fixed.

*Comment: In Yoga Sutra II, 41, the concept of sattva-suddhi (mental
purity) is explained. It is stated that due to sattva-suddhi one acquires
cheerfulness, one-pointedness of mind, control of the senses, vision of
the self, and gains fitness. Further, sutra III, 38 explains that when the
obstacles in the way of samadhi are turned outward, one achieves siddhi
(perfection in controlling the power of the mind).*

45.

यदा संहरते चायं कूर्मोऽङ्गानीव सर्वशः ।
इन्द्रियाणीन्द्रियार्थेभ्यस्तस्य प्रज्ञा प्रतिष्ठिता ॥

yadā saṁharate cā 'yaṁ
kūrmo 'ṅgānī 'va sarvaśaḥ
indriyāṇī 'ndriyārthebhyas
tasya prajñā pratiṣṭhitā

When a person is able to withdraw his senses from sense objects, as
the tortoise withdraws its limbs, his wisdom becomes steady.

Comment: This is the result of observing the steps of yama and niyama.
See sutras 30–44.

46.

यततो ह्यपि कौन्तेय पुरुषस्य विपश्चितः ।
इन्द्रियाणि प्रमाथीनि हरन्ति प्रसभं मनः ॥

yatato hy api kaunteya
puruṣasya vipaścitaḥ
indriyāni pramāthīni
haranti prasabham manaḥ

Because, O son of Kunti, these whirling senses forcibly carry away
the mind of even the intelligent purusha, in an improper direction,
though he be striving (for controlling the senses).

Comment: Patanjali explained the principles of yama and niyama and
taught the practice of dharana, dhyana, and samadhi. The fluctuation
of the mind is controlled and the condition of one-pointedness achieved
through the practices of these steps.

47.

रागद्वेषवियुक्तैस्तु   विषयानिन्द्रियैश्चरन् ।
आत्मवश्यैर्विधेयात्मा   प्रसादमधिगच्छति ॥

rāgadevesaviyuktais tu
visayān indriyaiś caran
ātmavaśyair vidhcyātmā
prasādam adhigacchati

But the self-controlled person who moves among the objects of sense, with the senses under control and free from attachment and aversion, attains peace.

Comment: Krishna refers to sutras 46 and 48 and the result of practicing certain forms of samyama.

48.

प्रसादे   सर्वदुःखानां   हानिरस्योपजायते ।
प्रसन्नचेतसो   ह्याशु   बुद्धिः   पर्यवतिष्ठते ॥

prasāde sarvaduhkhānām
hānir asyo 'pajāyate
prasannacetaso hy āśu
buddhiḥ paryavatiṣṭhate

When the mind is serene, all his sorrow (dukha) is destroyed and prasanna chetasah (happiness) arises. The intellect soon becomes steady.

Comment: Patanjali's views on sattva-shuddhi are found in sutras II, 41–42.

49.

नास्ति बुद्धिरयुक्तस्य न चायुक्तस्य भावना ।
न चाभावयतः शान्तिरशान्तस्य कुतः सुखम् ॥

nā 'sti buddhir ayuktasya
na cā 'yuktasya bhāvanā
na cā 'bhāvayataḥ śāntir
aśāntasya kutaḥ sukham

The person, who is not yukta (that is, who has not become Yoga-yukta as mentioned above) has no singleness of purpose; the one who is not yukta has no power to bring things about; and he who does not bring things about knows no serenity. And how can a man without serenity know happiness?

Comment: In Yoga Sutra III, 15 the cause-effect concept is discussed, and in sutra III, 17, the cause and resolution of confusion. It is obvious that without gaining the ability of concentrating the mind, one would not be able to control the senses and thereby would not achieve sukha (peace of mind).

50.

इन्द्रियाणां हि चरतां यन्मनोऽनुविधीयते ।
तदस्य हरति प्रज्ञां वायुर्नावमिवाम्भसि ॥

indriyāṇāṁ hi càratāṁ
yan mano 'nuvidhīyate
tad asya harati prajñāṁ
vāyur nāvam ivā 'mbhasi

When the mind runs after the wandering senses, it carries away the understanding, just as the wind carries away a boat on the waters.

Comment: Here, the nature of mind is explained. The reference is to sutras II, 33–34 in which it is stated that when the mind is disturbed by improper thoughts, constant pondering over the opposite is the remedy. Further, there are definite methods provided in Yoga Sutra for controlling this wandering nature of mind. The system of practicing dharana (concentration), dhyana (meditation), samadhi (deep meditation), and their combined form, samyama, all are recommended for controlling the fluctuations of mind. The nature of mind being as it is, Patanjali has given much attention towards disciplining it.

51.

तस्माद्यस्य महाबाहो निगृहीतानि सर्वशः ।
इन्द्रियाणीन्द्रियार्थेभ्यस्तस्य प्रज्ञा प्रतिष्ठिता ॥

tasmād yasya mahābāho
nigṛhītāni sarvaśaḥ
indriyāṇī 'ndriyārthebhyas
tasya prajñā pratiṣṭhitā

Therefore, O mighty-armed, he whose senses are completely restrained from sense-objects, his knowledge is firmly set.

Comment: In Yoga Sutra III, 9–10, nirodha parinama (the result of control) and its practice are explained. It is stated in these two verses that when the outgoing impression of the mind is controlled, at that moment of control, the mind is permeated with an impression, whose flow becomes abundant and peaceful.

52.

या निशा सर्वभूतानां तस्यां जागर्ति संयमी ।
यस्यां जाग्रति भूतानि सा निशा पश्यतो मुनेः ॥

yā niśā sarvabhūtānām
tasyām jāgarti samyamī
yasyām jāgrati bhūtāni
sā niśā paśyato muneḥ

What is night for all beings is the time of waking for the one
disciplined in Yoga; and what is the time for waking for all beings
is night for him.

*Comment: Here the distinction between knowledge and ignorance is
shown. Ignorance means darkness and knowledge means light. The knowledgeable can see what is not seen by the ignorant. According to Yoga Sutra,
by mastering the technique of samyama (nirodha, samadhi, and ekagrata
forms of samayama), one acquires the power of seeing and knowing the
past and future (sutra III, 16). And hence, the person disciplined in Yoga
can see what is commonly not seen by others.*

53.

आपूर्यमाणमचलप्रतिष्ठं   समुद्रमापः प्रविशन्ति   यद्वत् ।
तद्वत्कामा यं प्रविशन्ति सर्वेस शान्तिमाप्नोति न कामकामी ।।

āpūryamāṇam acalapratiṣṭham
samudram āpaḥ praviśanti yadvat
tadvat kāmā yam praviśanti sarve
sa śāntim āpnoti na kāmakāmī

He attains peace into whom all desires enter as waters enter the ocean, filling from all sides yet remaining unmoved; but not Kamkami, the man who hankers after the objects of the senses.

Comment: In Yoga Sutra III, 53–54, it is explained that through the practice of samyama one acquires discriminatory knowledge of things which otherwise cannot be distinguished by class, characteristic, or position. Further, due to mastery of samyama and due to the practice and observance of the steps of the Yoga system, one not only acquires knowledge but also becomes capable, physically and mentally, of remaining unmoved in unfavourable conditions and life-stressing situations. The problems arising out of society, self, and nature are understood in their proper perspective, and solutions are found. In all these circumstances, the one disciplined in Yoga remains undisturbed. The desires do not cause any disturbance to him. Nor does he run after passion or the objects of senses.

54.

अर्जुन उवाच

उयायसीं चेत्कर्मणस्ते मता बुद्धिर्जनार्दन ।
तत्कि कर्मणि घोरे मां नियोजयसि केशव ॥

arjuna uvāca:

> *jyāyasī cet karmaṇas te*
> *matā buddhir janārdana*
> *tat kiṁ karmaṇi ghore mām*
> *niyojayasi keśava*

Arjuna said:
O Janardana! If you consider that knowledge is superior to action, O Keshava, why then do you urge me to engage in this terrible action (warfare)?

Comment: Since both the philosophy of Samkhya and Yoga were explained to Arjuna, he was not sure whether the path of Jnana (knowledge) or Karma (action) was superior. Therefore, he asked Krishna to clarify which of the two would be superior for him.

55.

व्यामिश्रेणेव वाक्येन बुद्धिं मोहयसीव मे ।
तदेकं वद निश्चित्य येन श्रेयोऽहमाप्नुयाम् ॥

vyāmiśrene 'va vākyena
buddhiṁ mohayasī 'va me
tad ekaṁ vada niścitya
yena śreyo 'ham āpnuyām

With quite contradictory words, you seem to be confusing my understanding. Therefore, tell me definitely which is the course by which I will attain to the supreme good.

Comment: Arjuna is again pointing out his difficulty in selecting one of the two paths explained to him.

56.

कृष्ण उवाच

लोकेऽस्मिन्द्विविधा निष्ठा पुरा प्रोक्ता मयानघ ।
ज्ञानयोगेन सांख्यानां कर्मयोगेन योगिनाम् ॥

krishna uvāca:

> *loke 'smin dvividhā niṣṭhā*
> *purā proktā mayā 'nagha*
> *jñānayogena sāṃkhyānāṃ*
> *karmayogena yoginām*

Krishna said:
O Arjuna! As I have said before, there are two paths, in this world:
the path of knowledge is that of Samkhyas, and the path of action
is that of yogins (practitioners of Yoga).

*Comment: Krishna explains that there is a twofold path: the path of
knowledge and the path of action. It should be remembered that Samkhya
philosophy gave equal importance to both samyak jnana (proper knowledge) and satkarya (right action) for eliminating dukha (sorrow) and
achieving sukha (happiness). But these teachings of Samkhya remained
primarily in the category of acquiring knowledge. Therefore, Samkhya
teachings are considered, on the whole, following the path of knowledge.
On the other hand, the system of Yoga requires practicing on the physical
as well as on the mental levels. And therefore, the Yoga is considered to
follow the path of action.*

*This verse, again, is internal evidence concerning the original verses of
the Gita. In subsequent verses, the emphasis is on taking action, achieving
excellence in action, Samkhya Yoga, and on the norms of the Indian
tradition. It should be obvious that that which does not belong to Samkhya
and Yoga is not a part of the original Gita.*

57.

न   कर्मणामनारम्भान्नैष्कर्म्यं   पुरुषोऽश्नुते ।
न   च संन्यसनादेव   सिद्धिं समधिगच्छति ॥

na karmaṇām anārambhān
naiṣkarmyaṁ puruṣo 'śnute
na ca saṁnyasanād eva
siddhiṁ samadhigacchati

By non-performance of actions, a man does not attain actionlessness, nor does he attain siddhim (success) by giving up actions.

Comment: Here Krishna is explaining the importance of action in life. Life compels us to act. Action is life. Non-action is death. No one can be actionless and be alive. Those who lead a life of renunciation can never be actionless, nor can they claim to achieve self-mastery and control over the senses by merely rejecting actions. And hence, superiority of action is proclaimed. The word 'siddhim' may mean perfection or self-mastery.

58.

न हि कश्चिरक्षणमपि जातु तिष्ठत्यकर्मकृत् ।
कार्यते ह्यवशः कर्म सर्वः प्रकृतिजैर्गुणैः ॥

na hi kaścit kṣanam api
jātu tiṣṭhaty akarmakṛt
kāryate hy avaśah karma
sarvah prakṛtijair guṇaih

Because no one can remain even for a moment without performing some form of action. The gunas of prakriti compel every person to helplessly perform action.

Comment: Krishna refers to the concept of gunas (sattva, rajas, and tamas). Since these gunas are opposed to one another, are everlasting and constantly active, and are the constituents of nature, they affect and activate constantly those organs of the purusha (person) which develop through contact with prakriti (nature). For example, buddhi (intellect), ahamkara (consciousness), and the tanmatras (subtle elements) of our bodies emerge through interaction with nature. Also, they function as nature because they, too, produce other elements (see the chart of 25 tattvas in chapter one).

Since the gunas are the constituents of nature, and nature itself is present on our mental level, the gunas cause constant activation of our bodily system (see Karika 22 and 23).

59.

कर्मेन्द्रियाणि संयम्य य आस्ते मनसा स्मरन् ।
इन्द्रियार्थान्विमूढात्मा मिथ्याचारः स उच्यते ॥

karmendriyāṇi saṁyamya
ya āste manasā smaran
indriyārthān vimūḍhātmā
mithyācāraḥ sa ucyate

He who merely controls the faculties of action but keeps continually thinking of the objects of the senses in his mind, is called a mithyachara (self-deceiving hypocrite).

Comment: Here Krishna is very critical of those who pretend to have renounced the worldly life and claim to abstain from action. Because even after so doing, their senses keep attaching to the objects of the world and thereby induce their action-organs and other faculties to act—voluntarily or involuntarily. Therefore, the message here is that one must act without deluding, either oneself or others, and not be deceptive.

60.

यस्त्विन्द्रियाणि मनसा नियम्यारभतेऽर्जुन ।
कर्मेन्द्रियैः कर्मयोगमसक्तः स विशिष्यते ॥

yas tv indriyāni manasā
niyamyā 'rabhate 'rjuna
karmendriyaih karmayogam
asaktah sa viśiṣyate

But he who controls the senses by the mind, O Arjuna, and engages his action faculties in the discipline of action without attachment, is superior.

Comment: Here the value, significance and superiority of action is exalted. A person who has acquired the ability to control the senses (as discussed in the earlier verses) and engages in action without being attached to it, is an honourable person. It should be recalled here (as pointed out in the first chapter of this book) that all Indian rational thinkers from Kapila to Patanjali have advocated action. Vyasa is emphasizing action by declaring the superiority of those who act.

61.

नियतं कुरु कर्म त्वं कर्म ज्यायो ह्यकर्मणः ।
शरीरयात्रापि च ते न प्रसिद्ध्येदकर्मणः ॥

niyataṁ kuru karma tvaṁ
   karma jyāyo hy akarmaṇaḥ
śarīrayātrā 'pi ca te
   na prasidhyed akarmaṇaḥ

Perform action which you are obliged to do or which is niyatam (obligatory), for action is superior to inaction. Moreover, if you do not perform action, even your body will not be maintained.

Comment: According to Karma Yoga, even a wrong action is better than no action at all. One must therefore perform acts for which one is responsible, as an individual. Only by performing action, can one learn to eliminate errors in future actions. Refinement and excellence can be achieved only by action.

62.

यज्ञार्थात्कर्मणोऽन्यत्र   लोकोऽयं   कर्मबन्धनः ।
तदर्थं   कर्म   कौन्तेय   मुक्तसङ्गः   समाचर ॥

yajñārthāt karmano 'nyatra
loko 'yam karmabandhanaḥ
tadartham karma kaunteya
muktasaṅgaḥ samācara

This world is bound by actions, other than those performed for the sake of yajna (sacrifice) or rituals; therefore, O son of Kunti (Arjuna), perform action for that sake, mukta sangah (freedom from bondage).

Comment: Here again, the value and significance of action is pointed out. The functioning of world order depends on action. In the absence of action, whether manifested by nature (prakriti) or performed by purusha, this world would perish. The life on Earth depends upon our actions. Therefore, Krishna advises Arjuna to act in order to keep the world order functioning.

Vyasa is here critical of those who consider sacrificial (Vedic) ceremonies as action. According to Vyasa, the world order operates not due to the performance of rituals and ceremonies, but by work done with a sense of responsibility, obligation, and duty.

63.

एवं प्रवर्तितं चक्रं नानुवर्तयतीह यः ।
अघायुरिन्द्रियारामो मोघं पार्थ स जीवति ॥

evaṁ pravartitaṁ cakraṁ
nā 'nuvartayatī 'ha yaḥ
aghāyur indriyārāmo
moghaṁ pārtha sa jīvati

He who does not keep rolling the wheel that has been set in motion, indulging his senses in a lifespan of evil, lives for nothing, O Partha.

64.

यस्त्वात्मरतिरेव   स्यादात्मतृप्तश्च   मानवः ।
आत्मन्येव च संतुष्टस्तस्य कार्यं न विद्यते ॥

yas tv ātmaratir eva syād
  ātmatṛptaś ca mānavaḥ
  ātmany eva ca saṁtuṣṭas
   tasya kāryaṁ na vidyate

On the other hand, an individual who delights in the self, is satisfied
with the self, is completely contented with the self alone, has nothing
left to do (he finishes his work).

*Comment: This verse explains the characteristics of the purusha who has
acquired proper knowledge and works according to the theory of action
(satkaryavada) of Samkhya philosophy. No work is unworthy for him. Nor
does he leave any task undone. Being disciplined in the Yoga system, by
observing the principles of yama and niyama and by practicing samyama
he is satisfied with his own being and finds pleasure in his action. Thus, for
a person trained and disciplined in Samkhya Yoga, no task, once begun,
remains undone. He achieves excellence in whatever he chooses to engage
in.*

65.

नैव तस्य कृतेनार्थो नाकृतेनेह कश्चन ।
न चास्य सर्वभूतेषु कश्चिदर्थव्यपाश्रयः ॥

nai 'va tasya kṛtenā 'rtho
nā 'kṛtene 'ha kaścana
na cā 'sya sarvabhūteṣu
kaścid arthavyapāśrayaḥ

For him there is no concern for what is done or what is not done nor does he depend on any being for any object.

Comment: The man who has acquired proper knowledge (Samyak-Jnana) and performs action according to the theory of right action (satkaryavada), knows what to do. He is not dependent on this or that person. He sets his own course. His work is not conditioned by what others have done or are doing or not doing.

66.

तस्मादसक्तः सततं कार्यं कर्म समाचर ।
असक्तो ह्याचरन्कर्म परमाप्नोति पूरुषः ॥

tasmād asaktaḥ satataṁ
kāryaṁ karma samācara
asakto hy ācaran karma
param āpnoti pūruṣaḥ

Therefore, without attachment, ever perform work that has to be done. The purusha achieves the highest good by performing action without attachment.

Comment: The lesson here is not to be bound in the act itself. The act (work) is separate from the purusha (man). Thus, the purusha should always remain as a performer, keeping the target of work separate from himself.

67.

कर्मणैव हि संसिद्धिमास्थिता जनकादयः ।
लोकसंग्रहमेवापि संपश्यन्कर्तुमर्हसि ॥

*karmanai 'va hi samsiddhim
āsthitā janakādayah
lokasamgraham evā 'pi
sampaśyan kartum arhasi*

For it was by acting alone that Janaka and others achieved success, so you too must act while keeping an eye to universal welfare.

Comment: Reference here is to the life story of King Janaka (of Mithila, Bihar, and father-in-law of Rama, the hero of the Epic Ramayana). Janaka is acknowledged as symbolizing excellence in action (perfection). The word samsiddhim means one who has acquired self-mastery in any endeavour. Here Krishna points out the importance of setting a good precedent by acting for and serving the cause of universal welfare (goodness of the common people).

68.

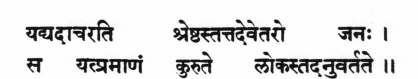

*yad-yad ācarati śresthas
tad-tad eve 'taro janaḥ
sa yat pramāṇaṁ kurute
lokas tad anuvartate*

Whatever a great man does, others do the same. Whatever he sets up as a standard, the world (mankind) follows.

Comment: The message here is that great men should set examples by their deeds and performances. All thinkers of the Indian philosophic age, from Kapila to Vyasa, have emphasized self-mastery, self-perfection, and self-achievement in order to inspire and guide others. Instead of forcing others to do what one wishes, these Indian thinkers advocated persuasion through example. Being inspired by such precedents, the people would adopt and follow them of their own volition.

69.

यदि ह्यहं न वर्तेयं जातु कर्मण्यतन्द्रितः ।
मम वर्त्मानुवर्तन्ते मनुष्याः पार्थ सर्वशः ॥

*yadi hy aham na varteyam
jātu karmany atandritah
mama vartmā 'nuvartante
manusyāh pārtha sarvaśah*

If I did not perform action, giving up idleness, people all around
would follow my path, O Partha.

*Comment: This refers to the impact and influence of the lifestyle of those
who are held in high esteem by the people of a particular land. The ignorant
(men without proper knowledge) follow the path of great men blindly.
Therefore Krishna advises Arjuna to give up indecisiveness, to take action
and set an example so that others would be inspired to follow him.*

70.

उत्सीदेयुरिमे लोका न कुर्यां कर्म चेदहम् ।
संकरस्य च कर्ता स्यामुपहन्यामिमाः प्रजाः ॥

utsīdeyur ime lokā
na kuryāṁ karma ced aham
saṁkarasya ca kartā syām
upahanyām imāḥ prajāḥ

If I did not perform action, these worlds would fall in ruin, and I would be the cause of disordered life and destruction of these people.

Comment: Krishna says that if he did not act, he would set a ruinous example, causing disorder and the destruction of the whole society.

Let it be noted here that by altering the original Gita, all the philosophical teachings about the value, significance, and importance of action in one's life, were changed and turned upside down. In countless ways, action was made insignificant. Inaction was glorified. Due to the influence of the Bhagavadgita, people came to believe in and followed the philosophy of inaction in their lives. This perpetuated misery and impoverishment. This aspect of the Bhagavadgita has proven suicidal to the Indian culture.

71.

सक्ताः कर्मण्यविद्वांसो यथा कुर्वन्ति भारत ।
कुर्याद्विद्वांस्तथासक्तश्चिकीर्षुर्लोकसंग्रहम्   ।।

saktāḥ karmaṇy avidvāṁso
yathā kurvanti bhārata
kuryād vidvāṁs tathā 'saktaś
cikīrṣur lokasaṁgraham

Ignorant men perform action from attachment to their work.
Learned men should act without any attachment, but with a desire
to achieve universal welfare.

Comment: The ignorant man does not differentiate the work from himself.
He thinks that his work and he are one and the same. The learned men
should not do that. Rather, without binding himself to the performable
act, the wise man should work with a desire for universal good.

72.

न बुद्धिभेदं जनयेदज्ञानां कर्मसंगिनाम् ।
जोषयेत्सर्वकर्माणि विद्वान्युक्तः समाचरन् ॥

na buddhibhedaṁ janayed
ajñānāṁ karmasaṅginām
joṣayet sarvakarmāṇi
vidvān yuktaḥ samācaran

The wise man should not sow dissension in the minds of the ignorant who are attached to work; rather he should perform all actions with yukta (excellence), and make others perform them willingly.

Comment: Here again Vyasa is pointing out that learned men should perform their actions with skill to achieve excellence. Instead of trying to unsettle the minds of the ignorant, they should let them perform their work willingly and freely. Being inspired and encouraged by the excellence of the learned, the ignorant will be motivated to learn those skills and techniques.

73.

प्रकृतेः क्रियमाणानि गुणैः कर्माणि सर्वशः ।
अहंकारविमूढात्मा   कर्ताहमिति   मन्यते ॥

prakrteh kriyamānāni
gunaih karmāni sarvasah
ahamkāravimūdhātmā
kartā 'ham iti manyate

Though all actions take place as a result of the gunas (sattva, rajas, and tamas) of prakriti, the ignorant man, being overwhelmed by self-consciousness (ahamkara) thinks: 'I am the doer.'

Comment: The purusha, who is a witness, seeing the manifestation of prakriti (nature) thinks as if he is the doer. This refers to Samkhya philosophy, Karika 65–66.

74.

तत्त्वविन्तु   महाबाहो   गुणकर्मविभागयोः ।
गुणा गुणेषु वर्तन्त इति मत्वा न सज्जते ॥

*tattvavit tu mahābāho
guṇakarmavibhāgayoḥ
guṇā guṇesu vartanta
iti matvā na sajjate*

But he who knows the characteristics of gunas and the tattvas (25 elements), and the divisions of their qualities and functions, does not become attached to them (manifestations of nature), O mighty-armed.

Comment: Here the significance of proper knowledge about the working of prakriti (nature), the gunas (rajas, tamas and sattva), and the emergence and functioning of the 25 tattvas (elements) is stated. Those who are knowledgeable do not become attached to the various manifestations of nature. He (the purusha) remains like the spectator of a stage play (see Karika, 66).

75.

प्रकृतेर्गुणंसंमूढाः   सज्जन्ते   गुणकर्मसु ।
तानकृत्स्नविदो मन्दान्कृत्स्नविन्न विचालयेत् ॥

prakrter gunasammūdhāh
sajjante gunakarmasu
tān akrtsnavido mandān
krtsnavin na vicālayet

Those who are confused by the functions of the constituents of
prakriti become attached to the works produced by them. He who
knows the whole should not upset these dull men who know only a
part.

Comment: This verse points out the difficulty in understanding the princi-
ple of 25 elements as stated in Samkhya philosophy. The ignorant do not
fully comprehend the marvel of nature, the gunas, and their interrelation.
   Karika 20 clarifies this aspect well by saying that due to the sanyogat
(proximity) of purusha and prakriti, the unconscious one appears conscious
and the indifferent one appears to be characterized by activity. But the fact
is that this happens because of the working of the gunas. The ignorant
person, not understanding this, becomes attached to various manifestations
of nature.

76.

ये त्वेतदभ्यसूयन्तो नानुतिष्ठन्ति मे मतम् ।
सर्वज्ञानविमूढांस्तान्विद्धि   नष्टानचेतसः ॥

ye tv etad abhyasūyanto
nā 'nutisthanti me matam
sarvajñānavimūdhāms tān
viddhi nastān acetasah

Those who do not act according to my teaching, finding fault with it with a fault-finding vision, are to be considered blind to all wisdom, thoughtless, and lost.

Comment: Here the importance of the teachings of the original Gita is emphasized. Since the teachings of the original Gita include the basic thoughts and philosophical tenets of all the rational thinkers of Indian civilization, those not knowledgeable will lack in proper understanding of things (of self, society, and nature) and will fail to act skillfully and properly. In the absence of proper knowledge and right action, a man will not achieve proper results from his actions and performance. As a consequence, he will face dukha (sorrow) and will be lost.

77.

सदृशं चेष्टते स्वस्याः प्रकृतेर्ज्ञानवानपि ।
प्रकृतिं यान्ति भूतानि निग्रहः किं करिष्यति ।।

sadṛśaṁ ceṣṭate svasyāḥ
prakṛter jñānavān api
prakṛtiṁ yānti bhūtāni
nigrahaḥ kiṁ kariṣyati

Even the man of knowledge acts in accordance with his own nature. All beings act according to their natures. Such being the case, what can restraint or pressure do?

Comment: This refers to the concept of bhavas (motivations) of man. These bhavas are: dharma (duty), raga (attachment), aishvarya (power), Jnana (knowledge), and their respective opposites, a total of eight. Everyone works according to his bhava (motivation) for the fulfillment of his desire. Therefore, repression, compulsion, or the forcing of people to work differently will not be fruitful. This refers to the futility of those who try to impose their own mode of thought and action on others.

78.

इन्द्रियस्येन्द्रियस्यार्थे रागद्वेषौ व्यवस्थितौ ।
तयोर्न वशमागच्छेत्तौ ह्यस्य परिपन्थिनौ ॥

indriyasye 'ndriyasyā 'rthe
rāgadveṣau vyavasthitau
tayor na vaśam āgacchet
tau hy asya paripanthinau

Attachment and aversion lie waiting in the sense and its object. A
man should not be carried away by this affection and repulsion, for
they are his two enemies.

*Comment: Here, the reference is to the concept of raga (attachment) and
viraga (non-attachment) and the effect of involvement of the sense organs
to their respective objects. These are natural motivations of man. But both
raga and viraga act as enemies when there is uncontrolled involvement
of the senses towards either. Therefore, the message here is that there
should be neither complete attachment nor total non-attachment of the
senses towards the objects. A balance or harmony should be maintained
in involvement of the senses.*

79.

श्रेयान्स्वधर्मो   विगुणः   परधर्मात्स्वनुष्ठितात् ।
स्वधर्मे   निधनं   श्रेयः   परधर्मो   भयावहः ॥

śreyān svadharmo viguṇaḥ
paradharmāt svanuṣṭhitāt
svadharme nidhanaṁ śreyaḥ
paradharmo bhayāvahaḥ

Better is one's own duty, even when imperfectly done, than another's
duty well performed. Better is death in one's duty: the duty of
another is fraught with fear (productive of danger).

*Comment: Here the emphasis is on attending to that for which one is
responsible and to that which is his swadharma (duty). To try to fulfill the
responsibility and duty of someone else (paradharma) is not only wrong
but also full of danger. And hence, undesirable.*

*According to Karma Yoga, even a wrongful (unintentional) action is
better than taking no action at all. The errors and mistakes of an action
can only be known and realized when one performs it. Improvements and
refinements in action, therefore, can result only by taking action. Then, in
due course, perfection in action will be mastered and excellence in action
will be a certainty.*

*Here, the advice is that one should never be afraid to take action. It
is better even to risk death in working with the bhava (motivation) of
swadharma (duty).*

80.

धूमेनाव्रियते वह्निर्यथादर्शो मलेन च ।
यथोल्बेनावृतो गर्भस्तथा तेनेदमावृतम् ॥

dhūmenā 'vriyate vahnir
yathā 'darśo malena ca
yatho 'lbenā 'vrto garbhas
tathā tene 'dam āvrtam

Just as fire is covered by smoke, or a mirror by dust, or the embryo
is covered by the caul, so this wisdom is covered by that (passion).

81.

आवृतं ज्ञानमेतेन ज्ञानिनो नित्यवैरिणा ।
कामरूपेण कौन्तेय दुष्पूरेणानलेन च ॥

āvrtaṁ jñānam etena
jñānino nityavairiṇā
kāmarūpeṇa kaunteya
duṣpūreṇā 'nalena ca

O Kaunteya (Arjuna)! wisdom is covered by this insatiable flame of passion (kama rupen), which is the constant foe of the wise.

Comment: It is pointed out that wisdom at times gets obscured by the feeling of passion in the individual. This happens when one of the gunas (rajas) becomes predominant over the other gunas (sattva and tamas). The over-domination of rajas causes restlessness and uncontrolled activation. As a result, harmony and equilibrium get lost. This condition acts like an enemy even for wise men. Therefore, it must be kept under control through Yogic discipline.

82.

इन्द्रियाणि मनो बुद्धिरस्याधिष्ठानमुच्यते ।
एतैर्विमोहयत्येष ज्ञानमावृत्य देहिनम् ॥

indriyāṇi mano buddhir
asyā 'dhisthānam ucyate
etair vimohayaty eṣa
jñānam āvṛtya dehinam

The senses, the mind, and the intellect are said to be its seat; through these it obscures knowledge and deludes his wisdom.

Comment: Krishna refers to the mode of perception and its impact on the bodily limbs and organs, as discussed in Samkhya philosophy and Yoga. It has been explained by Karika 35 that the senses perceive the objects indeterminately (not precisely) and bring such percepts to the mind, which synthesizes them and takes them to the self-consciousness (ahamkara). This faculty, in turn, refers percepts to the self, and as objects of self-consciousness they come before buddhi (the intellect), which ascertains their nature.

When the object of involvement of the senses is ascertained by the intellect, a visualization of that object occurs in the mind. This visualization of the image causes conditioning of the whole bodily system, in accordance with the nature of that which is held. When the visualization occurs, due to the domination of passion it affects the whole bodily system causing disturbance, restlessness, and stress. It follows that unless the state of over-domination of passion is controlled, it will obscure knowledge and delude wisdom.

83.

इन्द्रियाणि पराण्याहुरिन्द्रियेभ्यः परं मनः ।
मनसस्तु परा बुद्धिर्यो बुद्धेः परतस्तु सः ॥

indriyāni parāny āhur
indriyebhyaḥ param manaḥ
manasas tu parā buddhir
yo buddheḥ paratas tu saḥ

The senses, they say, are superior to their objects; higher than the senses is the mind, and higher than the mind is the buddhi (intellect); but higher even than the intellect is the purusha (self).

Comment: Here we find a reference to the concept of 25 tattvas of Samkhya philosophy. When the purusha comes in proximity to prakriti, the various internal faculties emerge, such as intellect, self-consciousness, mind, and the senses. Though perception occurs by means of these various faculties, the ultimate master and controller of them all is the purusha (the person or self). Therefore, the purusha is higher than all his internal and external faculties.

84.

एवं बुद्धेः परं बुद्ध्वा संस्तभ्यात्मानमात्मना ।
जहि शत्रुं महाबाहो कामरूपं दुरासदम् ॥

evaṁ buddheḥ paraṁ buddhvā
saṁstabhyā 'tmānam ātmanā
jahi śatruṁ mahābāho
kāmarūpaṁ durāsadam

Thus, knowing the purusha which is higher than the buddhi and controlling the self by the self, O mighty-armed, destroy this enemy which, like passion (kama rupam), is difficult to conquer.

Comment: In this concluding verse Vyasa combines the teachings of Samkhya philosophy and Yoga discipline both by referring to the 25 elements (of Kapila) and the samyama process (of Patanjali). Based on this understanding of the process of the senses and internal-external faculties, Krishna advises Arjuna to fight the war and conquer the enemy, who, like passion, is obscuring his knowledge and deceiving his wisdom.

APPENDIX

THE TRADITIONAL LINE OF DESCENT
OF THE LUNAR DYNASTY

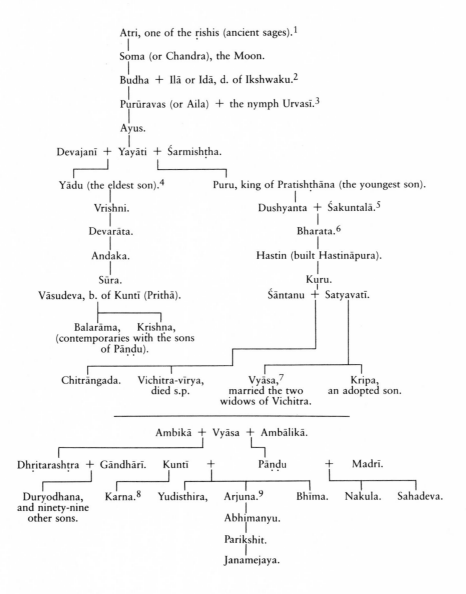

Atri, one of the ṛishis (ancient sages).[1]

Soma (or Chandra), the Moon.

Budha + Ilā or Idā, d. of Ikshwaku.[2]

Purūravas (or Aila) + the nymph Urvasī.[3]

Ayus.

Devajanī + Yayāti + Śarmishṭha.

Yādu (the eldest son).[4]   Puru, king of Pratishthāna (the youngest son).

Vrishni.   Dushyanta + Śakuntalā.[5]

Devarāta.   Bharata.[6]

Andaka.   Hastin (built Hastināpura).

Sūra.   Kuru.

Vāsudeva, b. of Kuntī (Pritha).   Śāntanu + Satyavatī.

Balarāma,   Krishna,
(contemporaries with the sons
of Pāndu).

Chitrāngada.   Vichitra-vīrya,   Vyāsa,[7]   Kripa,
               died s.p.   married the two   an adopted son.
                                  widows of Vichitra.

Ambikā + Vyāsa + Ambālikā.

Dhṛitarashtra + Gāndhārī.   Kuntī   +   Pāndu   +   Madrī.

Duryodhana,   Karna.[8] Yudisthira, Arjuna.[9]   Bhīma.   Nakula.   Sahadeva.
and ninety-nine
other sons.   Abhimanyu.

                                       Parikshit.

                                       Janamejaya.

The line down to Sāntanu has many omissions. The full line is given in Professor Dowson's "Classical Dictionary of Hindū Mythology," s.v. Chandra-vanśa. Bhīshma was a son of Sāntanu by a former wife, the goddess Gangā, whence he is sometimes called *Gāngeya*. Another name, *Sātanava,* is from his father, Sāntanu.

[1] They are usually numbered as seven, and are represented by the seven stars of the Great Bear (Ursa Major). The hymns of the Vedas were revealed to them.

[2] Son of the Manu Vaivasvat, who was the son of Vivaswat, the Sun. Founder of the Solar dynasty.

[3] A celestial nymph mentioned in the Rig Veda. The loves of Purūravas and Urvasī are the subject of the Vikramorvasī, a drama by Kālidāsa.

[4] From Yadu, Krishna is called Yādava, as being a descendant.

[5] The heroine of Kālidāsa's drama of that name.

[6] From him India is sometimes called Bhārata-varsha, the kingdom of Bharata.

[7] Vyāsa was the son of Satyavatī, but not of Sāntanu. His father was the sage Parāsara: he was therefore the half-brother of Vichitravīrya.

[8] Karna was the son of Kuntī, also called Prithā, by Surya, the Sun, before her marriage with Pāndu.

[9] Arjuna visited Krishna at Dwārakā, and there he married Subhadrā, the sister of Krishna. Abhimanyu was her son from this marriage. He was killed in the great contest of the rival princes, but the kingdom of Hastināpura descended to his son Parikshit. The city of Hastināpura was about fifty-seven miles northeast of Delhi, on the banks of an old bed of the Ganges. It is now in ruins.

Source: John Davies, *The Bhagavad Gita* (London: Trubner & Co., 1882), pp. 202–203.

GLOSSARY OF SANSKRIT TERMS

Adharma Vice, one of the eight basic motivations (bhavas) of man, evil.

Ahamkara Self-consciousness, self-awareness, a basic principle (tattva) of the Samkhya system, one of the 25 principles of Samkhya. It emerges from buddhi and in turn produces the group of 16 elements (see the chart of 25 principles, chapter 1).

Aishvarya Power, supremacy, affluence, one of the eight basic motivations of man.

Ajnana Ignorance, lack of knowledge of the eight basic motivations of purusha (man).

Anaishvarya Impotence, feebleness, one of the eight basic motivations (bhavas) of man.

Antahkarana The internal organ, consisting of buddhi (intellect), ahamkara (self-consciousness), and manas (mind).

Aptavachana The trustworthy verbal testimony, one of the three reliable means of acquiring knowledge.

Anumana Inference, one of the three means of acquiring proper knowledge.

Asana Body posture, body form, pose, physical practices of Yoga, one of the eight steps of Yoga.

Autasukya Ardent desire, eagerness, zeal.

Avyakta The unmanifest state of prakriti, primordial condition of prakriti (nature).

Bhava Motivation, basic striving, predisposition. According to the Samkhya system, bhavas are eight in number *(dharma, adharma, jnana, ajnana, viraga, raga, aishvarya, and anaishvarya)*.

Buddhi Intellect, emerges due to proximity of purusha and prakriti. See the chart of 25 elements, chapter 1, under Samkhya philosophy.

Buddhi-indriyas Sense organs, five in number (eyes, ears, nose, tongue, and skin).

Dharana Concentration, fixing the mind on an object, spot, or place within a limited area. One of the eight steps of the Yoga system; one of the three constituents of samyama.

Dharma Virtue, duty, responsibility, justice, one of the eight basic motivations or predispositions (bhavas) of man.

Dhyana Meditation, uninterrupted attachment or flow of the mind towards the object of observation; one of the eight steps of the Yoga system; one of the three constituents of samyama.

Dukha Sorrow, pain, suffering, unhappiness, misery.

Guna Constituent of prakriti, everchanging and everlasting quality of nature, three in number (sattva, rajas, and tamas).

Ishtha Desired, wished, aimed at.

Jnana Knowledge, one of the eight basic motivations (bhavas) of purusha (man).

Kaivalya Freedom, liberation, emancipation, the concept used by Kapila and Patanjali.

Karma-indriyas Action-organs, five in number (hands, feet, speech, excretory organ, and generative organ).

Mahabhuta Gross element, five in number (space, wind, fire, water, and earth), emerges from tanmatras (subtle elements). See the chart of 25 elements in chapter 1 under Samkhya philosophy.

Manas Mind, works as a sense-organ and also as an action organ. According to Samkhya, it emerges from self-consciousness (ahamkara).

Mulaprakriti Primal nature, *pradhana*; primordial nature in its unmanifest conditon.

Niyama Rules, principles, code of conduct. According to Yoga Sutra, it involves developing or mastering the five qualities (cleanliness, contentment, austerity, self-study, and self-perfection).

Parartha For the interest of others.

Pradhana The principal one, in Samkhya philosophy the term used for prakriti and mulaprakriti (primal nature).

Prakriti Nature. It is singular, eternal, unconscious, and uncreated by any power or entity. It has three constituents (sattva, rajas, and tamas) and two states: *avyakta* (unmanifest) and *vyakta* (manifest).

Pranayama Control of breath by interruption in the flow of inhalation and exhalation, a Yogic breathing exercise.

Pranidha Pranidhanani, pranidhana; endeavour, meditation, to resolve upon, determined, having the mind fixed upon, apply, exertion.

Pranidhanama Applying, employing, application, great effort, profound meditation.

Pratyahara Visualizing the opposite of what is presently held as undesirable, one of the eight steps of Yoga. For detail see chapter 1, under Patanjali.

Pratyaksha Perception, the act of ascertaining objects through contact with sense organs. It involves operation of five sense organs and three internal organs (buddhi, ahamkara, and manas).

Purusha The man, person, self, individual, is numerous, conscious, mortal, intelligent, and the knower. Purusha has been used for both male and female by Kapila, Patanjali, and Vyasa.

Purusartha Self-effort, self-endeavour, on one's own action, an achievement by self-action.

Raga Attachment, affection, joy, passion, desire, one of the eight basic motivations (bhavas) of purusha (man).

Rajarshi A royal sage, a saint-like prince, a sage and kshatriya king.

Rajas One of the three gunas (constituents of nature), characterized by activation, mobility, stimulation, passion, and pain.

Samadhi Contemplation, deep meditation, attachment of mind to the object without any distraction or consciousness of self. One of the eight steps of the Yoga system; one of the three constituents of samyama.

Samyama Mental discipline or perfection, mental mastery by combining concentration (dharana), meditation (dhyana), and deep meditation (samadhi).

Satkarya Right action, the Samkhya doctrine that the effect pre-exists in its cause, comprised of two words (sat + karya): *Sat* means true, real, existent, essential, best, excellent. *Karya* means work, action, performance.

Sattva One of the three gunas (constituents of nature), characterized by harmony, equilibrium, perfection, goodness, quietness, and illumination.

Siddhi Perfection, accomplishment, fulfillment, completion, complete attainment.

Sukha Happiness, pleasure, joyous life, satisfactory.

Sutra Verse, aphorism, a concise statement of a principle.

Swartha Self-interest, own affair or cause, personal matter or advantage.

Tamas One of the three gunas (constituents of nature), characterized by heaviness, darkness, torpor, and insensibility.

Tanmatra Subtle elements, five in number (sound, touch, form, taste, and smell). According to Samkhya, they are non-specific or imperceptible elements of prakriti from which five mahabhuta (gross elements) are produced.

Tattva An element, a primary substance, elementary property, constituent of everything in nature; has been referred as principle or basic component in the Samkhya system. See the chart of 25 tattvas in chapter 1.

Vijnana, Vijnanata Science, scientific knowledge.

Viraga Disinclination, disaffection, discontent, without desire, one of eight basic motivations of man.

Vyakta The manifest state or conditon of prakriti.

Yama Self-restraint, discipline, observance of certain principles. According to Yoga Sutra, it is fivefold (non-violence, truthfulness, honesty, continence, and freedom from greed).

Yoganga The eight steps of Yoga described by Patanjali in his Yoga Sutra (*yama, niyama, asana, pranayama, pratyahara, dharana, dhyana, and Samadhi*); the eight limbs of Yoga, or branches of Yoga.

SELECTED BIBLIOGRAPHY

Agarwala, G.C. (Ed.). *Age of Bharata War*. Delhi: Motilal Banarsidass, 1979.

Allchin, Raymond and Bridget. *The Birth of Indian Civilization*. Harmondsworth, England: Penguin Books, 1968.

Bahadur, K.P. *The Wisdom of Yoga*. New Delhi: Sterling Publishers, 1977.

Ballantyne, J.R. and Deva, Govind Sastri. *Yoga Sutra of Patanjali*. Delhi: Indological Book House, 1971.

Bazaz, Prem Nath. *The Role of Bhagavad Gita in Indian History*. New Delhi: Sterling Publishers, 1975.

Belvalkar, S.K. and Ranade, R.D. *History of Indian Philosophy*. New Delhi: Orient Books Reprint Corp., 1974.

Bhave, Acharya Vinoba. *Talks on the Gita*. New York: Macmillan, 1960.

Buch, Maganlal A. *The Philosophy of Shankara*. Baroda: Vidya Vilas Press, 1921.

Butterfield, H. *The Study of Modern History*. London: G. Bell and Sons, 1944.

Catalina, Francis V. *A Study of the Self Concept of Sankhya Yoga Philosophy*. Delhi: Munshiram Manoharlal, 1968.

Chandler, Wayne B. 'The Jewel in the Lotus', *African Presence in Early Asia*. U.K.: Transaction Books, 1985.

Chakravarti, Pulinbihari. *Origin and Development of the Samkhya System of Thought*. New Delhi: Orient Books Reprint Corp., 1975.

Chattopadhyaya, D. *Lokayata: A Study in Ancient Indian Materialism*. Delhi: People's Publishing House, 1959.

Chidbhavananda, Swami. *The Bhagavad Gita*. Madras: Tapovanam Publishing House, 1965.

Davies, John. *The Bhagavad-gita*. London: Trubner and Company, 1882.

Dani, A.H. (Trans.). *Alberuni's Indica*. Pakistan: University of Islamabad, 1973.

Dasgupta, Surendranath. *A History of Indian Philosophy*. Cambridge: The University Press, 1932.

―――. *Yoga Philosophy*. Delhi: Motilal Banarsidass, 1974.

―――. *Religion and the Rational Outlook*. Delhi: Motilal Banarsidass, 1954.

Deshmukh, P.S. *Religion in Vedic Literature*. London: Oxford University Press, 1933.

Deussen, Paul. *The System of the Vedanta*. Translated by Charles Johnston. New York: Dover Publications, 1973.

Deutsch, E. *The Bhagavadgita*. U.S.A.: University Press of America, 1968.

Dhar, Pandit Murli. *Gems of Bhagavatgita*. New Delhi: Amrit Books, 1940.

Dikshit, K.N. *Prehistoric Civilization of the Indus Valley*. Madras: University of Madras, 1967.

Dutt, Romesh Chunder. *Ancient India: 2000 B.C. to 800 A.D.*. London: Longmans, Green and Company, 1893.

Edgerton, Franklin (Trans.). *The Bhagavadgita*. Massachusetts: Harvard University Press, 1972.

Fairservis, Jr., Walter A. 'The Script of the Indus Valley Civilization', *Scientific American*, March 1983.

Feuerstein, G.A. *Introduction to the Bhagavad-Gita*. London: Rider and Company, 1975.

_____. *The Philosophy of Classical Yoga*. New York: St. Martin's Press, 1980.

Feuerstein, G.A. and Miller, J. *A Reappraisal of Yoga*. London: Rider and Company, 1971.

Gambhirananda, Swami (Trans.). *Brahma-Sutra-Bhasya of Sankaracarya*. Calcutta: Adaita Ashram, 1965.

Gandhi, M.K. *Gita the Mother*. Edited by Jag Parvesh Chander. Lahore: Indian Printing Works, 1947.

_____. 'Neither Fiction Nor History', *Young India*, May 1928.

_____. *The Teaching of the Gita*. Edited by Anand T. Hingorani. Bombay: Bharatiya Vidya Bhavan, 1962.

Garbe, Richard. *Introduction to the Bhagavadgita*. Translated by D. Mackichan. Bombay: The University of Bombay, 1918.

_____. *India and Christendom*. Translated by Lydia G. Robinson. Chicago: Open Court Publishing Company, 1959.

_____. *Die Samkhya Philosophie*. Leipzig: H. Haessel Verlag, 1917.

_____. *The Philosophy of Ancient India*. Chicago: Open Court Publishing Company, 1897.

Ghosh, Anil Chandra. *Swami Vivekananda: His Life and Message*. Calcutta: Presidency Library, 1963.

Ghosh, J. *Samkhya and Modern Thought*. Calcutta: The Book Company, 1930.

Gollancz, Israel (Ed.). *Mahabharata: Epic of Ancient India*. London: Ballantyne, Hanson and Company, 1898.

Gupta, S.P. and Ramachandran, K.S. (Eds.). *Mahabharata Myth and Reality*. Delhi: Agam Prakashan, 1976.

Habermas, Jürgen. *Legitimation Crisis*. Translated by Thomas McCarthy. Boston: Beacon Press, 1975.

———. *Theory and Practice*. Translated by John Viertel. London: Heinemann, 1974.

———. *Toward a Rational Society*. Translated by J.J. Shapiro. Boston: Beacon Press, 1972.

Hauer, J.W. *Der Yoga*. Stuttgart: W. Kohlhammer Verlag, 1958.

Hill, William Douglas P. *The Bhagavadgita*. London: Oxford University Press, 1928.

Hopkins, E.W. *The Great Epic of India*. Calcutta: Punthi Pustak, 1969.

———. *The Religions of India*. New Delhi: Munshiram Manoharlal, 1970.

Hutton, J.H. *Caste in India*. London: Oxford University Press, 1963.

Jha, Ganganath. *Gautama's Nyayasutras*. Poona: Oriental Book Agency, 1939.

Kapoor, J.C. *Bhagavadgita: An International Bibliography*. New York: Garland Publishing, 1983.

Keith, A.B. *A History of the Samkhya Philosophy*. Delhi: Nag Publishers, 1975.

Khair,G.S. *Quest for the Original Gita*. Bombay: Somaiya Publications, 1969.

Kufi, Ali. *The Chachnamah*. Translated by Mirza Kalich Beg. Karachi: The Commissioners Press, 1900.

Kulkarni, B.R. *The Bhagavadgita and the Bible*. Delhi: Unity Books, 1972.

Lal, R.B. *The Gita in the Light of Modern Science*. Bombay: Somaiya Publications, 1970.

Lamotte, E. *Notes Sur La Bhagavadigata*. Paris: Librairie Orientaliste Paul Geuthner, 1929.

Larson, Gerald James. *Classical Samkhya*. Delhi: Motilal Banarsidass, 1979.

Lord, J. Henry. *The Jews in India and the Far East*. Connecticut: Greenwood Press, 1976.

Macdonell, A.A. *A Vedic Reader*. London: Oxford University Press, 1965.

———. *A History of Sanskrit Literature*. New York: Haskell House Publishers, 1968.

Macnicol, Nicol. *Indian Theism*. Delhi: Munshiram Manoharlal, 1969.

———. *Hindu Scriptures*. London: J.M. Dent and Sons, 1938.

Mahadevan, T.M.P. *Sankaracharya*. New Delhi: National Book Trust, 1968.

Mahajan, Vidya Dhar. *Ancient India*. New Delhi: S. Chand and Company, 1962.

———. *Political and Cultural History of Ancient India*. New Delhi: S. Chand and Company, 1962.

Majumdar, A.K. *Concise History of Ancient India*, Vol I. New Delhi:

Munshiram Manoharlal Publishers, 1977.

Majumdar, R.C. *Readings in Political History of India*. S.P. Gupta (Gen. Editor). New Dehli: B.R. Publishing Corp., 1976.

Majumdar, R.C. and Altekar, A.S. (Eds.). *A New History of Indian People*. Vol. VI. Lahore: Motilal Banarsi Dass, 1946.

Mainkar, T. G. *The Samkhya Karika of Isvarakrishna*. Poona: Oriental Book Agency, 1964.

Mehta, J.L. (Ed.). *Vedanta and Buddhism*. Varanasi: Banaras Hindu University, 1968

Minor, R.N. *Bhagavadgita*. New Delhi: Heritage Publishers, 1982.

Modi, P.M. 'Meaning of Smriti in the Brahma-Sutras', *Indian Historical Quarterly*, December 1936.

_____*A Critique of the Brahmasutra*, Part I. Bhavnagar: P.M. Modi, 1943.

Monier-Williams. *Brahmanism and Hinduism*. London: John Murray, 1891.

_____. *Indian Wisdom*. Varanasi: Chowkhambha Sanskrit Series Office, 1963.

Mookherji, Sudhansu Bimal. *India's Empire of Mind*. Agra: Lakshmi Narain Agarwala, 1973.

Müller, F. Max. *A History of Ancient Sanskrit Literature*. Edinburgh: Williams and Norgate, 1860.

Nehru, Jawaharlal. *Glimpses of World History*. London: Lindsay Drummond Limited, 1949.

Otto, Rudolf. *India's Religion of Grace and Christianity Compared and Contrasted*. Translated by F.H. Foster. New York: Macmillan, 1930.

_____. *The Original Gita*. Translated by J.E. Turner. London: George Allen and Unwin, 1939.

Paranjpye, R.P. *The Crux of the Indian Problem*. London: Watts and Company, 1931.

Parrinder, E.G. *The Significance of the Bhagavadgita for Christian Theology*. London: Dr. Williams' Trust, 1968.

Pendse, S.D. *Pouranika Bhagawata Dharma*. Poona: Venus Prakashana, 1967.

Phukan, Radhanath (Ed. and Trans.). *The Samkhya Karika of Isvarakrsna*. Calcutta: Firma K.L. Mukhopadhyay, 1960.

Prakash, Shanti. *The Adi Bhagwad Gita*. Fyzabad: The Sadharana Dharma Sangha, 1936.

Puri, B.N. *India in the Time of Patanjali*. Bombay: Bharatiya Vidya Bhavan, 1957.

Radhakrishnan, Sarvepalli. *The Bhagavadgita*. London: George Allen and Unwin, 1948.

_____. *Indian Philosophy*. London: George Allen and Unwin, 1966.

Ramanujacharya (Ed.). *Ahirbudhnya Samhita of the Panchratra*. Madras: Adyar Library, 1916.

Ramesam, N. *Sri Sankaracharya*. Ponnur: Bhava Narayana Swami Temple, 1971.

Rangachar, S. *Early Indian Thought*. Mysore: Rao and Raghavan, 1964.

Rao, N.J. *The Age of the Mahabharata War*. Varanasi: Bharat-Bharati, 1978.

Riepe, D.M. *The Naturalistic Tradition in Indian Thought*. Seattle: University of Washington Press, 1961.

Roy, S.C. *The Bhagavad-Gita and Modern Scholarship*. London: Luzac and Company, 1941.

Sardesai, N.G., 'The Bhagavadgita from the Island of Bali', *Modern Review* (Calcutta), July 1914.

Sastri, S.S. Suryanarayana (Ed. and Trans.). *The Samkhya-Karika of Isvara Krsna*. Third revised edition. Madras: University of Madras, 1948.

Schrader, F. Otto, *Introduction to the Panchratra and the Ahirbudhnya Samhita*. Madras: The Adyar Library, 1916.

Sharma, C. *Indian Philosophy*. Banaras: Nand Kishore and Bros., 1952.

Senart, Emile. *La Bhagavadgita*. Paris: Société D'édition, 1967.

Shilotri, P.S. *Indo-Aryan Thought and Culture*. New York: The Evening Post Job Printing Office, 1913.

Singh, Waryam. *History of Ancient India: From the Earliest Times to the Muslim Conquest*. Lahore: Sikh University Press, 1943.

Sinha, Nandalal. *Vaisesika Sutras of Kanada*. India: The Panini Office, 1911.

————. (Trans.). *The Samkhya Philosophy*. Bahadurganj, Bihar: The Panini Office, Bhuvaneswari Asrama, 1915.

Sinha, Phulgenda. *Yoga: Meaning, Values and Practice*. Patna: Indian Institute of Yoga, 1970.

————. *Yoga for Total Living*. New Delhi: Orient Paperbacks, 1977.

Sivananda, Sri Swami. *The Bhagavad Gita*. India: The Divine Life Society, 1969.

Slater, Gilbert. *The Dravidian Element in Indian Culture*. New Delhi: E.E. Publications, 1976.

Sorensen, S. *Index to the Names in the Mahabharata*. London: Williams and Norgate, 1904

Sovani, V.V. *A Critical Study of the Sankhya System*. Poona: Oriental Book Agency, 1935

Steiner, Rudolf. *The Bhagavadgita and the Epistles of Paul*. New York: Anthroposophic Press, 1971.

Sunderlal, Pandit. *The Gita and the Quran*. Translated by Syed Asadullah. Hyderabad: Institute of Indo-Middle East Cultural Studies, 1957.

Taimni, I.K. *The Science of Yoga.* Madras: The Theosophical Publishing House, 1967.

Tambimuttu, E.L. *Dravida.* Bombay: International Book House, 1945.

Telang, K.T. *The Bhagavadgita.* Oxford: The Clarendon Press, 1882.

Tilak, Bal Gangadhar (Trans.). *Sri Bhagavadgita-Rahasya.* Vol I and II, First Edition; Poona: Tilak Bros., 1935.

Upadhyaya, K.N. *Early Buddhism and the Bhagavadgita.* Delhi: Motilal Banarsidass, 1971.

Vaidya, C.V. *The Mahabharata: A Criticism.* Delhi: Mehar Chand Lachhman Das, 1967.

Vaidya, R.V. *A Study of Mahabharat (A Research).* Poona: A.V.G. Prakashan, 1967.

Van Buitenen. 'The Critical Edition of the Bhagavadgita', *Journal of the American Oriental Society,* March 1965.

Vireswarananda, Swami (Trans.). *Brahma-Sutras.* Calcutta: Adviata Ashrama, 1965.

Vivekananda, Swami. *Thoughts on the Gita.* Calcutta: Advaita Ashrama, 1967.

————. *The Complete Works of Swami Vivekananda.* Vol IV. Calcutta: Advaita Ashrama, 1978.

Warshaw, Steven and Bromwell, C. David. *India Emerges.* California: Diable Press, 1974.

Weber, Max. *The Hindu Social System.* Translated by Hans Gerth and Don Martindale. Minnesota: University of Minnesota Press, 1950.

————. *The Religion of India.* Translated by Hans Gerth and Don Martindale. Illinois: The Free Press, 1958.

————. *The Sociology of Religion.* Translated by E. Fischoff. Boston: Beacon Press, 1922.

Wilson, H.H. (Trans.). *Sankhya Karika by Iswar Krishna.* Bombay: Tookaram Tatya, 1887.

Wolpert, Stanley A. *A New History of India.* New York: Oxford University Press, 1982.

Wood, Ernest E. *Practical Yoga: Ancient and Modern.* New York: E.P. Dutton and Company 1948.

Yardi, M.R. *The Yoga of Patanjali.* Poona: Bhandarkar Oriental Research Institute, 1979.

Zaehner, R.C. *Hindu Scriptures.* London: J.M. Dent and Sons, 1966.

————*The Bhagavad-Gita.* Oxford: The Clarendon Press, 1969.

Zeuner, F.E. *Prehistory of India.* Poona: Deccan College, 1951.

INDEX